HILLS

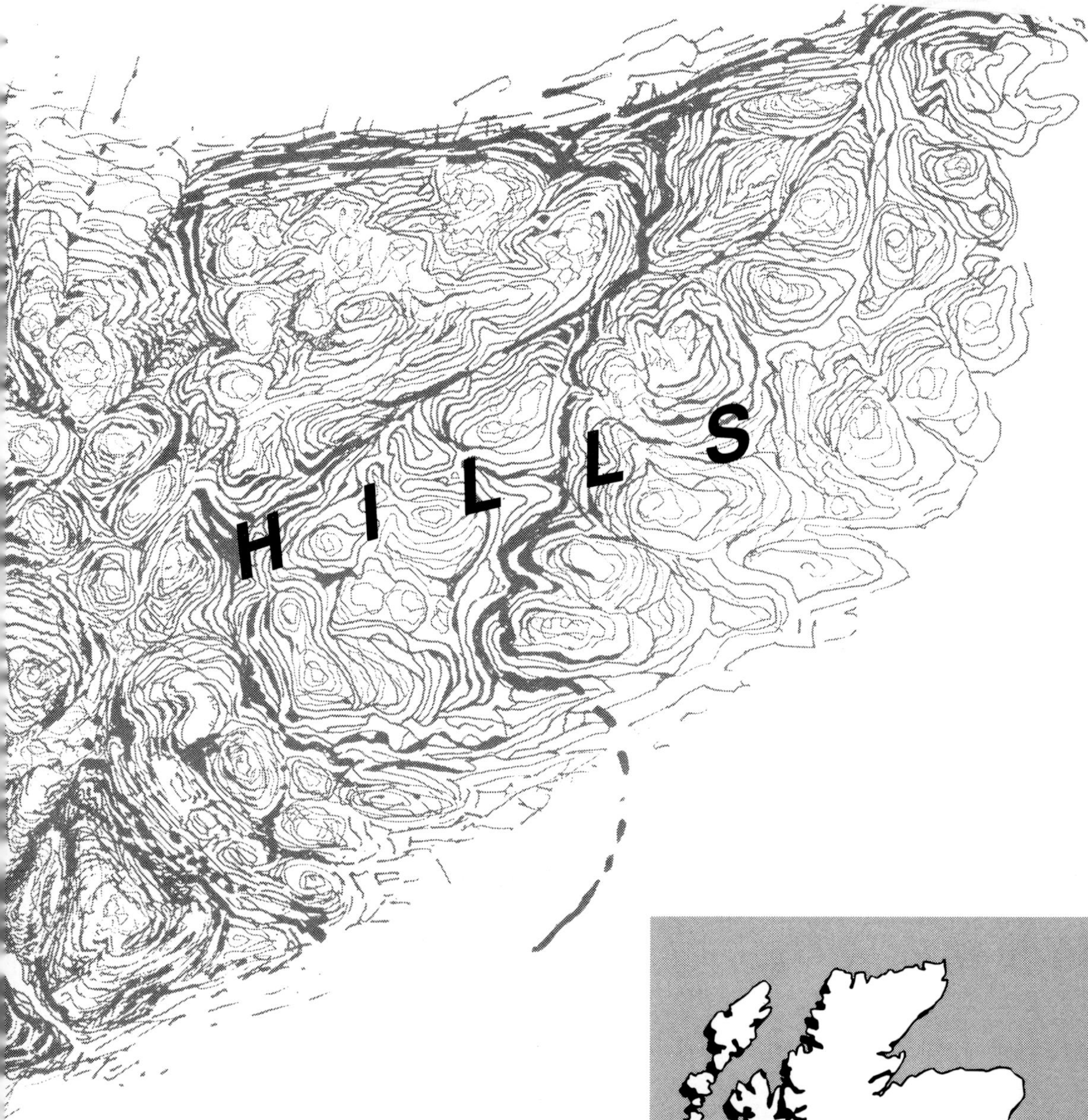

The Ochils

Placenames, History, Tradition

Angus Watson

Perth and Kinross District Libraries
1995

Published by
Perth and Kinross District Libraries

ISBN 0 905452 16 X

Printed by
Cordfall Ltd
0141 332 4640

"Fanciful etymologies can never yield satisfaction to the judicious antiquary, and therefore when nothing rational can be offered, it seems better to acknowledge ignorance, than to offer what can neither amuse nor inform."

The Reverend John Duncan, Old Statistical Account for Alva Parish, 1790-95.

Contents

Acknowledgements

The reader of this book will quickly spot my indebtedness to the two foremost Scottish placename scholars of this century, Professor W J Watson (1865-1948) and Professor W F H Nicolaisen. With them the study of Scottish placenames comes of age, and their writings are indispensable to anyone with an interest in the subject.

I also made extensive use of the splendid *Concise Scots Dictionary* edited by Mairi Robinson for the Aberdeen University Press.

A good number of individuals gave generously of their time, interest and knowledge, or made documents available to me. I would like to express my thanks to Professor Geoffrey Barrow, Mr Richard Bernard, Coalsnaughton, Mrs Janet Carolan of Dollar Local History Society, Mr Brodrick Haldane, Mr John Haldane, Foswell, Mr Richard Haldane, Cloan, Mrs Kennard, Coul, Mr Laurie MacLean, Geography Department, University of Aberdeen, Rennie McOwan FSA Scot, Mrs Naomi Mitchison, Professor W F H Nicolaisen, Mr George Ritchie, Dunning, and Mr Kenneth Young of Auchterarder and District Local History Society, as well as to Mr F J Guthrie, District Librarian Perth and Kinross District Libraries, for acting as publisher.

I would not have tracked down much of the information in the following pages without the courteous and efficient help of the staff of: Aberdeen University Library, Alloa District Library, the Map Library of the National Library of Scotland, Perth and Kinross District Archives, Perth Museum and Art Gallery, the Sandeman (now the A K Bell) Library Perth, St Andrews University Library, the Scottish Records Office and Stirling University Library.

Finally I would like to express my gratitude to Ken Laing, Dunning, and Dr Colm O Baoill of the Celtic Department, University of Aberdeen. Ken not only contributed the fine drawings but also showed an enthusiastic and encouraging interest in the project from its earliest beginnings. Colm was never too busy to oblige me with answers to my interminable queries, and without his wise counsel this book would have been considerably less sound than it is.

Any errors and shortcomings are mine entirely.

Angus Watson
Forgandenny

Foreword

Some would say that the Ochils area proper excludes Sheriffmuir and extends no further East than Glen Farg. Others call Norman's Law, well into Fife, the last of the Ochils. The area I finally settled on for study is the elongated oval shown on the location map on the front endpaper. Though it contains a variety of types of environment it nonetheless forms a single physical mass neatly circumscribed by the road and rail system. I have normally excluded sites lower than 200 to 300 ft, 70 to 100 metres, approximately. The towns and villages on the periphery, such as Dunning or Dollar, have generally speaking only been mentioned when they are the source of secondary names which fall within the area chosen: 'Dunning Burn' or 'Dollar Glen' for example.

As far as I am aware, this is the first detailed study of the placenames of the Ochils area and it is hoped that for this reason it will be of value to students of placenames in general. Local historians and hillwalkers should also find something of interest between these covers. For linguists the Scots component of the name list will, I hope, throw a little new light on Scots usage in the area.

Less is known about the Gaelic language in the few centuries during which it was spoken here than is known about the history of Scots. It would be gratifying if the material in this book were to add a little new knowledge about the intensity of Gaelic penetration into the area, or at least confirm through placename evidence some of what is known from other sources.

But this book has no particularly high scholarly ambitions. My aim has been to set out a substantial body of basic information for the interest and pleasure of all who feel affection for the hills and are intrigued by the intrinsically fascinating subject of placenames. It would be particularly pleasing if people living and working in the Ochils were to discover in these pages old names for features now unnamed, and were to find it useful or satisfying to bring some of them back into use.

I would be delighted to receive comments, corrections and additional information from those who use this book and I would be very interested to hear of the whereabouts of old maps of the area, particularly estate maps and other such locally made maps and plans. Readers who so wish are welcome to write to me c/o Perth and Kinross District Libraries who have kindly agreed to forward any correspondence.

Introduction to the Gazetteer

The Gazetteer entries are put together in such a way as to give as much information as possible in the space available. Readers will find it worthwhile to spend a little time familiarising themselves with the explanations and comments on the following few pages.

Types of Placenames

When describing placenames we distinguish between the specific and the generic. In 'Dunning Burn' for example, 'Burn', denoting the type of feature, is the generic, while 'Dunning', the specific, distinguishes that burn from other burns. Entries in the Gazetteer are arranged in alphabetical order of the specific, which is enlarged and emboldened on its first appearance. Eg '**Arlick** Hill' or 'Craig **Bakie**'. The latter example shows that the specific can come after the generic and this is often a characteristic of names of Gaelic origin.

In addition, placenames can be primary or secondary names. 'Dunning', 'Craigentaggert' and 'Bald Hill' are examples of primary names because that village, that crag and that hill are the features that these names first identified. 'Dunning Common', 'Craigentaggert Hill', 'Baldhill Burn' are secondary names because that common, that hill and that burn were named not for themselves but from another feature. Their naming represented a subsidiary use of a name already in existence.

As a general rule, where there is a group of two or more related names as in the examples above, I have put first in the entry the name that seems likely to be the primary name, though it must be said that the primary name cannot always be identified with certainty.

Scope of the Name List

The list of names at the beginning of an entry gives all the names I have been able to find, both current and disused, which contain the specific in question. Exceptions to this are cases where some very early or short-lived secondary names may be listed only among the earlier forms and references which are quoted further on in the entry (see below).

All names appearing in the Gazetteer which have not been found on Ordnance Survey maps, ie from the first edition of c1860 onwards, are marked with an asterisk when they first appear in the entry for their specific. Where they appear again in their own or other entries the asterisk is not present.

Grid References and Accuracy

The six-figure numbers used in entries are six-figure OS grid references and are preceded by 'GR'. Four-figure references to the OS grid are preceded by 'OS square', to avoid the possibility of their being confused with dates. Occasionally AD is appended to a date to avoid ambiguity.

Most of the area covered in the Gazetteer appears on Sheet 58 of the OS 1:50000 Landranger Series. To the West and East it extends a little way onto sheets 57 and 59 respectively.

Stobie's map of 1783 is the earliest major map on which I have found it possible to estimate a location to the nearest OS grid square with any confidence. With some later pre-OS maps however I felt the standard of accuracy was such as to merit the attempt at six-figure grid references in some cases. The standard of accuracy of smaller estate maps and plans varied considerably and so the standard of accuracy with which locations are estimated from them varies accordingly. In general the reader must bear in mind that where a four- or six- figure grid reference is derived from a pre-OS map, and particularly if marked 'approximate' or 'approximately', close accuracy cannot be taken for granted. Even grid references given for the 6" OS maps of c1860 must be regarded as approximate since of course those maps did not carry grid squares.

Dating

The Gazetteer entries also set out to convey any information I have on the dating of names. If a name has been found at only one date the phrase 'on record in' or 'recorded in' will indicate this. 'On record since' gives the earliest date I have for names still current, while 'on record between' will give a bracket of dates for names now disused.

Names found on recent Ordnance Survey maps ("recent" here meaning OS maps since c1970) are regarded for the purposes of this book as current. It is not of course the case that all names on recent OS maps are in general local use, but it was not feasible to check the currency of all the 700 or so specifics that appear on recent OS series.

Type of Feature

The head entry also indicates, if known, the type of feature each name represents, unless this is obvious from the name itself. 'Settlement' in this context stands for any inhabited site, whether a single dwelling or a substantial village.

Other short items of topographical information may immediately follow the head entry.

Earlier Forms and References

Next comes a very important section of the entry, that is a list of earlier recorded forms of the name concerned, introduced by the words 'Earlier', 'Earlier forms' or 'Earlier references'. The entries here are in chronological order.

Dating

One function of this section is to give information on dating, and so the first item in each list of earlier forms is always the earliest reference I have found to the specific concerned. At the same time I have also aimed to supply in the lists of earlier forms the first and last dates I have for all secondary names mentioned in an entry unless that information has been given in the head entry.

Status of the Dates Given

It should be stressed that the dates I give cannot claim to be the earliest or indeed the latest at which a given name was in use or a given settlement in existence. It is inevitable that there will be references that I have not unearthed, some of which would show new information. Thus the dating to be deduced from the entries claims only to provide a bracket of dates between which I have evidence that the name concerned was in use.

History of the Site

The earlier forms quoted are also intended to give a glimpse of the history of the site in question; for instance if a farm or estate name is involved they will often indicate divisions and subdivisions the holding may have undergone and may well indicate links with other holdings &c that existed from time to time. Eg 1793 'Knowhead or half of Souther Balquhandies' implies that the present Knowehead, OS square 0309, evolved from part of a component holding of Balquhandy OS square 0311.

In the earlier forms quoted for a number of former baronies, large estates &c, the reader will sometimes find the names of related holdings at a given date. Eg: 1808 'parts of the Barony of Ogilvy, viz lands of Cockplay, Biggs & Carrim, Biggs arable farm, Heldrick, Knowhead, Whack, Burnside & Wester Drumcairn'.

Evolution of the Name

The selection of earlier forms and references included in a Gazetteer entry is also intended to show in general terms the stages the name concerned has passed through in changing from its earliest to its latest form.

Source of the Derivation

In addition the earlier forms quoted in an entry include, where applicable, a form or forms on which the suggested derivation is based.

Surnames

At the end of the list of earlier forms, in cases where a surname is thought to have arisen from the placename concerned I have given dated early forms of that surname. This information is derived almost exclusively from Black's *Surnames of Scotland* (see Bibliography).

Historical Information and Tradition

A number of entries contain a little historical information about the site concerned. In addition, popular theories and traditions about the places and their names are sometimes quoted, as I feel that what people have believed in the past can often be as fascinating as the 'facts'.

Derivations

The concluding item in most Gazetteer entries is an indication of the derivation of the name concerned.

Scots Derivations

In the case of Scots placenames, I have normally set down English translations and explanations close to the form they have in *The Concise Scots Dictionary* (see Bibliography). The dates quoted from that dictionary show the earliest period at which the word involved is recorded in Scots, indicating that, whatever other circumstances might apply, the name concerned is unlikely to have been coined before the date given.

Though Scots names can of course be obscure, generally speaking they have been used throughout their history in a Scots-speaking environment. For this reason they have not become as obscure as many names of Gaelic origin have, since they have not been subject to the same degree of distortion and/or reinterpretation. The derivations given in the Gazetteer for Scots names are therefore offered with a reasonable degree of confidence.

Gaelic Derivations

To help the reader to appreciate the status of the Gaelic derivations offered in this book, it might be useful to give a little historical background and to outline some of the problems involved in the analysis of placenames of Gaelic origin.

The movement of Gaelic-speaking Scots from Ireland to what is now Argyll culminated in the foundation of the kingdom of Dalriada c500 AD. From this bridgehead the Gaelic language moved outwards with the result that there is virtually no part of Scotland, excluding the Northern Isles and the extreme North East mainland, where it was not spoken at some time.

The vicinity of the Ochil Hills was a Pictish stronghold during the early centuries of Gaelic expansion in Scotland. J.D. Mackie for example (see Bibliography) writes:- "later [than about 565 AD] the core of the Pictish monarchy was in Strathmore and Perthshire, and Scone eventually became the capital". Forteviot too was an important Pictish centre. After the amalgamation of Picts and Scots c843 under Kenneth Mac Alpin, Scone became the main administrative and political centre of the new Kingdom of the Scots, and Kenneth in fact died at Forteviot in 858. It can be seen from these few details that South East Perthshire was a key area for the expansion of the Gaelic language.

Professor WJ Watson (see Bibliography) was of the opinion that Pictland must have been largely Gaelic-speaking by the mid 9th century. However for the purposes of this book I have taken 900 AD as a cautious working assumption for the earliest date of durable Gaelic naming on any significant scale in the Ochils area.

When it comes to trying to establish a date for the end of the Gaelic period in our area, we have Withers' judgement (see Bibliography) that Gaelic was probably extinct as the native vernacular in Fife, Kinross and Clackmannan by about 1350. *An Historical Atlas of Scotland c400-c1600* (see Bibliography under McNeill) shows the western half of the area covered in this book as still Gaelic-speaking c1400.

As it seems unlikely that durable naming of places would occur to a significant degree in a language that was not in a culturally confident situation, it seems prudent to suggest that durable Gaelic naming was unlkely to occur in the Ochils area much later than, say, 1300 AD.

It seems then that a Gaelic name from our area is likely to have been coined no less than seven centuries and perhaps as many as eleven centuries ago.

A number of Gaelic names have remained surprisingly intact over this long period. 'Craigentaggert' and 'Drumfin', for example. Many, though, have changed to the extent that their present-day form is a very unsure guide to the original form of the name. 'Auchlinsky', for example, like multitudes of other Gaelic names, begins straightforwardly enough with a product of Gaelic 'Achadh'. We have to go back to 1483 however before we find a form, 'Auchinlesky', that begins to make sense of the second part. Other Gaelic names are no longer even recognisable as Gaelic names at all. 'Whaik', for example, looks like a good Scots name, and it is only forms of it prior to the 18th century such as 'Aquhaick' that reveal it as very probably Gaelic.

It is obvious from what has just been said that early forms of Gaelic names are indispensable if the original name is to be reconstructed with any certainty.

Where major natural features such as large rivers are concerned, or major settlements such as towns, villages, feudal baronies and other important land holdings, the early documentation may well provide forms which give a very feasible etymology.

Smaller holdings, or component holdings within larger units, are often less well documented. The biggest problem comes however when the name is that of an obscure hill, a remote burn, or lochan, or crag. If such a feature was used as a boundary marker at some time, the researcher may be lucky enough to light upon a document describing those boundaries and thus find an early form for the name. Failing that however there will have been little reason in early times to record the names of the vast majority of natural features, particularly in out-of-the-way locations. In many cases we have to wait until the early 18th century, when men like Sibbald and Macfarlane were collecting topographical material, before we find mention of natural features on even a modest scale.

The Ochils area does have a good number of quite well documented Gaelic names. There are also, however, a large number for which I have not been able to find really early forms and it follows from this that on the whole it is wise to regard the Gaelic etymologies in this book as informed suggestions. At best the analysis of old

Gaelic names is rather like a game of Chinese Whispers, but a game where we cannot go back to the first person in the line of transmission and ask what the original was. It would be a brave or foolhardy delver into Gaelic placenames who claimed that all his or her derivations were correct.

Nevertheless it seems to me worthwhile in itself to try to establish which names are of Gaelic origin, and it is often the case that one element at least of a name will be certain enough to establish the name's Gaelic credentials, even if there is not the evidence to hand to reconstruct the complete original form of the name beyond reasonable doubt. Even a simple numerical count of Gaelic names is of value as it helps to establish the degree of penetration of the language into the area. In the Appendices I have gone a little further and ventured some conclusions based on the suggested Gaelic etymologies that appear in the Gazetteer.

Even if we can be sure of the Gaelic words that originally made up a name, we cannot always be certain of the exact grammatical form that linked them together. For instance, modern forms of some Gaelic names such as Craigentaggert or Ashentrool, or early forms of others such as 'Carnibo' (now Carnbo) or 'Peticarne' (now Pitcairns) are a strong indication that some Gaelic names were formed in the Ochils area using the various forms of the Gaelic genitive definite article, meaning "of the". That being so, even where no trace of a genitive article is found in a name's recorded history we cannot assume that it was not originally present in that name. The genitive article is an unstressed syllable in the middle of the name and would in many cases be one of the first elements to be lost when the Gaelic language system broke down in our area. Thus 'Ben Buck', for example, could in theory have been 'Beinn Bhuic', buck mountain, 'Beinn Bhoc', bucks mountain, 'Beinn a' Bhuic', the mountain of the buck, or 'Beinn nam Boc', the mountain of the bucks.

Etymologies of Gaelic names are given in modern Gaelic except in the case of obsolete words and of so-called 'locatives'. An example of a locative is to be found in the name 'Clunie'. Here 'Cluanach', or 'Cluaineach', meadowy, meadowy place, from 'Cluan' or 'Cluain', a meadow, seems to have been used in the form 'Cluainich' with the 'locative' sense 'at meadowy place'. Another example is 'Drunzie', from 'Droigheann' or 'Druidheann', thorn, 'Druidhneach', thorny place, 'Druidhnich', at thorny place. Because this usage does not exist in modern Gaelic - and it seems to have been unique to placenames - the endings of locatives quoted in the Gazetteer are given the older spelling '-igh' to indicate their archaic character.

The Gazetteer

A

Abdie Church, in ruins, & **Abdie House**, both GR 259163. According to MacGibbon & Ross (see Bibliography) this is St Magridin's Church, consecrated in 1242. It was founded by adherents of the early Scoto-Irish Church, the Culdees, and was one of the earliest religious settlements in Scotland. Earlier called Lindores, it gave up that name to the more important foundation beside Newburgh. The church currently used for worship is at GR 256166.

Earlier forms include: 1248 'Ebedyn', 1595 'Ebdy Kirk', 1694 'Ebdie', 1775 'Abdie', 1860 'Abdie Cottage'.

Derivation: 'Abdie' is related to Old Irish 'Apdaine', abbot's jurisdiction and territory: compare Modern Irish 'Abdhaine', abbacy.

Abdie Kirk. Drawing by Ken Laing.

Abernethy Glen GR 186150, **Abernethy Hill** GR 190154. These are secondary names from Abernethy, OS square 1816.

Derivation: Abernethy is 'Abur-nethige' in the Pictish Chronicle, meaning confluence of the Nethy Burn. According to WJ Watson (see Bibliography), 'Nethy' may originally have meant 'pure one'.

Hill of Aithrey, GR 798980. A secondary name from Aithrey, now Airthrey, OS square 8196.

Earlier forms include: 1142 'Atherai', 1675 'Athra', 1688 & 1783 'Ethra'. Earliest surname form: 1432 'Athera(y)'. These spellings show that the first 'r' in the modern form of the name was not original.

Derivation: Gaelic 'Aithre', locative 'Aithrigh', at place of cows.

***Aitkenhall** GR 110067 approximately, on record between 1796 & 1828.

Derivation: From the surname? Scots 'Hall' was usually applied to a reasonably substantial dwelling.

Alva Burn & **Alva Glen**, both GR 884980, **Alva Moss** GR 888015. ***West Hill of Alva**, OS square 8798, is on record in 1790. The foot of Alva Glen appears as 'Strude Glen' on Morrison's map of 1848 and was the site of Upper & Lower Strude Mills in 1860.

Derivation: These are secondary names from Alva, OS square 8797, which is probably from Gaelic 'Allmhagh', rock-plain, crag-plain.

Andrew Gannel Hill GR 919006, **Andrew Gannel Burn**, which rises at GR 917002, & **Gannel Burn** GR 915990.

The Old Statistical Account for Tillicoultry claims that no trout were ever found in Gloomingside, later Gannel, Burn, but Gibson (see Bibliography) says this has been proved to be a fallacy.

Earlier references: In 1769 'Andr Ganhill' & 'Andrew Gan hill' are given for the hill, 'Cannel(l)'s Burn' is given for modern Gannel Burn, and 'Burns of Tillicoultry' is also marked along modern Gannel Burn. 1848 'Andrew Gannel Burn', 'Gannel Burn', 1860 'Andrew Gannel Hill'.

Derivations: The Gaelic derivation 'An Sruth Gainmheil', the sandy (bottomed) burn, has been suggested, but even if that was an accurate description of the stream bed, the pattern 'article + noun + adjective' is not a common one in Gaelic watercourse names. The 1860 OS Name Book reports that the site was locally said to be named for a man who lost his life close by in a storm.

Between 1792 & 1845 at least, Gannel Burn was called 'Gloomingside Burn'. 'Glooming' and 'Gloomingside' appear in the later 18th century to have been areas of ground, and Gloomingside Burn may well have taken its name from them (see further under Gloomingside Burn).

In the sources I have come across prior to 1848 all the 'Ganhill' &c names apply to the hill only, so 1769 'Cannell's Burn' may well represent a totally unrelated name, but which later became assimilated to 'Gannel'. For 'Cannell's Burn' a comparison with Glen Cannel in Strath Fillan, derived by WJ Watson (see Bibliography) from the Saint's name 'Cainer', could perhaps be borne in mind.

Ardargie House in 1903. The house is now demolished. Reproduced by permission of Perth Museum and Art Gallery.

***Andrewsfold**. A holding on record in 1788, when it formed part of Easter Ballieliesk, OS square 0001.

Annafreich Brae OS squares 0504 & 0604, the South slopes of Drumgarland Hill. I take this to be a secondary name from Annacrioch near Cleish, GR 115987, just over 4 miles away, which from the 14th century occurs in charters in conjunction with several holdings close to our site, including Brockley, OS square 0805, and Touchie, OS square 0605.

Earlier forms: 1860 'Annafreich Brae'. Earlier forms for the primary site near Cleish include: c1346 (transcribed c1622-32) 'the lands of Enachrache', 1521 'Anaquhrytht', 1616 'Ennecreich vulgo Annacroich', 1637 'Annacroich', 1828 'Annafriech'.

Derivation: The earliest forms suggest that the modern 'f' derives from an aspirated Gaelic 'c', pronounced 'ch' as in 'loch'. Gaelic 'Eanach', a marsh, is likely for the first element – note that Bog Burn is near the primary site. The final syllable could be Gaelic 'Ràth', as 'c' for 't' is a frequent misreading in the transcription of early documents. This would give a sense 'marsh dwelling'. A possibility that takes account of the 1521 spelling would be Gaelic 'Eanach Raoic', marsh of the bellowing of deer or cattle.

Glen Anny GR 880053. Earlier: 1654 'the burne of Glenany'. This name is discussed under Danny Burn.

Ardargie Hill GR 088151, **Ardargie Mains** GR 083148, **Ardargie House** GR 074159.

Sadly, Ardargie House has now been demolished.

Earlier forms: 1483 'Ardargy', 1505 'Ardargze', 1860 'Ardargie Mains', 'Ardargie Hill'.

Derivation: Gaelic 'Airde', height or point. '-argie' may be from a form such as Gaelic 'Fheirge', the genitive of an earlier form of the name of the River Farg, which rises about 1.8

miles from Ardargie Hill. The 1505 form quoted above is consistent with this suggestion, and compare Culfargie, OS square 1617, which is 'neuk of Farg', and Aberargie, OS square 1615, which is 'confluence of Farg'.

***Ardgowny**, a settlement, approximate OS square 0912, last on record in 1750. The name is presumably related to Auchengownie, in the same OS square.

Earlier form: 1659 'Ardgownie'.

Derivation: Gaelic 'Airde Gamhnaigh', height or point of stirk place, from 'Gamhainn', a stirk.

Arecaria Wood GR 192126. This may be from the botanical term 'Araucaria', "a genus of lofty coniferous trees native to the southern hemisphere" (OED).

***Argyle**, a settlement, approximate OS square 2113, on record in 1783. This was perhaps named for the chief of Clan Campbell. The nearby barony of Abernethy was held by the Earl of Argyll from 1528 to 1543 at least.

Arlick Hill GR 093105. Earlier: 1827 'Arlick Hill'.

Derivation: Gaelic 'Airde Lice', rock or stone slab height.

Arlick Burn GR 060055, **Arlick Hill** GR 064055.

Earlier: c1796 'Arlick Burn', 1860 'Arlick Hill'.

Derivation: Gaelic 'Airde Lice', rock or stone slab height.

***Crook of Arnbathie** GR 096146 approximately. ***Crook D** is seemingly the burn at GR 095143. They are both on record in 1774.

Derivation: Scots 'Cruik', 'Cruke' &c, a bend, in placenames from the late 13th century. 'Arn-' could be for either Gaelic 'Airde', height or point, or Gaelic 'Earrann', portion of land, but '-bathie' is not clear to me. Crook 'D' is for Scots 'Digh' &c, shallow gully, watercourse.

***Arnfald**, a settlement, approximate OS square 8105, on record in 1783. This is perhaps close enough to The Arns, OS square 7903, to have been a secondary name from that holding?

Derivation: Scots 'Fa(u)ld', field, fold, pen &c, late 14th century on.

Arngask GR 138105, also the name of a parish and a former barony, **Arngask House** GR 139106. ***Arngask Miln**, GR 136110 approximately, was on record from 1628 to 1724 and was later known as 'Hay's Mill'.

Earlier forms: 1250 'Ardgrosc', 1287 'Ardengrost', 1388 'Arncorst', 1628 'Mill of Arngosk', 1654 'Arngosk Kirk', 1742-4 'Arngask Miln', 1761 'the barrony of Balvaird or Arngask', 1855-6 'Part of the Mill Lands of Arngask called Hay's Mill', 1860 'Arngask House'.

Derivation: Gaelic 'Earrann na gCrasg', division of land at the crossings, or 'Airde na gCrasg', height of the crossings. The 13th century forms quoted above appear to authenticate 'r' in the final syllable. Gaelic 'Gasg', a tail-like piece of land, may have influenced a later reinterpretation of the name.

See also Hay's Mill.

***Arniedike**. In 1783 the name for what is now Easter Balquhandy. See Balquhandy.

The Arns GR 794034. Earlier: 1750 'Arns'.

Derivation: Possibly Gaelic 'Earrann', division or portion of land, with the Scots plural. A Scots plural ending is commonly present when a holding is, or has been, composed of more than one unit, or when an earlier Gaelic name taken over into Scots was understood as a plural form.

Ashentrool GR 826999, a hillside.

Earlier references: 1451 'Lessyntrule', 1635 'Ashintrule', 1784 'Ashintrule or Loss'.

Rennie McOwan, that prolific writer on the Ochils, names 'Auld Meg of Ashintrool' as one of the Logie witches.

Derivation: There appear to have been two closely related sites: Gaelic 'Ais an t-Sruthail' & 'Lios an t-Sruthail', hill, and enclosure, of the wee burn. See also Luss.

Athron Hall & **Athronhall Cottage** both GR 097067. Given in c1796 & 1828 as 'Hawthorn Hall', but if this was a reinterpretation or an error, the derivation might be Gaelic 'Ath Shròin', point ford, ford at the point.

Auchengownie GR 091122, a settlement. Earlier form: 1502 'Auchingouny'.

Derivation: Gaelic 'Achadh Gamhnaigh', 'field' at stirk place, from 'Gamhainn', a stirk, with locative '-aigh' ending. See also Ardgowny & Gowenyhall which seem to be related sites.

In this and other 'Auch-', 'Auchen-', 'Auchin-' &c names, Gaelic 'Achadh' should probably be understood as a piece of land cleared for grazing or cultivation, the modern notion 'field' being misleading in the context.

Auchenharry Burn GR 876987. The ground is too high and steep for a permanent settlement to be likely, so this may well be from a lost primary name along the lines of Gaelic 'Achadh na h-Airigh', 'field' of the shieling. For sense of 'Achadh' see previous entry.

***Auchinbie**, a settlement, approximate OS square 7902, on record between 1442 & 1815.

Earlier forms: 1442 'Achinvy', 1506 'Auchinbie', 1713 'Knows of Auchinbae', 1766 'Achnbee Mill Kippendavie'.

Derivation: From Gaelic 'Achadh', 'field' (for sense see Auchengownie), perhaps followed by the Gaelic genitive article 'of the'. For the last syllable Gaelic 'Bigh', pillar, post, is one possibility, though if the 'v' of 1442 is reliable a masculine noun such as 'Biadh', food, fodder, is more likely.

Nether Auchlinsky GR 002026, **Auchlinsky House**, on record in 1860, GR 990044 approximately, **Auchlinsky Hill** GR 987024. **Auchlinsky Burn** rises at GR 986018.

Earlier forms: In a document of 1251-1258 a name taken to be this item is only legible as '[ ]clasky' and a late 13th to early 14th century endorsement reads 'Hachlasky'. 1483-4 'Ovir Auchinlesky', 1496 'Nether Auchlanesky', 1507 'Over Auchinlensky', 1569 'Auchlanskyburne', 1860 'Auchlinsky Hill'

The charter from which the 1569 form comes indicates that a cross had earlier stood at the source of the Auchlinsky Burn.

Derivation: On the evidence of the 15th century forms, the position of 'n' and 'l' was inverted from the late 15th century onwards. Gaelic 'Achadh an Fhleasgaich', 'field' of the young man or hero, is a possibility. For the sense of 'Achadh' see Auchengownie.

Auchtenny GR 069103, a settlement, ***Aughtenny Hill**, on record between 1796 & 1828, GR 057098 approximately.

Earlier forms: 1371 'Achteveny', 1505-10 'Auchtewny', 'Auchtewinny' &c, 1595 'Achteny', 1616 'Auchteveny', c1796 'Aughtenie Hill', 1860 'Auchtenny Wood'.

Derivation: Gaelic 'Achadh', 'field' (for sense here see Auchengownie) seems certain enough. The 'v' and the 'w' in the second syllable of the 1317 & 1505-10 forms imply a 'v' sound, written 'bh' or 'mh' in Gaelic. 'Achadh Taobh (an) Aonaich', field beside the hill-slope or moor, with subsequent loss of stress on 'Aonaich', would fit the location.

Auchtermuchty Common is marked on recent OS maps as parts of OS squares 2412 & 2413, & an area South of Glassart Den centred on GR 227134. Also **Auchtermuchty Burn** GR 233130, **Auchtermuchty Bleachfield**, on record in 1860, & **Bleachfield House**, both GR 234129.

The areas in OS squares 2412 & 2413 now marked 'Auchtermuchty Common' were earlier part of Whitefield Common (q.v.). In 1591 the extent of Auchtermuchty Common was approximately equivalent to OS squares 2111, 2211, 2012, 2112, 2212, the W half of 2312, 2013, 2113, the SW half of 2213 & the SW corner of 2313. Macfarlane (1722, see Bibliography) calls the common 'Auchtermuchty hill' and continues: "in some parts of that hill there are caves supposed to be digg'd by the ancient Picts, but for the most part filled up with earth".

Earlier forms: 1591 'frie commoun in monte de (ie in the hill of) Auchtermuchtie', 1654 'the Hills of Auchtermuchtie', 1769 'Auchtermuchty Common', 'Auchtermuchty Burn'.

Derivation: These are secondary names from Auchtermuchty OS square 2311, from Gaelic 'Uachdar' and Gaelic (Old Irish) 'Muccatu', upland at swine place.

The present Backhills. (AW)

B

Baadhead GR 005127, a settlement.

Earlier forms: 1783 'Badhead', 1855 'Bandhead', 1905 'Boadshead'.

Derivation: Perhaps a hybrid from Gaelic 'Bad', spot, place, or clump of trees, and Scots 'Heid' &c, upper part of rising ground, top of a hill or brae, late 15th century on. 1855 'Bandhead' is perhaps influenced by Scots 'Band', a ridge, early 19th century.

Back Burn GR 973047, on record since 1860. This name commonly refers to the position of a burn in relation to some other feature. There are also burns with this name at GR 898080, at GR 000001, at GR 026080 (on record since 1860), in approx OS square 0715 (recorded in 1860 only), and in OS square 9298 (recorded, as far as I know, only by Gibson – see Bibliography – who also calls it 'Tillicoultry House Burn'). Finally, yet another Back Burn, on a map of 1829, appears to rise at GR 002079.

Back Hills, on record between 1769 & 1819, and named because of their position on the North boundary of Tillicoultry parish, in contrast to Fore Bank and Forehills (q.v.). Also **Backhill** GR 911045, a farmhouse on record since 1860 but which has since 1952 been under Upper Glendevon Reservoir, and is replaced by **Backhills** GR 912035.

Backhill farmhouse lies under Upper Glendevon Reservoir, approximately in the centre of the photograph. (AW)

Earlier forms: 1769 'Back Hill of Broich', 1792 'the back hills', 1860 'Backhill' (a settlement).

The earlier sources refer to "the Back Hills" as if this was the name of an area: in 1819 it stretched from Ben Buck OS square 8901 to the Broich Burn. The earlier farm and dwelling appear to have been called 'Bruach' &c until the mid 19th century – see Broich Burn.

***Badds**, a settlement, approximate OS square 0512. I have come across record of this only between 1771 & 1783. Earlier form: 1771 'Baads'.

Derivation: Gaelic 'Bad' in the sense of a spot, place, clump of trees, with the Scots plural probably indicating division of the holding at some time.

Upper Badenheath. See Banheath, the more recent form of the name.

Bain Craig GR 230120, now a settlement name.

Derivation: Gaelic 'Bàn Chreag', white crag, but in the absence of early forms the surname 'Bain', or even Scots 'Bane', bone, with the Scots loanword 'Craig', crag, are also possible.

White Stane of Tam Baird GR 941991.

Earlier form: 1769 'White stone of Tombaird'.

The 1860 OS Name Book says this is something of a mixture of whinstone and white marble, that the local tradition was that it had been erected to commemorate a battle between Wallace and the English, and that there was "no doubt whatsoever" that it was "druidical"!

Derivation: Gaelic 'Tom Bàird', bard's knoll, may well be behind 'Tam Baird'.

Craig Bakie GR 026089, a crag, **Craigbakie Hill** GR 026094, **Craigbakie**, a settlement on record between 1530 and 1860.

Earlier forms: 1530 'Cragbake', 1630 'the Rig of Craigbakie', 1799 'Craigbaikie including the pendicle called Rigg', 1860 'Craig Bakie', 'Craigbakie Hill'. Macfarlane (1723 – see Bibliography) describes Craigbakie as a "room", ie a subsidiary or rented holding, of Kippen OS square 0112.

Derivation: Gaelic 'Creag' plus, possibly, Gaelic 'Bacaidh', giving 'crag of hindrance', referring to tethering of animals. Note also Scots 'Baikie' &c, an iron or wooden peg to which a tether was fastened, 19th to early 20th centuries, but this is much too late in Scots to be possible here, and in any case the word order makes a Gaelic original more likely.

***The Bala Slap**. See The Balloch, for which this is an alternative name.

***Balcalk**, described as a pendicle in 1821, approximate OS square 9611. I have found this on record only between 1783 & 1821.

Earlier form: 1783 'Balchalk'.

Derivation: Gaelic 'Baile Chalcain', Calcan's steading, might be a possibility here.

Balcanquhal House GR 159107, **Newton of Balcanquhal** GR 158106, **Balcanquhal** GR 162099, all settlements.

Earlier references: 1494 'Bawcanquell', 1505-10 'Balcancoll', 'Balcanquhale' & 'Balcankell', 1531 'Newtoun of Balcancoll', 1654 'N Balcanquell', 1827 'Balcanquhal', 1860 'Balcanquhal Plantation'. Earliest surname forms: 1340 'Belmacancolle', 1373 'Balcanko', 1395 'Balmacankow'.

Derivation: Gaelic 'Baile', a 'toun', a steading, unless the 1494 form quoted above indicates Gaelic 'Both', a cottage, a dwelling. For '-canquhal' Gaelic 'Ceann Coille', (at) wood end, has been suggested. Alternatively 'ma' in the early surname forms raises the possibility of a saint's name being present as these were commonly preceded by the affectionate Gaelic 'mo', my. Gaelic 'Baile' and 'Mac', 'toun of the sons of', plus a secular personal name, is also possible.

Bald Hill GR 933039, **Baldhill Burn** GR 934038. Both are on record since 1860.

Baldie's Burn GR 992007, **Baldiesburn**, a settlement, GR 993003. On record since 1860 and 1855 respectively.

Derivation: A reference to St Baldred could lie behind this name? Alternatively, Scots 'Ba(u)ldie' can be a diminutive of Archibald, or for that matter of Garibaldi!

Baldmony Knowe GR 993035. On record since 1860.

The 1860 OS Name Book points out that this hill was nearly covered by the plant 'Baldmony', Scots 'Bad-money', 'Bald-money' &c, the gentian, the spignel, 19th to early 20th centuries. Haldane (1944 – see Bibliography) mentions this plant as growing in the Ochils: "a flower known locally as 'bald mingie' or St Baldred's money, though I think the full name is Meum Athamanticum". The presence of the plant on this hill and of the settlement name 'Balmony' in the same OS square is one of those coincidences which help to make placename study unpredictable. Normally I would say with confidence that 'Balmony' is Gaelic 'Baile Monaidh', hill or moor steading, and that the hill took its name from the settlement, later being reinterpreted as 'Baldmony' because of the presence of the plant. However, as I have come across no reference to Balmony (the settlement) earlier than recent OS maps, this one must be considered not proven.

Balgower GR 868075, a settlement. Earlier forms: 1547 (perhaps this site) 'Ballegoir', 1830 'Bellgowan', 1855 'Balgour'.

Derivation: Gaelic 'Baile Gobhair', goat steading, or, if the 1830 form is reliable, Gaelic 'Baile Gobhainn', smith's steading.

Balhaldie GR 813053, **Inns of Balhaldie** GR 814052, **Burnside of Balhaldie** GR 818051, **Mains of Balhaldie** GR 822058, **Woodside of Balhaldie** GR 818061, all settlements. Also **Balhaldie Toll** GR 812053 approximately, with **Toll Wood** OS squares 8104 & 8105, both on record in 1863 but both now disappeared. ***Burn of Balhadie**, recorded in c1723, appears to be the burn at GR 818060.

Earlier forms: 1271 'Buchaldy', 1483 'Boithaldy', 1526 'Bochaldy', 1611 'Balhadie', 1650 'Balhadies & Mylne', 1666 'Balhaddies alias Bohaddies', 1720 'Woodsyde of Balhaldie', 1750 'Lairhill of Ballhadie' (ie Lairhill, OS square 8302), 1783 'Burnside', 1803 'Lairhill & Pittack, Broadleyside, Langbank & Muir, being parts of the Barony of Balhaldies', 1855 'Mains'.

Balhaldie was a seat of the Drummond clan, earlier MacGregor. Drummond (1851 p291 – see Bibliography) writes: "Duncan Drummond of Culcrieff and Balhadie was one of a tribe of the Clan Gregor ... On the proscription of the name of MacGregor, AD 1603 he took that of Drummond". By 1796 Balhaldie was again held in the name of a MacGregor: "Alexander McGrigor, formerly Drummond". The

MacGregors of Balhaldie were known as 'Clann Iain Mhalaich', the race of bushy-browed John, from Gaelic 'Malach', and Black (see Bibliography) says the surname Malloch originated from them.

Derivation: The early forms show that this is not a 'Baile' name – indeed alternative spellings in 'Bo-' appear well into the 19th century – but it had begun to be reinterpreted as 'Bal-' by 1611. By that date the second 'l' was, or was sometimes, silent, as it is today. Either Gaelic 'Both Choillte', woods dwelling, or Gaelic 'Both a' Challtainn', hazel dwelling, could be the derivation.

Ballieliesk GR 001013. ***Middle Ballieliesk** was the modern **Middlehall** GR 994007, so **Westerhall** GR 989005 may well represent the earlier ***Wester Ballieliesk**.

Earlier forms: 1540 'Bellilisk', 1574 'middle third of Bellelisk', 'east third of Bellelisk', 1650 'Bellilisk' ('wester', 'midle', 'easter'), 1800 'Easter Ballilisk', 'Wester Ballilisk', 1855 'Westerhall', 1860 'Middlehall'.

Derivation: My earliest forms do not confirm the expected Gaelic 'Baile', steading, but do not rule it out. The final syllable could be Gaelic 'Leisg', idle, unwilling, perhaps applied to the land in the same way as Scots 'Sweerie' was to the old holding at GR 230180?

Ballingall GR 104046. Earlier forms: 1372 'Estirbalnegalle', 1505 'Ballingall', 1654 'Hilton of Binnaga' (ie Hilton GR 108046). Surname forms: 1478 'Bangall', 1478 & 1489 'Ballingall'. Black (see Bibliography) says the surname from these lands was common in Newburgh in the mid 16th century.

Derivation: Gaelic 'Baile nan Gall', foreigners' or strangers' steading. 'Gall' often meant 'non-Gael' and so may indicate an Anglian or perhaps Norman presence here, as it may have done at Glassingall, OS square 7904.

Ballo Burn GR 180145, **Ballomill Hill** GR 183145, **Ballomill** GR 188162. Earlier forms: 1189 'terra de Belach', 1526 'Bello-mylne', 1650 'Ballo', 1722 'The Balou Water', 1792 'Ballo Burn', 1797 'Miln called Provost Miln or Ballomiln', 'ground on the West side of the Ballomiln called the Balloburnbrae'.

Derivation: Gaelic 'Bealach', a pass. The burn rises below a col which is crossed by a track.

The Balloch 836003. Described as "A Pass" by the 1860 OS Name Book.

Derivation: Gaelic 'Bealach', a pass. The site is also known as 'The Bala Slap' from Scots 'Slap', a pass or shallow valley between hills, making this a good example of a description duplicated in two languages.

***Ballyman**, on record between 1663 & 1829, approximate OS square 9709. Also ***Outtown of Balyeoman**, on record in 1783, an area around OS squares 9808 & 9908 to either side of Coul Burn: 'Outer Park' appears in that vicinity in 1829, possibly as a relic of this 'Outtown'.

Earlier forms: 1663 'Balzieman', 1747 'Balgeman', 1771 'Balyeaman'.

Derivation: Gaelic 'Baile Eamainn', Eamonn's steading.

The Balmanno Hill Rocking Stone. Drawing by Ken Laing.

Balmanno Hill GR 140145, a secondary name from Balmanno OS square 1415. There is a rocking stone on the SE extremity of the hill.

Derivation: Gaelic 'Baile Mhanach' or 'Baile nam Manach', monks' steading.

Balmony GR 993037. This is discussed under Baldmony Knowe.

Balquhandy GR 033117, called '**Middle Balquhandy**' in 1860, **Balquhandy Cottage** GR 036118, **Wester Balquhandy** GR 031117, **Balquhandy Hill** GR 032109, **Balquhandy Burn** GR 040121. Also **Easter Balquhandy**, recorded between 1855 & 1860, GR 037118 approximately.

Earlier forms: 1428 'Buchondy', 1487-8 'de duobus Buchquhandiis', 1513 'Bouchondy', 1610 'North & South Balquhandie', 1683 'Buquhandie', 1699-1701 'Over Balquhandie', 1792 'Boquhandies' & 'Balquhandie', 1855 'Balquhandy' ('Easter', 'Middle' & 'Wester'), 1860 'Balquhandy Burn', 'Balquhandy Hill'.

The Scots plural in earlier forms of the name arose from the holding being multiple. Mr G Ritchie says Wester Balquhandy was formerly 'Westerdele' and Easter Balquhandy 'Arniedike', names which are given on Stobie's map of 1783.

Derivation: I have no 'Bal-' form earlier than

the early 17th century so Gaelic 'Both', a hut, a cottage, a dwelling, is probably behind the first syllable. It seems likely that this was reinterpreted from the late 15th or early 16th century by analogy with the numerous 'Bal-' names. 'quh' – in Scots orthography often interchangeable with 'wh' – here probably represents an aspirated Gaelic 'c', pronounced 'ch' as in 'loch'. It is tempting then to identify the second part of our name with Condie (q.v.), some 2 miles distant; ie 1428 'Buchondy' could be for 'Both Chondaigh', cottage, or dwelling, belonging to Condy. I have no external evidence to support this possible connection, though the lie of the land between the two sites would have made communication relatively easy.

Balquharn GR 866973, ***Balquharn Glen**, on record in 1848, & **Balquharn Burn**, both GR 866975.

Earlier forms: 1315-21 'Balecharn', 1621 'Balquharne'.

Derivation: Gaelic 'Baile a' Chàirn', cairn steading.

Balvaird Castle GR 170115, **Balvaird** GR 173123, which appears as 'Meikle *Bein*' (q.v.) on the OS 1" map of 1901, **Balvaird Cottage** GR 182127. Earlier forms: 1295 'Baleward', 1507 'Balvarde', 1671 'Milne of Balvaird', 1761 'the barrony of Balvaird or Arngask', 1860 'Balvaird' (ie site of castle), 'Balvaird Cottage'. Black (see Bibliography) says a surname came from these lands, his earliest surname reference is 1530 'Balvaird'.

The castle has been restored in 1991-2.

Derivation: Gaelic 'Baile a' Bhàird', the poet's steading, probably indicating the site of land granted to a poet when Gaelic custom was still being observed in the area. Only later did the name become attached to a centre of feudal power when the castle was built in the 15th century, probably after the Gaelic period.

***Ban**, a settlement, approx OS square 0113, which I have come across only once, in 1783.

Derivation: Perhaps Scots 'Ban', a range of hills, a ridge of a hill, early 16th & early 19th centuries.

Banekist Burn runs from GR 992114 to the Duncrub Burn. Earlier: On record in 1860. It passes through ***The Bein Kist**, OS square 9912, a steep gully on the face of Rossie Law.

Derivation: It seems likely that gully and burn once had the same name but that the name of one of them was later reinterpreted. Scots 'Bane Kist', coffin, dates from the late 14th century. Scots 'Bein', 'Bien', with the senses 'cosy', late 15th century on, and 'well-stocked', 18th century on, seems a less likely original!

Banheath GR 906077, a settlement, **Benheath Quarry** GR 909081. Earlier forms: 1373 'Bardynhathe', 1608 'Nether Badinheith', 1636 'Banheath', 1667 'Over Bedinheth', 1783 'Upper Banheath' (ie modern Banheath), 1824 'Nether Banheath', 1855 'Badenheath', 'Banheath Quarry', 'Banheath Park', 1860 'Upper Badenheath'.

Balvaird Castle after restoration. Drawing by Ken Laing.

Derivation: The 14th century form 'Bardynhathe' (if reliable) is perhaps a hybrid from Gaelic 'Bàrd', meadow, followed by the Gaelic genitive article, 'of the', and Scots 'Heath', with 'Bàrd' later reinterpreted by analogy with 'Bad-' names and intervocalic 'd' disappearing to give the doublet 'Banheath'.

***Bank Burn** GR 940005. This is said by Beveridge (see Bibliography) and others to be a 19th century name for the Burn of Sorrow (see Burn of *Care*). The presence of Bank Hill OS sq 9599 and the Bank Muir OS sq 9300 seems to lend credibility to this, though Mr. Richard Bernard, whose knowledge of the Southern Ochils is very detailed, gives the name 'Bank Burn' to a small stream feeding the Sorrow, rising W of Bank Hill, OS sq 9599.

***The Bank Muir**, on record in 1779, lies SW of Priest Goat Burn, around OS sq 9300. It was described as a "Commonty", ie common land.

West Bank Burn is the burn at GR 131070. Earlier: On record since c1796.

***Bank Head**, on record in 1775, was a settlement at GR 251123 approximately.

Bank Hill GR 953992. Earlier: On record since 1860.

Bankfold, a settlement, GR 972097. Earlier: On record since 1855.

Bankfoot, a settlement, GR 092074. Earlier: On record since c1796.

Easter Bankhead GR 072110. Earlier: 1837 'Bankhead', 1855 'Easter Bankhead', 1860 'Bankhead'.

Bannaty GR 162085, a settlement, **Bannaty Mill** GR 178087. ***Bannetty Bank**, on record in 1750, appears to be modern Yellow Hill OS sq 1509.

Earlier forms: 1358 'Banochtyne', 1505 'Bannachty', 1621 'Bannatye Mill'. Earliest surname reference: 1536 'Bannaty'.

Derivation: From Gaelic (Middle Irish) 'Bendachtu', blessing, in the sense of a blessed place. Eclmurghuall (q.v.) was nearby.

***Craig Banochy** GR 962116. This appears as a field name on a plan of Cloanden Estate of 1862, but is surely from the tree-grown rocky mound or roundel clearly visible from the road leading up to Cloan.

Derivation: Gaelic 'Creag Bheannachaidh', blessing rock.

Barclayfield GR 167145, a settlement. Earlier: 1812 'Barclay-field'. According to Mackie (see Bibliography) "From 1332 to 1507 the Barclay family occupied the seat of power in the Barony of Fourgie", now Fargie OS square 1512, little more than a mile away.

Craig Banochy beside Cloan House. (AW)

Derivation: Feasibly from the surname, which itself probably originates from the town of Berkeley in Gloucestershire. Black (see Bibliography) records the surname in Scotland in 1165.

Bardrill GR 912080, a settlement, **Bardrill Burn** GR 918080.

Earlier forms: 1172 'Barderal', 1234 'Barderel', 1483 'Berdrale-Haldane', 1604 'Bairdrell', 1791 'Over Bardrell', 1824 'town and lands of Over & Nether Bardrills', 1855 'East Bardrill', 'West Bardrill' (ie seemingly modern Bardrill), 1860 'Bardrill Burn'. The 'Bardrill' of 1860 was at GR 918082 approximately.

Derivation: Gaelic 'Bàrd', meadow. It is suggested in Appendix III of the Inchaffray Charters (see Bibliography) that 'erel' of the 1234 form quoted may be the same as modern Welsh 'erwyll', gloomy, dusky.

***Bargain Meadow**, on record to 1736, is an area between Core Hill OS square 8804 and Greenforet OS square 8601, approximately. Earlier: 1654 'Bargan Medow'.

Derivation: This area lies between approximately 400 and 630 metres above sea level and so the 'meadow' may have been summer hill pasture. There are old shielings near Core Hill. For Scots 'Bargan' DOST has 'Contention, conflict, combat, struggle', 1560, and 'a bargain or business transaction', 1571. OED gives 'Bargain' as an obsolete term for a small farm holding, c1600 to late 19th century, though with no Scottish examples.

Barley Mill, disused, GR 126103. Earlier: 1790 'the mill lands of Barleymill of Glendy', 1812 'Barleymiln'.

This was a farm belonging to the estate of Paris OS square 1312.

Barnaigh GR 877973. "An 1860's mansion at the foot of Carnaughton Glen" (Swan – see Bibliography). Johnston (see Bibliography) has this as 'Barnaich' which he explains as Gaelic 'Bâirneach', a limpet, the name of a house clinging to the hillside.

Barnbrae, a dwelling at GR 160084, on record from 1860 to 1901.

***Barnhill** GR 082119 approximately. Earlier forms: This was 'Beirnhill' in 1627 and I have last seen it on record in the late 19th century when it was 'Barnhill of Struie', from Struie OS square 0711.

Barroway Burn GR 210106. Earlier: 1722 'a water called Barroway'.

Derivation: Perhaps the same as the Irish river 'Bearbha', the Barrow, whose Gaelic name is related to the idea 'to boil'. More likely perhaps is Gaelic 'Allt a' Bharrach Mhaigh', burn of the dominating plain, from some prominent site near which the burn flows.

Baulk Hill GR 077091. A secondary name from Baulk of Struie OS square 0709. Derivation: Scots 'Baulk', a dividing ridge or dyke.

Baw Hills GR 227162, on record since 1860. The Bow Burn rises close by so the names could originally have been connected.

Beatie Burn GR 143075. Earlier: c1796 'Beatie Burn', 1860 'Beatie Bridge'.

Derivation: From the surname?

Glen Bee GR 900053. Earlier: 1783 'Glenbee'.

Derivation: Note the Gaelic word order. One possibility might be Gaelic 'Gleann na Bìghe', glen of the post or pillar.

The Head of Glen Bee, with a glimpse of the Upper Glendevon Reservoir. (AW)

Beggars Burn GR 210141. Earlier forms: 1590 'Colsay-burne alias Auchtermuchtie-burne' (named from Colzie OS square 2114), 1860 'Beggars Burn'. Also known as Glassart Burn (q.v.) which may well be from an earlier Gaelic name. Snoddy (see Bibliography) says it is 'the Colzie' in its upper reaches (compare the 1590 form quoted) and 'Loverspool Burn' where it flows through Auchtermuchty.

***The Bein Kist**. See Banekist Burn.

***Meikle Bein**, a settlement, on record between 1775 and 1901. This appears, from OS 1" 1901, to be on the site of the present Balvaird, GR 172122. It was "much resorted to" as a preaching venue at the time of the Seceders. Mackay (1896 p158 – see Bibliography) quotes an eye-witness in 1776: "The same spirit that assembled the Covenanters at Loudon Hill draws together the Seceders of this day annually to the Muckle Ben, generally in June and July".

Derivation: Scots 'Muckle', 'Meikle', was applied to the larger of two farms of the same name, from the 14th century on. The smaller farm in this case was Little Binn. See also Binn Hill.

Beins Law GR 185123, a hill, though it appears as a settlement name in 1636.

Derivation: Presumably named from one of the Binn holdings, perhaps Meikle *Bein* (q.v.) OS square 1712. See also Binn Hill.

Beld Hill GR 983112, **Beldhill Burn** GR 986110. Also **Nether Beldhill** GR 983108 approximately & **Upper Beldhill** GR 985107 (both last on record in 1860 and marked "in ruins"). Earlier forms: 1539 (perhaps our site) 'Beldhill', 1829 'Nether Beld Hill', 1860 'Beld Hill', 'Beldhill Burn'.

Derivation: Scots 'Beld', bald, 15th century on.

Bellshill 963103, a settlement. ***Pendicle of Billshill** is on record in 1800.

Earlier forms: 1635 'Beleshill', 1681 'Bellhill', 1800 'Bills Hill', 1855 'Bellshill'. See also Connel's Spout.

***Belly Slack**, on record in 1801, GR 093151.

Derivation: Scots 'Slack', a hollow between hills, a pass, frequent in placenames from the late 14th century. Where Scots 'Slack' is present there is often the possibility that it represents an earlier Gaelic 'Sloc', a hollow.

Bengengie Hill GR 869002.

Derivation: Gaelic 'Beinn na Teangaidh', tongue hill, hill of the tongue of land, is possible here.

***How of the Bent**. An unidentified site on Sheriffmuir on record in 1766. It may be connected with Howe OS square 8105.

Bentie Knowe GR 960027, a hill. Earlier: On record in 1860.

Derivation: Scots 'Benty', covered in bent grass, late 16th to 19th centuries.

***Berclayishauch** and ***Berclais-landis**, last found in 1541 and 1532 respectively and both in Forgandenny barony.

Earlier: 1482-3 'Barclayshaugh', 1512-3 'Barkclaisland'.

Derivation: Not unlikely to be connected with the Barclays of Fourgie, like Barclayfield OS square 1614 (q.v.).

***The Berry Bank Moss**, on record in 1769. It extended from GR 928003 to GR 923994, approximately.

Berry Hill GR 889054, on record since 1860.

Berry Hill GR 952044, **Berry Burn** GR 958034. Earlier: 1860 'Berry Hill'.

Berry Hill GR 117126, **Berry Wood** and **Berryhill Wood** both OS square 1112. **Berryknowe**, a settlement at GR 119120, has been on record since 1736. I do not know if it is the same as the farm of 'Berryhill', found between 1742 and 1856.

***Berryden**, a settlement, occurs in 1783 in OS square 0716 approximately.

Berryhill Farm GR 258159. Earlier forms: 1558 'Berry-hill', 1565 'Berryholl', 1593 'Berryhill' & 'Berryholl', 1595 'Berryhall', 1617 'Berriehoill', 1699 'Berrieholl', 1860 'Berryhall'. 'Hill', 'Hall' and 'Hole' are not uncommonly interchanged in earlier placenames, as they are here. We cannot always be sure whether we are seeing inconsistent transcription, or genuine alternative names for the site.

The Bein Inn photographed by Magnus Jackson in the late 1800s. The building behind, at the other side of the Balvaird road, is now the inn. Reproduced by permission of Perth Museum and Art Gallery.

Big Knowe 051117. Earlier: On record since 1860.

Easter Biggs GR 869067, **Wester Biggs** GR 865061.

Earlier: 1666 'Biggs', 1669 'Biggs of Kincardine', 1761 'Biggs of Ogilvie', 1808 'parts of the Barony of Ogilvy viz ... Biggs & ... Biggs arable farm', 1824 'Biggs Hillfarm, Biggs arable farm', 1860 'Easter Biggs', 'Wester Biggs'.

Derivation: Perhaps related to Scots 'Biggins', buildings, 14th century on.

The Bike GR 801996. A "cascade" (1860 OS Name Book).

Earlier: On record since 1860.

Derivation: Note Scots 'Byke' in the sense of a wasps' or bees' nest, here perhaps with reference to the noise of the water?

Billage Brae GR 236154. This is possibly to be compared with Bialaid in Badenoch which WJ Watson (see Bibliography) relates to Gaelic (Old Irish) 'Belat', a cross road, a path. It overlooks the route from Auchtermuchty to Newburgh.

Binn Hill GR 172138, **Binn Wood** GR 163135, **Binn Burn** GR 170130, **Binn**, a settlement, GR 172134, **The Bein Inn** GR 161131. ***Cotton of Binn** is on record between 1683 and 1791. **Beinsnook** TP (ie Turnpike), found in 1860 at GR 159131, was known as 'Waterloo Toll' in 1828. See also **Beins Law** GR 185123 & ***Meikle *Bein*** GR 172122.

Earlier forms: 1295 'Beyn', 1507-8 'Bene', 1636 'Bennslaw', 1643 'Binn', 1683 'Cottoune of Binne', 1750 'House of Binn', 'Little Binn', 1775 'Binn', 'Little Beans', 'Mickle Beans', 1783 'Cottown of Bein', 1825 'Beansnook', 1827 'Binnhill', 1828 'Glen Farg Inn' (later the Bein Inn), 1855-6 'Bein Inn', 1860 'Bein's Law', 1901 'Meikle Bein' (now Balvaird).

Derivation: From Gaelic 'Beinn', a hill. *The Concise Scots Dictionary* has 'Bin(n)' as a loanword in Scots since only the late 18th century. The senses of Scots 'Bein' or 'Bien', cosy, comfortable, well-stocked, make of 'The Bein Inn' a neat play on words. For 'Cotto(w)n' &c in earlier forms see Cottown OS square 0615.

Binzian GR 074153, **Binzian Mill** (for corn & barley in c1860) GR 076149, **Over Binzian** GR 073141, all settlements, and **Binzian Burn** GR 060125.

Earlier forms: 1473 'le Bunyane' & 1488 'Benzane', 1505-6 'Binzeane', 'Byngzane', 'Bynzean' & 'Bynzeane' , 1623 'Binzian Milnes', 1720 'Binging', 1750 'Bingin Burn', late 19th century 'Over Binzian'.

Derivation: Gaelic 'Binnean' or 'Beinnean', a small hill, perhaps from the spur of ground at the end of which Binzian stands. Haliburton (see Bibliography) says the pronunciation in his time (c1900) was "Bingen", as it still is. 'z', 'y' and 'g' in earlier Scots orthography were all used to represent the semi-vowel [j] and in the case of this name a spelling pronunciation seems to have developed based on 'g' spellings.

Birken Glen GR 877009. Derivation: 'Glen', the Scots loanword from Gaelic 'Gleann', in placenames from the 12th century; plus Scots 'Birken', having birch trees, in placenames from the late 12th century.

***Birne Hill**. An unidentified site on Sheriffmuir recorded in 1766. The name may be related to Burniepark Burn OS square 8301? For possible derivations see the next entry.

Birniehill GR 126078, a settlement on record since 1750.

Derivation: Scots 'Hill of the wee burn' is the obvious possibility. Alternatively '-birnie' can be for St Brénnainn or Brendan, or for Gaelic 'Braonaigh', the locative of 'Braonach', meaning 'at moist place'.

***Bishops Boug** (ie Bog) is found in 1736. It was East of Lairhill GR 833026.

Black Cairn GR 233172, **Black Cairn Hill** GR 234169.

Earlier: 1722 'the Black Kairn', 1860 'Black Cairn Hill'. According to Macfarlane in 1722 (see Bibliography), Black Cairn was considered to be the beginning of the Ochil Hills.

Black Craigs GR 084108. On record since 1860.

***Black Dub** GR 965080? Found on a plan of Foswell estate of c1800.

Derivation: Scots 'Dub', a pool, especially of muddy or stagnant water, late 15th century on.

***Black Dub** GR 034138.

Derivation: Scots 'Dub', a pool, especially of muddy or stagnant water, late 15th century on.

Black Hill GR 839032. Earlier: 1736 'Black Hill' & 'Orchals Black Hill' (ie belonging to Orchill OS square 8711), 1855 'Blackhill' (a settlement), 1860 'Black Hill'.

Black Hill GR 966047, **Blackhill Burn** GR 967043. Both are on record since 1860.

Black Hill GR 066072. On record since c1796.

Black Law occurs in 1860 in OS square 0006 approximately. It may be the same as 'Black hill' on Stobie's map of 1783, in the same vicinity.

Black Law GR 028070. Earlier: 1615 'Blaklaw'. In 1615 this was part of the lands of Carnbo OS square 0503.

Black Linn is recorded in the OS 1860 Name Book and is a waterfall on the River Devon a little distance South of Downhill village OS square 9904. **Blacklinn Bridge** GR 994042 and **Linn Hill** GR 993042 have taken their name from it. Earlier: 1860 'Blacklinn Bridge'.

Black Linn GR 055043 is one of the Golland (q.v.) Linns and is on record from the early 19th century.

Black Loch GR 262150, **Black Burn** GR 265147.

Earlier references: 1510 'Blakloch', 1860 'Black Burn'. According to Macfarlane (see Bibliography), Black Loch was supposed to be very deep and full of springs. Wilkie (see Bibliography) says it was "supposed to be bottomless". He also calls it the 'Dhu Loch' (from Gaelic 'Dubh Loch', black loch) but I have seen no other confirmation that it had a Gaelic name. In 1614 the loch was part of the lands of Woodmill OS square 2715.

Black Rig GR 977030 and **Blackrig Burn** GR 975028, both on record since 1860.

Derivation: Scots 'Rig', a ridge, a hill crest, in place names from the late 12th century.

Black Wood GR 977052. Earlier: 1860 'Black Wood'.

Black Wood, which I have found only in 1860, was in OS square 1510 approximately.

***Blackberry Hill**. See Blaeberry Hill GR 028101, for which this was an alternative name.

***Blackfolds**, a settlement on record between 1766 and 1783 in approximate OS square 8001. Earlier: 1766 'Blackfold'.

Blackgoats Hill GR 997120, on record since 1860.

Derivation: As an alternative to the quadruped, this name could well contain Scots 'Goat', 'Gote', a ditch, drain, late 16th century on, or a watercourse, 17th century on. Interestingly, Dwelly (see Bibliography) has Gaelic 'Gobhar', goat, as also having in Perthshire the sense of watercourse, as a "sort of branching river".

Black-shed Wood GR 791996.

Derivation: Scots 'Shed', 'Shade', a strip of land, late 15th century on.

Blackthornduff Burn GR 939980, ***Whitehorn Duff**, in 1819 seemingly the burn at GR 935985.

Earlier forms: 1769 'Black horn Duff', 'White horn Duff', 1860 'Blackhornduff Burn'.

Derivation: Though we have no really early forms it is possible we have here a Gaelic original along the lines of 'Allt a' Chùirn Dhuibh', burn of the black horn, with horn in the sense of spur, promontory. The next stage would be for this to become 'Hornduff Burn' in Scots. Then, it is not uncommon for adjacent burns to have the same name and to be distinguished by 'White' and 'Black', and this may well have happened here. If this is correct then the final stage would be the reinterpretation of 'Blackhorn' as 'Blackthorn'.

Blaeberry Hill GR 028101, also known in the 18th century as **'Blackberryhill'**, **Blaeberry Toll**, now a dwelling, GR 024103, and **Blaeberryhill**, c1860 the ruins of a steading on Wester Balquhandy OS square 0311.

Blaeberry Toll served the drove road across the hills from Dunning to Muckhart. 1860 OS Name Book calls it 'Blaeberry TP' (ie Turnpike) and it is also known as 'Sky Toll'. Skymore Hill is close by.

Earlier references: 1574 'terras de Blaberryhill et Fairney-Knowis', 1650 'Blaeberriehills', 1738 'sunny half of the hill called Blackberryhill', 1799 'Blackberryhill', 1800 'North & South Blaeberryhill', 1860 'Blaeberry', 'Blaeberry Hill'.

Blair Hill, GR 993128, has been on record since 1860.

Derivation: Possibly Gaelic 'Blàr', a piece of level ground. The site forms a relatively level spur in otherwise steeply sloping ground.

Blair Hill GR 107103, **Blair Burn** GR 110101, **West Blair** GR 110102, **East Blair** GR 116102.

Earlier: 1580 (perhaps our site) 'Blairhill', 1771 'East Blair', 'West Blair', c1796 'Blair Burn', 1860 'Blair Hill'. Derivation: Gaelic 'Blàr', perhaps with the sense here of 'level spot' – it may be no coincidence that the next holding to West Blair is Plains.

Blairdenon Hill GR 865018. Earlier: 1860 'Blairdenon Hill'.

Derivation: Gaelic 'Blàr', level ground, perhaps referring to the comparatively level top of the hill. '-denon' is obscure to me.

Blairlogie. See Logie.

Blairnathort GR 136069, **Blairfield** GR 142070, **Blairhead** GR 145077, all settlements. I take the latter two to be secondary names from the first.

Earlier forms include: 1536 'Blairfortht', 1539 'Blairforth', 1553 'Blair de Forth', 1615 'Blearathort', 1616 'Blair of Forth', 1650 'Blair of Forth', 'Blairhead', 1750 'Blair Athort', 1775 'Blair of Forth', c1796 'Blairathort', 1803 'Blairnathort', 1827 'Blairathort', 1828 'Blairathort', 'Blairfield', 1836 'Blairathort', 1860

Blaeberry Toll on the Dunning to Muckhart road. Drawing by Ken Laing.

'Blairathort', 'Blairfield Plantation', 1901 'Blairathort'.

Derivation: These Blairnathort forms and the Milnathort forms quoted below suggest that there were variants of both these names co-existing over a considerable period. Blairnathort would seem to be a related site to Milnathort OS square 1205 &c, just over a mile away, or at least to have come under that name's influence. The 'n' occasionally found in our name after the 18th century may well result from analogy with 'Milnathort' mistakenly analysed as 'Mil(l) Nathort', though this 'n' presumably belongs with the first syllable as the ending of either Gaelic 'Muileann' or Scots 'Miln'. I believe Gaelic 'Muileann a' Choirthe', mill of the standing stone, has been suggested as an etymology for 'Milnathort' and this is consistent with 'Quhorthe' &c in some 16th & 17th century forms. Earlier forms for Milnathort include: 1372 'Milnethort', 1507 'Mills of Forth', 1524-5 'le Mylne de Quhorthe', 1654 'Thuartmills', 1665 'Milnes de Quorth', 1741-1774 'Milnathort'. The date given by CSD for Scots 'Athort', across, late 15th century on, makes it too late to be involved here except as a reinterpretation. 'Blair-' is no doubt from Gaelic 'Blàr', plain, field or marsh.

Blair's Den GR 015075. A considerable hollow between Muckle Rig and Little Rig (1860 OS Name Book). Perhaps from the surname?

Blairstruie, a settlement, GR 139136, **Blairstruie Hill** GR 135136, **Blairstruie Cottage** GR 142130.

Earlier forms: 1493 'Blastrowe', 1530 'Blairstrowy', 1679 'Blayrstruie'.

Derivation: In 1537 Blairstruie was held by Robert Barclay of Struie and had earlier been incorporated in the barony of Barclay Struie. It is feasible then that the name was originally formed from Struie OS square 0711.

Bleachfield House 234129. In 1860 this was the site of 'Auchtermuchty Bleachfield' and both are secondary names from Auchtermuchty (see Auchtermuchty Common).

Blind Well GR 115058. There are two possibilities here. Some wells are reputed to cure blindness. Alternatively, in Scots 'Blind' can be applied to water running underground or hidden by dense plant growth. DOST has "Ane blind well", 1534, in the sense of a hidden well.

Blindwell, a settlement on record in 1860, approximate OS sq 1510. For possible derivations see the previous entry.

Blinkbonny GR 125065, a settlement.

Derivation: In the sense of having a pleasant appearance? Compare, from the *Scottish National Dictionary* (see Bibliography), "There let your charms blink bonnilie" R. Gall *Poems*, 1819.

Blueton, a settlement, GR 856080, **Blueton Burn** GR 853080.

Earlier: 1551 (Perhaps our site) 'terra ecclesiastica de Dunblane vocata Bleto-Buttergask', 1579 (& 1789-1825) 'Blew-Buttirgask alias Wester Buttirgask', 1654 'Blewtoun', 1723 'the burn of Blucton' (sic), 1759 'Blewtoune of Bittergask', 1860 'Blueton', 'Blueton Burn'.

Derivation: A descriptive name? 'Blew' is an attested older Scots spelling for the colour.

***Bluidy Well**. On Clatchard Crag OS square 2417. Wallace and his men are said to have washed their swords here after a fight.

***Boar's Den** & ***Boar's Knowe**. This is the form in which the names are given by Simpkin (see Bibliography) in 1914. The sites were located on Craiginnan Hill Farm OS square 9600.

Earlier: 1793 'Bears Den', 'Bears Knowe'.

Derivation: The Old Statistical Account for Dollar parish (see Bibliography) says that King's Seat Hill (OS square 9399) was where "according to tradition the Kings of Scotland, then residing at Dunfermline, sat and viewed the hunting of the wild bears which then haunted among these hills, whence several places ... are named ... the Bear's Den and the Bear's Know to this day".

I am grateful to the naturalist Ron Greer for the comment that bears would be unlikely to survive in this area as late as the 12th century (the time of the earliest royal connection with Dunfermline). He also points out that the word 'wild' in the Old Statistical Account would be superfluous if bears were meant, since virtually all bears were wild. The term 'wild boars' on the other hand was and is common, distinguishing them from the domestic variety.

Boat Stone is on record in 1860 at GR 872072 approximately.

***Bog**, a settlement, is on record in 1783 in OS square 8199 approximately.

Bog Wood GR 920091.

***Boggy Brae** was at GR 115085 approximately. My only reference dates from 1750.

Boghall, a settlement, GR 042135, **Boghall Hill** GR 047132, **Knock of Boghall**, a hill, GR 044132. The earlier references show that Boghall farm developed from the East Third of *Pitcairns* (q.v.) and in the 18th century included Longdrum OS square 0412. A 'Raw' (see the 1717 reference quoted) was a row of farmworkers' cottages.

Earlier: 1526 'Boghall', 1717 'Raw of Boghall', 1794 'East Third (ie of Pitcairns) called Boghall', 1829 'the Town and lands of Boghall sometimes known by the names of Boghall & Longdrum', 1860 'Boghall Hill'.

Boghall, a hillside, GR 232154. This looks like a lost settlement name now represented only by its one-time hill land.

Earlier: 1607 & 1713 'Boghall of Pitca(i)rlie' (ie Pitcairlie OS square 2314).

Bogie Wood GR 169122.

Bogle Burn GR 003050. Earlier: On record since 1860.

Derivation: Perhaps 'Hobgoblin', or 'Ghost', Burn. However, for a possible P-Celtic origin compare P-Celtic (Welsh) 'Bugail', herdsman. Finally, 'Bogle' is also a Scots surname.

Bogle's Quarry GR 185155. According to the 1860 OS Name Book the man who first worked this quarry was nicknamed 'Bogle' because of his eccentricities.

***Boirhead**, a settlement recorded in 1775, just North of Dumbarrow which is at GR 197127.

Derivation: Scots 'Bore', a hole, a crevice, late 15th century on, perhaps here referring to a declivity in the ground.

***Boll Knoll** on record in 1801 at GR 091154 approximately. Derivation: Scots 'Bow', a stock or herd of cattle, 15th to early 19th century.

***Boonafrie**. See Ben *Effray*.

Boreland GR 884092.

Earlier: 1507 'Bordland', 1618 'Boirland of Ogilvie' (ie Ogilvie sq 9008), 1855 'Boreland'.

Derivation: Scots 'Bordland' &c, the name given to a farm charged with supplying the laird's table or 'board', in this case at Ogilvie.

***The Borestane**, on record in 1591. This was a stone near Demperston, OS square 2211, which marked the boundary of Auchtermuchty Common.

Derivation: Scots 'Bore', a hole, thus 'stone with a hole in it'. The *Concise Scots Dictionary* (see Bibliography) gives 'Borestane', boundary stone, as from the late 19th century only but here is an example from over 200 years earlier.

Borland GR 986048, **Borland Glen** GR 992060.

Earlier references: 1358 'ly bordland de Glendovan', 1443 'Dundovane-Bordland', 1618 'Boirland', 1699 'Borland', 1860 'Borland Glen'. 'Le Bordland de Glencoy' (ie Glen Quey OS squares 9803 &c), found in 1511, may have been a different though nearby 'Borland'.

Derivation: Scots, the name given to a farm charged with supplying the laird's table or 'board'.

Bothie Burn GR 950025. Earlier: On record since 1860.

Looking down Borland Glen into Glen Devon. Auchlinsky Hill is in the background. Drawing by Ken Laing.

Derivation: Scots 'Bothy', hut, shepherd's hut, late 18th century on, a loanword from Gaelic 'Bothan', hut, cottage.

Bow Burn GR 230165. **Glenbow**, a settlement, was in 1860 on the site of modern Whinnybank GR 228167.

Derivation: The progress of the burn could be said to form a distinct bow-like curve. Alternatively, though I have no references earlier than 1860, the word order of 'Glenbow' implies a Gaelic origin and a lost glen name. Gaelic 'Allt nam Bò' and 'Gleann nam Bò', cattle burn and cattle glen, are possible. The nearby Baw Hills may have the same origin.

*__Bowie Hole__, in 1800 a settlement at GR 958103 approximately. Mr John Haldane, Foswell, tells me this was also known as 'Headdyke' (q.v.).

Derivation: Scots 'Bowie', a broad shallow dish, 16th century on, perhaps here referring to an indentation in the ground; Scots 'Howe', 'Hole', a hollow, a low-lying piece of ground, 16th century on.

*__Boyak Burn__. In 1617 & 1625 this was an alternative name for Craig Burn (q.v.). The burn emerges from Clevage Loch OS square 0513 and passes to the North East of Easter Clevage.

Derivation: It is tempting to see this as Gaelic 'Bòidheach', bonny, beautiful. Note also though that 'Boyack' is a Fife surname on record in 1614.

*__Braefoot__, a settlement on record in 1783 in OS square 0812 approximately.

Derivation: Scots 'Brae', a bank, a hillside, 13th century on.

Braeside Villa GR 228124.

*__Braidloch__, on record in 1614, is an earlier alternative name for Lindores Loch OS square 1725. In 1627 it is referred to as 'the loch of Wodmyln' (from Woodmill OS square 2715).

Derivation: Scots 'Braid', broad, in placenames since the 13th century.

Braidmyre Wood GR 083035.

Derivation: Scots 'Braid', broad, in placenames since the 13th century; Scots 'Myre', mire, peat bog, late 14th century on.

Bramblebrae Quarry, on record in 1860 in OS square 1409, and not unlikely to be the disused quarry marked at GR 147090 on recent OS maps.

Craig Bran GR 914037, described by the 1860 OS Name Book as a small craig.

Derivation: Gaelic 'Creag Bhrain', Bran's Craig, possibly from Fionn MacCumhaill's dog Bran, or Raven Craig. This is one of the very few surviving Ochils Gaelic names that may contain a mythological reference.

*__Branders__ or 'Brander' is on record between 1750 and 1820 as the name of the present Culteuchar GR 082159. It was becoming known as 'Wester Culteucher' by 1801 and was 'Culteucher' by 1860. For further details on the history of these holdings see Culteuchar.

WJ Watson (see Bibliography) gives Gaelic 'Cumhang a' Bhrannraidh' for the Pass of Brander in Argyll, from 'Brannradh', an obstruction, a narrow place. There are small glens and declivities in the vicinity of Branders which this derivation might perhaps suit, but in the absence of really early forms it cannot be assumed that this is a Gaelic name.

Branders, now known as Culteuchar. (AW)

*__Braside__, a settlement on record in 1783 in OS square 8398 approximately.

Derivation: Scots 'Bra', 'Brae', a bank, a hillside, 13th century on.

Braughty GR 042036, a settlement, **Braughty Hill** GR 035040, **Braughty Burn** which rises at GR 039041.

Earlier forms: 1491-2 'Brauchti', 1511 'Brachty', 1663 'Brauchtie', 1750 'Coll of Brachty' (perhaps GR 036042?), 1828 'Braughty Hill', 1860 'Braughty Little Burn' (ie Braughty Burn).

Derivation: Possibly Gaelic 'Brochdach', locative 'Brochdaigh', at badger place.

*__Breackless Knowe__ is on record in 1774 at GR 108146 approximately.

Derivation: Gaelic 'Breac Lios', chequered enclosure, with the later addition of Scots 'Knowe', knoll. Gaelic 'Breac' when applied to landscape can refer to the visual effect of a mixture of vegetation; bracken and grass for example.

*__Bread Green__ or 'Broad Green' (not clearly legible to me), an area on record in 1800 near the burn which rises at GR 951083.

Derivation: Scots 'Green' in this context would designate an area where grass grew well, perhaps even where hay would be made. In areas like this however, where steep land is dissected by branching burns, 'Green' can be a reinterpretation of Scots 'Grain', the place where two burns meet, and by extension the promontory of land which divides them, in placenames from the late 15th century.

*__Brendi's Well__. Once known as 'Brendan's Well' this is said by Morris (see Bibliography) to be near the Gattaway Burn, South East of Abernethy OS square 1916. Note that one suggested derivation of the name of the neighbouring parish of Dunbarney involves the name of St Brendan.

*__Brewer's Knowe__. At the foot of Dollar Glen, approximate OS square 9698. Drummond (1953 – see Bibliography) and other writers report a tradition that the brewer here was charged with supplying the King of Scots with 15 gallons of ale whenever he passed this way.

Brewlands 963994, a settlement. Earlier: 1783 'Browland', 1819 & 1836 'Brewlands', 1848 & 1860 'Browlands'.

Derivation: Explained locally from its being on the 'Broo' (ie brow) of the hill.

Bride's Burn GR 931070, on record since 1860.

Derivation. This could be from St Bride or Brigit, but note also the tradition of washing brides-to-be in certain wells or burns on the eve of their wedding day, as reported by Morris and Mackinlay (see Bibliography).

*__Saint Bride's Seat__. On the Hill of Gattaway OS square 1915. According to Butler (see Bibliography) the church at Abernethy was dedicated to St Brigit (St Bride) from the 5th century. It is possible, but no doubt unprovable, that this is a translation of an older Gaelic name 'Suidhe Brighde'.

*__Broad Greens__. An unidentified site on Sheriffmuir on record in 1766.

Derivation: Scots 'Green' in this context would designate an area where grass grew well, and possibly where hay would be made.

Broad Wood GR 041146.

*__Broadfold__, a settlement on record in 1808, seemingly near Wester Glensherup OS square 9605.

Broadgate, a settlement I have last found on record in 1860, GR 956116 approximately. It is now a ruin, replaced by a new house 'Broadgates'.

Earlier forms: 1667 'Bredgett of Fossuell', 1687 'Broadgate of Fossaway' (sic). The last quoted reference illustrates the uncertainty found in some earlier records in distinguishing between 'Fossoway', 'Fossakie' and, occasionally, 'Foswell' (qq.v.). Derivation: Scots 'Gate', a way, road, path, late 14th century on.

Broadhead GR 029045, a hill. Earlier: c1796 'Broad Head'. Derivation: Scots 'Heid' &c, a hilltop, late 15th century on.

Broadheadfold GR 041105. Abandoned as an independent holding, I am told, in the late 1920s.

Earlier forms: 1650 'Broadiesfauld & Mylne', 1664 'Breadhead-Fauld', 1667 'Broadfolds', 1699-1701 'Bryddiesfauld', 1718 (Perhaps) 'Broadridgefolds', 1781 & 1783 'Broadheadfold'; 1816 'Bradiesfauld or Brydiesfauld', 1860 'Broadheadfold'.

In spite of the variety of forms, this represents, as far as I can see, a single holding. It is not unknown for alternative names for a site to co-exist over a long period.

Broadley GR 831041, a settlement.

Earlier forms: 1766 'Broad Leys', 1803 'Broadleyside' (ie modern Side OS square 8204), 1860 'Broadley'.

Derivation: Scots 'Lea', grassland, in place names since the 16th century.

*__East Broadlies__ GR 229125 approximately & *__West Broadlies__ are on record in 1775.

Derivation: Perhaps Scots 'Lea', grassland, in place names since the 16th century.

Brockley GR 084054, a settlement, **Brockley Knowe** GR 086055.

Earlier forms: c1346 (transcribed c1622-32 as 'Wroclache'), 1371 'Brochelache' & 'Brochlache', 1519 'Broklaw', 1649 'Brokloche', 1654 'Bracley', 1673 'Braklaw', 1860 'Brockley', 'Brockley Knowe'. Black (see Bibliography) says the surname "perhaps" came from these lands.

Derivation: Gaelic 'Broclach', a shortened form of 'Broc Thulach', badger knoll. In the light of this it is possible that the Knowe was the primary name. The 1519 & 1673 forms quoted imply a reinterpretation or translation of '-(thu)lach' as Scots 'Law', comparable to Gaelic 'Garbhlach' becoming 'Garb Law' (q.v.).

Broich Burn GR 916030. *__Bruich__ (also 'Bruach' & 'Broich'), on record as a settlement until 1836, was at or near the site of the now submerged Backhill (q.v.) OS square 9104. Earlier forms: 1769 'Broich' & 'Broich Burn', 1779 'Back Hill of Broich' (ie hill land between Ben Buck OS square 8901 and the Broich Burn), 1783 'Bruach' (the farm), 1792 'the farms of Bruich and the back hills', 1819 'Bruich' (the farm) & 'Bruich Burn', 1836 'Broich' (the burn), 1848 'Foot of Broich' (this may well be 'Burnfoot' OS square 9104 – q.v.), 1860 'Broich Burn'. The 1860 OS Name Book has 'Broich' from one informant and also has the spelling 'Brooch'.

Derivation: Gaelic 'Bruthach', hillside or bank, no doubt from one of the nearby steep hillslopes.

Broombrae, a settlement, GR 241124. On record in 1769 are ***Broom Braes**, a hillside, centred on GR 238126 approximately, ***West Broombraes** GR 239124 approximately & ***East Broombraes**, which seems to be the modern Broombrae.

Earlier: 1695 'Broombrae', 1722 'Broombreas'.

Broom Hill GR 204138, **Broomhill**, a settlement at GR 203138 on record since 1860. Snoddy (see Bibliography) describes Broomhill as a ruin in 1966, saying it was known locally as "Lady Miller's" in memory of an occupant who kept a shebeen there some 100 years previously.

***Broom Know Meadows** recorded in 1829. Seemingly at Pothill OS square 9611.

Broomfield GR 217170, a settlement on record since 1860.

***Broomhill Cottage** was in 1885 in approximate OS square 8297.

Brown Hill GR 834001.

Brownie Knowe GR 029123, on record since 1860. Derivation: Scots 'Brownie', "a benevolent spirit or goblin" (OED).

Brownies Chair GR 207121. A boulder of whinstone. Snoddy (see Bibliography) gives the location and a photograph.

Earlier forms: 1775 'Broonies chair', 1801 'James Clunie, Weaver, Brunies Chair', 1828 'Bruno's Chair', 1860 'Brownies Chair'. The 1801 reference quoted indicates the presence of a settlement.

Derivation: Scots 'Brownie', "a benevolent spirit or goblin" (OED).

***Browster's Well Stripe**. A small burn on record in 1800 that appears to rise at GR 964087.

Derivation: Not unlikely to be named from a well that was used for brewing or named from the surname. Scots 'Brewster' & 'Browster', a brewer, 15th century on; Scots 'Stripe', a small stream, 15th century on.

Brunt Knowe GR 063127, on record since 1860.

Derivation: Scots 'Brunt', burnt, late 15th century on.

***Brunt Rig**, a hill on record 1615-20 and situated somewhere between Carnbo OS square 0503 and the Dunning to Muckhart road OS squares 0105 & 0106. In the 17th century it was part of the lands of Carnbo.

Derivation: Scots 'Brunt', burnt, late 15th century on; Scots 'Rig', a ridge of high ground, a long narrow hill, a hill-crest, in placenames since the late 12th century.

***Brunton Hall** was at GR 243167 approximately, recorded in 1775.

***Sanct-Brydes-Well**. This was in Auchtermuchty, or between Auchtermuchty and GR 232132. In 1591 it marked the West or South West boundary of Whitefield Common (q.v.).

***Buchthill** is on record between 1666 & 1799. It was a holding forming part of the barony of Gleneagles and was absorbed into the Mains of Gleneagles c1799.

Earlier: 1666 'Buchthill of Gleneglis'. Derivation: Scots 'Boucht', 'Bucht' &c, a sheepfold, 15th to early 20th centuries.

Ben Buck GR 896015, **Benbuck Burn** GR 889010.

Earlier: 1769 'Height of Benbuck', 1819 'Ben Buck'.

Derivation: Gaelic 'Beinn', mountain, hill; Gaelic 'Buc', 'Boc', a roebuck.

Buittle GR 234123. Compare 'Buittle', Castle Douglas, probably from Old English 'Botl', a dwelling. I have come across no early forms so this could well be a name fairly recently borrowed from elsewhere.

Burleigh Burn GR 129050. This is a secondary name from Burleigh OS square 1204.

Burnfoot GR 989042, a settlement. Also **Burnfoot Mill** (Woolspinning) same GR, Milltown Check TP (ie Turnpike) GR 989047 and Mill-Leas Plantation GR 990055, all on record in 1860.

Earlier references: 1662 'Burnfoot of Auchansley' (ie Auchlinsky OS square 9904 &c), 1750 'Burnfoot', 1780 'Burnfoot of Glendevon', 1783 'Milltown', 1855 'Burnfoot Wool Spinning Factory'.

***Burnfoot**, a settlement on record in 1783 in approximate OS square 9104, may be the same as 'Foot of Broich' found in 1848 (see Broich Burn). Also **Burnfoot Hill** GR 901034. Earlier: 1769 'Knows of Killsprott' (ie modern Burnfoot Hill), 1783 'Burnfoot' (a settlement), 1836 'Kilsprot Hill' (modern Burnfoot Hill?).

*__Burnhouses__, a settlement found in 1796 at GR 044043 approximately.

Burniepark Burn GR 830012. This burn flows past Park Cottage OS square 8201, so the same 'park' may be involved in both names. There is also a chance that 'Burniepark' is related to 'Birne Hill', unidentified but also on Sheriffmuir.

Earlier: On record since 1860.

Derivation: This name appears to derive from a lost 'Burnie Park', which could of course be 'park of the wee burn'. Alternatively Scots 'Burnie', 'Birnie' can derive from Gaelic 'Braonach', locative 'Braonaigh', at damp oozy place.

Burnside GR 889075, a settlement, formerly part of the barony of Ogilvie – Ogilvie Castle was in OS square 9008. Earlier: 1632 'Burnesyde of Ogilvie', 1650 'Burnssyde', 1824 'Lands & Barony of Ogilvie viz Burnside (&c)'.

Burnside GR 117158. Earlier: 1668 'Burnesyde of Wester Dron'.

Burnside, a settlement, GR 163080. Up to the end of the 18th century this was also known as 'Burngrange'.

Earlier references: 1577 'Cuthill Burngranys alias Burnsyde', 1614 'Burngrange', 1860 'Burnside TP' (ie Turnpike). 'Cuthill' in the 1577 reference, a feudal barony, is now represented by Cuthill Towers OS square 1508. 'Grange' in Scots can indicate tenure of a farm by an ecclesiastical foundation – note that Bannaty and Eclmurghuall (qq.v.) are or were nearby.

*__Burnstanners__, a settlement on record between 1783 and 1855 in OS square 8908 approximately. It is described in 1824 as part of the Barony of Ogilvie – Ogilvie Castle was in OS square 9008.

Derivation: Scots 'Stanners', shingle, gravel, 16th century on.

Burnt Hill GR 002062, on record since 1860.

Burntlaw GR 115098, on record since 1796.

Burnwarroch GR 835973. According to the 1860 OS Name Book this is a rugged ravine carrying a burn.

Earlier: 1848 'Warrock Glen'. The interchanging of '-och' and '-ock' is not uncommon in placenames.

This site is also that of *Warlock Glen, also known as *Warrick Glen, and these may well be reinterpretations of 'Warrock Glen'.

Derivation: The order of the elements of the primary name implies a Gaelic original and it could be significant that St. Moroc, patron of nearby Lecropt parish, appears there as 'Maworrock'.

Butend GR 954114 is on record since 1860, ***Wester butt-end** between 1794 & 1820. Both are settlements.

Derivation: 'At the end of a butt': Scots 'Butt', a ridge or strip of ploughed land, a small piece of ground cut off in some way from adjacent land, in placenames since the 13th century.

Butler Linn GR 143118, on record since 1860.

Butter Road GR 060052, on record since 1860.

Derivation: If this is not as simple as it looks, Gaelic 'Bothar', a road, is very possible, giving a hybrid name where the second part translates the first.

Butter Well GR 212165, on record since 1860.

Derivation: Butter-making used sometimes to involve washing the product in burns, wells and springs, and wells were sometimes used to store butter.

Buttergask, Set, GR 877085, **Buttergask Burn** GR 850053, **Buttergask Bridge** GR 877085, **Buttergask Mill**, on record in 1860 GR 877085. Also **Buttergask Pendicle** & **Buttergask Cottage**, recorded in 1862, approximately 225 and 350 yards respectively South West of Topfauld OS square 8708.

Earlier forms: 1304 'Buthyrgaske', 1442 'Buthirgask', 1512 'Buttergask', 1642-1824 'Blew-Buttergask alias Wester Buttergask', 'Eister Buttergask' (ie modern Buttergask?), 1664-1759 'Bittergask', 1783 'Mill of Bittergask', 1789 'Easter Buttergask', 1860 'Buttergask Burn', 'Buttergask Bridge', 'Buttergask Mill'. For 'Blue (&c) Buttergask' see also Blueton.

Derivation: The earliest forms imply that 'Butter' & 'Bitter' are reinterpretations. Gaelic 'Bothar Gaisg', 'tail' road, with 'tail' in the sense of spur of land.

C

*__Cadger__ **Linn** on record 1796 to 1828, GR 082063 approximately.

Derivation: Scots 'Cadger', a pedlar, late 15th century on.

*__Cadger__ **Road** GR 099140 approximately, on record in 1774. It ran roughly North West to South East.

Derivation: Scots 'Cadger', a pedlar, late 15th century on.

Cadgeracre Wood GR 174102. Derivation: Scots 'Cadger', a pedlar, late 15th century on.

*__Cadgergate__ **Head** GR 987073, the highest point on ***Cadger's Walk**, the track between Coulshill and Glendevon which was taken by pedlars allegedly to avoid tolls in Glen Eagles and on the Muckhart-Dunning road. ***Cadger's Brae** OS square 9807 is sometimes said to be the same as Cadgergate Head, or the slope leading to it. ***Cadger's Yett** was the name given to an old wicket gate at Cadgergate Head. The Cadgergate is named 'Coal Road' on a map of 1800.

Derivation: Scots 'Cadger', a pedlar, late 15th century on; Scots 'Gate' &c, a way, road, path, late 14th century on; Scots 'Yett', a gate, late 14th century on.

Cadgergate Head with Ben Thrush in the haze behind. (AW)

*__Cadron__ **Linns**. Unidentified waterfalls on the Old Wharry Burn on record in 1766.

Derivation: Scots 'Caldron', 'Caddroun' &c, cauldron, 14th century on.

*__Cairn__. A pendicle on record in 1801 and forming part of the Mains of Kincardine OS square 9411.

*__Cairn__ **Burn**. An 18th century name for the Burn of Sorrow, discussed under Burn of *Care.*

Cairn Hill GR 049036. See Carnbo.

Cairnavain, site of a cairn, GR 069083, **Cairnavain Burn** GR 060081.

Earlier: c1790 'Cairnie-ven', c1796 'Cairnavain', 'Cairnavain Burn'. For a traditional rhyme indicating that the cairn was formerly believed to contain treasure, see Dryburn Well.

Derivation: Gaelic or P-Celtic 'Càrn', cairn, perhaps with P-Celtic 'Maen', 'Faen', a stone. Alternatively, though few mythological references seem to survive in Ochils names, this could be one as Gaelic 'Càrn na Fèine', cairn of the warriors (of Fionn MacCumhail).

*__Cairndrowan__ was a settlement on record in Dunning parish in 1717. Derivation: Gaelic 'Càrn', cairn, with an unknown second element.

Cairnmorris Hill GR 934017. This name may have some connection with the 'Cairn', an earlier name for the Burn of Sorrow – see further under Burn of *Care.*

Earlier forms: 1779 'Moris Carn', 1819 'Cairn Morris', 1848 'Cairn Mirris', 1860 'Cairnmorris Hill'.

Derivation: The earlier forms are inconclusive but could imply a Gaelic etymology: Gaelic 'Càrn', cairn, with a second element reinterpreted out of recognition.

***Cairnquarter**. A holding forming part of the barony of Gleneagles from the late 16th century at least, and absorbed into the Mains of Gleneagles c1799.

Earlier references: 1587 'Carnequarteris Over et Nethir', 1604 'Cranequarter of Glenegeis', 1663 'Kearnquarter', 1685 'Cairnquarter'.

***Caldrons**, on record between 1769 & 1819, seemingly at GR 939990 approximately. ***Caldron Burn**, on record in 1769, rises at GR 939992. Derivation: Scots 'Caldron', 'Caddroun' &c, cauldron, 14th century on.

Caldwells GR 268132, a settlement. Earlier: 1752 'Coldwells', 1775 'Caldwells', 1827 'Coldwells', 1828 'Cold Wells', 1860 'Caldwells'. A well is marked on OS maps.

The earlier forms quoted are a good illustration of the uncertainty of earlier mapmakers and others about using Scots forms, and of the 1860 Ordnance Survey's frequent practice of reinstating them.

Calf Craig GR 898996.

Calfford Brae GR 138096, **Calfford Bridge** GR 138097. Earlier: 1860 'Calfford Bridge'.

East Cameron Burn GR 879010, **Middle Cameron Burn** GR 875010, **West Cameron Burn** GR 870005. Earlier: 1860 'East Cameron Burn', 'Middle Cameron Burn'.

Derivation: From the surname, unless it is from some feature past which one of the burns runs. Gaelic 'Cam Shròn', bent nose, or in topography, bent point or spur of land.

Castle Campbell GR 961993. MacGibbon & Ross (see Bibliography) date the castle from the 14th century. Billings (see Bibliography) gives a transcript of the Act of Parliament of 1489 by which the castle's name was changed from Castle Gloom, after its acquisition through marriage (c1465) by the chief of Clan Campbell, Colin 1st Earl of Argyll. It remained Argyll's main Lowland stronghold until the 17th century. For the legend of the captive princess see Burn of *Care.* The first Earl and his cousin Sir Duncan Campbell of Glenorchy were accomplished Gaelic poets, as was at least one member of the Earl's close family, either his Countess or his daughter, or perhaps both of them. It seems possible then that some kind of Gaelic literary ambiance may have existed at Castle Campbell during the years of the Earl's ownership.

A print of Castle Campbell by J Hooper, dated 1791. Reproduced by courtesy of Perth and Kinross District Libraries.

Earlier references: 1497 'terras ecclesiasticas de Campbel, alias Dolare seu Gloum nuncupatus' (the church lands of Campbel, otherwise called Dolare or Gloume), 1525 'terras de Gloume cum castro Castel Campbell nuncupato' (the lands of Gloume with the castle called Castel Campbell), 1569 'Castle Campbell', c1680 'Cambel Castle', 1688 'Castle Campbell', 1745 'Castle Campbell', 1779 'Campbell Glen' (ie the Glen of Sorrow).

Derivation: The word order of the castle name suggests a Gaelic form, and it is likely that 'Caisteal Chaimbeul' would be used by the Gaelic speakers among the castle's inhabitants and visitors. A Gaelic name given in the 15th century seems on the face of it unlikely to be adopted by the local population at large and it should be noted that Adair's map of c1680 and Crose *Antiquities of Scotland* (1797) have 'Campbel(l) Castle', suggesting that an alternative form may have existed. The Gaelic word order won the day no doubt through the prestige of the site and its owners, helped also by such models as Castle Sween &c.

Campbell's Hill Plantation GR 135140. From a lost hill name, derived from the surname? It is worth noting that the Earl of Argyll, chief of Clan Campbell, held the Barony of Abernethy, some 4 miles away, from 1528 to 1543 at least. Compare Argyle OS square 2113.

Candy GR 118098, a settlement, **Candy Hill** GR 118101. Jack (see Bibliography) says that in the mid 18th century Candy consisted of four distinct farms. The 18th century forms quoted below associate this holding or one of its parts with the Deuglie names in OS square 1011 &c.

Earlier: 17th century 'Candy', 1650 'Qundiehill', mid 18th century 'Candy Dewglie', 1771 'Candydeuglie'.

Derivation: Note the slight possibility of P-Celtic 'Cand', white, being present in the name.

Cap Law GR 012081, ***Caplaw Bent**, on record in 1829, was an area centred on GR 012083.

Earlier: 1860 'Caplaw'. Derivation: Scots 'Bent', a stretch of open ground covered in bent grass, a moor, late 15th to 17th centuries.

Caplawhead GR 010012, a settlement on record since 1789. In 1800 it was part of Ballieliesk OS square 0001.

Earlier: 1789 'Caplahead'.

Cardingoats GR 057056. A craggy defile.

Earlier: On record since 1860. Derivation: P-Celtic 'Cardden', a thicket. The second element could be either a translation of Gaelic 'Gobhar', goat, or Scots 'Goat' &c, a ditch or a watercourse, in placenames in these senses since 1568 & 1627 respectively.

Burn of Care GR 963000, **Burn of Sorrow** & **Glen of Sorrow** both GR 950999.

Earlier forms: c1680 'Cair', 1771 'the glens of Care', 'the birns of Sorrow', 1779 'Campbell Glen & Burn that runs by Dollar' (ie Glen & Burn of Sorrow), 1791 'the Cairn', 'Glencairn' (ie Burn & Glen of Sorrow), 1819 'Burn of Care', 'Glen of Sorrow', 1836 'Easter Burn' (ie the Care), 'Wester Burn' (ie the Sorrow), 1848 'Burn of Care', 'Burn of Sorrow', 1888 'Turnpike Burn' (ie the Care), 'Bank Burn' (ie the Sorrow).

Derivation: As these forms show, the naming of these burns has a complex history. The traditional explanation (see for example the Old Statistical Account for Dollar or the 1860 OS Name Book) is that a daughter of one of the early Kings of Scots, languishing in Castle Gloom (later called Castle Campbell) as a punishment for falling for a man of too lowly station, gave melancholy names to surrounding features to reflect her own unhappiness. In some versions she names Gloom Hill and 'Dolour' (ie Dollar) as well as the burns. Haliburton (1905 – see Bibliography) says that her suitor was the same individual who subsequently pursued and killed the outlaw Kemp in order to commend himself to the King (see also Kemp's Score). According to Stewart (see Bibliography) 'Care' and 'Sorrow' are recorded in 1465. Pennant (see Bibliography) says that the Castle of Gloom was "bounded by the glens of Care and washed by the birns of Sorrow". Billings (see Bibliography) states that the castle "stands beside the stream of Griff or Grief". Beveridge (see Bibliography) says that 'Care' and 'Sorrow' were "now (ie 1888) in great measure discarded" in favour of 'Turnpike' and 'Bank' Burns respectively (qq.v.). I have found no evidence that these last two names are in use for the Care and the Sorrow today, and 1860 OS maps and the recent OS series give 'Care' and 'Sorrow' only. Evidence for names more rooted in the surrounding landscape however comes in the form of the Rev John Watson's entry for Dollar in the Old Statistical Account, 1791. He refers to the Sorrow as the 'Cairn' and has it running through 'Glencairn'. Glencairn Bridge OS square 9699 is no doubt a relic of this name. It appears that the lands behind the Banks of Dollar were known as the 'Lands of Glencairne' in the 16th & 17th centuries, and the Cairn (ie Sorrow) rises in the vicinity of Cairnmorris Hill and passes close to the sites of cairns including Innercairn (q.v.). In the early 19th century the Care and Sorrow were known as 'Easter Burn' and 'Wester Burn' respectively, possibly for Easter & Wester Dollar Burn, while the first stretch of the Sorrow is marked 'Priest Goat Burn' on estate plans of 1779 & 1836. The existence of so many alternatives over the past three centuries perhaps suggests that 'Care' and 'Sorrow' were not truly popular names, at least until they acquired greater currency and prestige by appearing on OS maps.

Castle Campbell seen from the North. Drawing by Ken Laing.

Carim Lodge GR 858052. See Mickle *Corum*.

Carleith Hill GR 096087. Earlier: On record since 1796. This was the site of an old circular stone structure near which stone coffins were found "not long ago" according to the 1860 OS Name Book. Stobie's map of 1783 shows a circular hill fort here.

Derivation: P-Celtic 'Caer', fort, plus, possibly,

an element related to 'Lite' – which is also Gaelic for the town of Leith – which WJ Watson (see Bibliography) tentatively compares to Welsh 'Llaith' meaning damp, moist.

Carlie Craig GR 816971, on record since 1784, when it appears to be a settlement name. The 1860 OS Name Book calls this a high and rugged cliff. It is also known as ***Carlin Craig** and latterly ***Witches' Craig.**

A story tells of an Elder of Logie Kirk, returning from a hunting trip, seeing the Devil here and shooting him with a silver button (in some versions a silver coin). On returning next morning he found the 'Devil' was in fact a pet goat. Shooting giants, ghosts, witches, devils with silver is a common folk theme relating to Stith Thomson motifs (see Bibliography) D1385.4, G303.14, G303.16 and G303.19.

Derivation: Scots 'Carlin', a witch, late 14th century on.

Carlownie Hill GR 961083, **Carlownie Burn** GR 950089.

Earlier references: 1595 'Glendowaly' (which appears to carry Carlownie Burn), 1799 (perhaps our site) 'Carselownie' (part of the barony of Gleneagles), 1800 'Carlownie Cairn' (ie the summit of Carlownie Hill), 1860 'Carlownie Hill'. Haldane (1944 – see Bibliography) calls Carlownie Burn 'the Cornhill Burn', from Cornhill OS square 9410.

Derivation: According to WJ Watson (see Bibliography) 'Carlownie' represents Gaelic 'Cathair Leamhnach', elm-fort, an early name for Tullibardine (though identified by Professor Barrow with Strageath, afterwards Blackford parish) which came to be used as a district name. On the map facing p316 of the *Charters of Inchaffray Abbey* (see Bibliography) the area labelled 'Cathirlauenache' (ie 'Cathair Leamhnach') runs from Tullibardine OS square 9214 to near Kincardine OS square 9511.

***Carlungie**, a settlement on record in 1775, GR 210136 approximately.

Carmodle GR 030053, a hill. In the 17th century it was part of the lands of Carnbo OS square 0503.

Earlier forms: 1615 'mons (ie hill) de Cormoddill', 1629 'Cormodill', 1666 'Cormodille', c1796 'Carmodle' (a settlement).

Derivation: For the first syllable the 17th century forms suggest Gaelic 'Còrr', tapering or horn-shaped hill. '-modle' is obscure to me.

Carmore GR 149093, a settlement, **Carmore Burn** GR 150096. Earlier references: 1494-5 'Carmore', c1796 'Carmore Burn'.

Derivation: Names in the vicinity such as Pitlochie, 'portion of land at loch place', suggest a poorly drained environment in earlier times. Gaelic 'Càrr Mòr', big moss or bog, perhaps with reference to the flattish stretch of land North East of the present dwelling, would make sense here.

***Carmore Hill** GR 094105, on record in 1796.

Derivation: This appears to be on or very close to Arlick Hill, 'rock or stone slab height'. Three names in the vicinity contain 'Craig-', implying crags or rocks, and there are quarries nearby. Gaelic 'Càrr Mòr', big rocky shelf or projecting rock, would therefore seem an appropriate name here.

***Carmosly Burn**, on record between 1800 & 1829, is the upper section of Cloan Burn. ***Greens of Carmossly**, found in 1800, is an area at the source of Carmosly or Cloan Burn GR 964082.

Derivation: The order of the elements of the name appears Gaelic. If the site was poorly drained in earlier times in spite of its height, Gaelic 'Càrr', bog or moss, would seem the best suggestion. '-mossly' is obscure to me. The nature of the country is such that 'Greens' of Carmossly could be for Scots 'Grain', the place where burns branch and by extension the promontories of land between them.

Carnaughton Burn & **Carnaughton Glen** both GR 878976. The burn descends extremely steeply from Craig Leith OS square 8798 above Alva. The name may well be from some rocky feature the burn passes: Gaelic 'Càrr Nochta', bare rock ridge.

Carnbo GR 054032, **Carnbo Farm** GR 053031, **Cairnbo Stewart** GR 046046, **Cairn Hill** GR 049036 (a cairn is marked on some OS maps).

Earlier: 1194-8 'Carnbo', 1370 'Carnbo' & 'Carnibo', 1511 'Nethir-Carnbo', 'Ovir Carnbo', 1539-47 'Carnibo', 1609 'Carnebo-Stewart', 1615 'Craigheid alias Wester Carniebo' (ie Craighead OS square 0403), 'Carnehill', 1629 'Over Carneboe' & 1671 'Nether Carnbo', 1775 'Cairnbowhill', 'Cairnbow Mill', 1860 'Cairn Hill'.

Derivation: Gaelic 'Càrn nam Bò, cairn of the cattle. The 'i' or 'e' in the middle of some earlier forms quite possibly represents the Gaelic genitive article 'nam', 'of the'.

Carpow Hill GR 207164. This is a secondary name from Carpow OS square 2017 which is probably P-Celtic, from 'Caer', fort, and 'Pwll', sluggish stream: the fort on the sluggish stream.

Cart Burn GR 053060 on record since 1860. If this name is not as simple as it seems, then WFH Nicolaisen (1976 – see Bibliography) derives the River Cart, an affluent of the Clyde, from an Indo-European root meaning 'hard, stone, stony'.

Casken Hill GR 015116, on record since 1860 when the OS Name Book explained the name as a diminutive of 'Cask', barrel (a form not confirmed by any Scots dictionary I have consulted), adding that a whisky still was worked here "formerly". However the hill forms a slight promontory so Gaelic 'Gasgan', a small tail of land, is a stronger possibility.

Castle Craig GR 976127.

Earlier forms: 1750 'Craig of Coul' (ie Coul OS square 9612), 1860 'Castle Craig'.

This and the following four hills carry, carried, or are reputed to have carried forts, or are close to forts. They illustrate the tendency for 'Castle' to be used in such contexts. The influence of similarly used Gaelic 'Dùn', fort, hill, castle, is not to be ruled out.

***Castle Craig** GR 912977. Now obliterated by a quarry, it used to carry the remains of a fort the stone from which was reputed to have been used in the building of Stirling Castle. According to Beveridge (see Bibliography) the remains were still visible in 1888 when they were known as 'Johnie Mool's House'.

Castle Hill GR 001036 also known as Downhill & Dunhill (see Downhill OS square 0003), **Castlehill Reservoir** GR 996035, completed in 1977. Earlier: 1860 'Castle Hill'.

Castle Law GR 100154. Earlier forms: 1722 'Castle Law', 1783 'Castle Hill', c1790 'Castle-law', 1801 'Little Castle Law'. Material submitted for the Old Statistical Account but not published mentions "a sort of half tower" still standing c1790, built by the previous Lord Ruthven (of Freeland OS square 0918) inside the fort on this hill. 'Little Castle Law' of the 1801 reference quoted above, may well be the distinct smaller hill just to the North West of Castle Law proper.

Derivation: Scots 'Law', a rounded hill, 12th century on. As hills of this shape were highly suitable for fortification, it is not uncommon to find forts on Laws.

Castle Law GR 179152. There is a tradition that the fort on this hill was the residence of Pictish Kings and the 1860 OS Name Book adds a tradition that the Picts threw a silver cradle into the loch on the summit of the Law when under attack from the Romans.

Earlier references: 1629 'common pasture on Castellaw', 1820 'Commonty of Castle Law'. For 'Law' see the previous entry.

Castleton GR 981000, **Castleton Hill** GR 979009, **Castleton Burn** GR 980002.

Earlier: 1543 'Casteltoun', 1593 'Casteltoun and Hill', 1800 'Castletown' (Easter & Wester), 1860 'Castleton Burn'. These are secondary names from Cowden Castle OS square 9899. 'Cowden' often derives from Gaelic 'Calltuinn', hazel.

Catochil GR 177134, a settlement.

Earlier forms: 1295 'Cathohill', 1507 'Catoichill', 1827 'Catochil'.

Derivation: According to WJ Watson (see Bibliography) the first part may be P-Celtic 'Cat', a bit, piece (of land). '-ochil', as in the name of the Ochil hills themselves, is probably related to P-Celtic 'Uxellos', high, giving a sense 'high-part'. Liddall however (see Bibliography) thinks Catochil is the 'Cindocellum' of the anonymous 7th century geographer of Ravenna, 'the head or end of the Ochils'. Its position doesn't really justify that description.

Cauldhame GR 825011, a settlement. Earlier: 1663 & 1728 'Caldhome', 1682 & 1720 'Coldhome', 1805 'Caldhame', 1812 'Coldhame'. A mixter-maxter of Scots and English forms!

Cauldhame GR 921079, a settlement, **Cauldhame Wood** GR 920084. Earlier forms: 1783 'Coldhame', 1855 'Cauldhame'.

Chapel Burn GR 074110, **Chapelburn Well** GR 071081. Meldrum (see Bibliography) thinks that 'Water of Whitburn' may have been an alternative name for the burn.

Earlier forms: c1790 'the chapel-water', 1792 'Chapel Burn'. Derivation: 1860 OS Name Book

Could this be the Loch on Castle Law Abernethy where the Picts threw the silver cradle? (AW)

says the burn was named from a chapel, no longer traceable, built near the burn's confluence with the Water of May GR 078119.

Chapel Hill GR 010097, on record since 1829, **Chapel Burn** GR 012092, on record since 1860.

Derivation: I have come across no evidence that there was ever a chapel in this locality. Gaelic 'Allt a' Chapuill' or 'Cnoc a' Chapuill', horse burn or horse hill, is a possible original.

***Chapel Well**, in ***Chapel Den**.

According to Wilkie (see Bibliography) these were at Gateside OS square 1809, where a chapel dedicated to the Virgin Mary was founded after 1249.

***Charleston**. Recorded in 1813 as an alternative name for Easter Rottearns OS square 8407.

Christie's Knowe GR 036092, on record since 1860.

Cin** Well**. Recorded c1796 at GR 092085 approximately. Partly illegible. 'Cin-' could well be for Gaelic 'Ceann', head, end.

Clamieduff Hill GR 198136, **Clamieduff**, a settlement on record in 1860, GR 203135 approximately.

Earlier: 1827 'Clammieduff'.

Derivation: Scots 'Clamm', damp, clammy, late 16th century on, plus Scots 'Duff', moss, peat, 19th century on. The fact that 'lie pait myre de Sanct Serf', Saint Serf's peat bog, was seemingly at the West end of the hill in the late 16th century gives some support to this derivation.

Clarkshill GR 073137, a settlement on record since 1826.

Clatchard Craig carried the remains of a fort in 1860. Fort and hill are now obliterated by **Clatchard Craig Quarry** GR 243177.

Earlier: 1595 (Perhaps our site) 'Craig', 1705 'Clatchartcraig'.

Derivation: Snoddy (see Bibliography) suggests the perhaps too ingenious Gaelic 'Clais Ard', high trench, with reference to the trenched fortifications of the fort. 'Clais Ard' in the sense of high stream or streambed is also possible, as perhaps is Gaelic 'Clach Ard', high rock.

Clatteringford Burn GR 027110, on record since 1860.

***Clattery(e)furd**, on record between 1569 & 1613 at the source of the 'Graneburne'. I have not identified ford or burn but they appear to be in the area between Glenquey OS square 9702 and Auchlinsky OS square 9904.

Ben Cleuch GR 902006.

Earlier: 1769 'Bencleugh', 1783 'Benclach', 1790 'Ben-Cloch', 1845 'Benclough', 1848 'Benclach', 1860 'Bencleuch'; 1869 'Bencloich', 1954 'Ben Clach'.

Derivation: There is lively disagreement about the derivation of the name of this hill, the highest in the Ochils. The seemingly obvious derivation, Scots 'Cleuch', gorge, ravine, in placenames late 12th century on, could be taken as referring to the steep descent towards the Daiglen Burn on the hill's South West slopes. However, the word order and the presence of 'Ben' surely make this name Gaelic, as 'Ben', a loanword from Gaelic 'Beinn', hill, mountain, does not appear to have been productive in Scots. The later 18th century forms quoted indicate Gaelic 'Clach', genitive 'Cloiche', stone, rock, as the origin, with 'Cleuch' as a perhaps longstanding reinterpretation. The hill does in fact have a stony top unlike many Ochil summits.

Cleuch Burn, on record in 1860, rises at GR 956045.

Derivation: Scots 'Cleuch', a gorge, a ravine, in placenames late 12th century on.

Cleuch Hill GR 971059 & **Cleuch Burn** GR 969063, both on record since 1860. **Cleugh Farm** GR 968054.

Derivation: Scots 'Cleuch', a gorge, a ravine, in placenames late 12th century on.

Wester Clevage GR 046147, **Easter Clevage** GR 050149, settlements, **Clevage Hills** GR 055137, **Clevage Loch** GR 053132. Also ***Middle Clevage**, ***Mill of Clevage** & ***Hill of Clevage**, all on record in 1783.

Macfarlane (1723 – see Bibliography) reports that a little above Clevage there was a fort where "there has been some Pictish weapons found by the country people in making their truff" (ie turf, peat).

Earlier forms: early 13th century 'Clethues', 'Cletheueis', 'Cletheues', 1603 'Clevaige', 1630 'Wester Clevege', 1809 'Roe of Clavage', 1860 'Clevage Hills', 'Clevage Loch'.

Derivation: The 13th century forms point to Gaelic 'Claidheamh Fhais', sword stance, sword station, a site acquired by force of arms. 'Roe' (see the 1819 form quoted) is probably for Scots 'Raw' &c, a row of farmworkers' cottages, 15th century on.

Clevitch 228157, a settlement. Earlier: 1860 'Clevitch'. The same derivation as Clevage OS square 0414 seems feasible, and that site appears as 'Clevetch' in 1686.

Inner Clints GR 039041, **Outer Clints**, GR 037042, forming the North side of Keerie Glen. Both are on record since 1860. Derivation: Scots 'Clint', a cliff, a crag, a precipice, 16th century on.

Cloan GR 962116, **Nether Cloan** GR 962119, **Upper Cloan** GR 969108, all settlements, **Cloan High Wood** GR 970114, **Cloan Burn** & **Cloan Glen** both GR 963110.

In 1800 and 1829 Cloan Burn in its upper reaches appears as 'Carmossly' Burn (q.v.). Mr. Richard Haldane, Cloan, tells me the name 'Cloanden' was used for Cloan from about the mid 1850s to the 1920s.

Earlier forms: c1260 'Clune', 1707 'Cloone', 1752 'Cloan', 1800 'Cloan Burn', 1855 'Overcloan' (ie modern Upper Cloan), 1860 'Cloanden', 'Upper Cloan'. It is possible that the surname 'Clune', 'Clone' came from these lands as Black (see Bibliography) says all the early references are to Fife and Perthshire. His earliest surname form is 'Clone', from 1337.

Derivation: Gaelic 'Cluan', meadow.

***Cloch Law** GR 967077?, on record in 1829, **Glencloch Burn** GR 976080, on record 1829 to the present.

Derivation: The order of 'Glencloch' appears Gaelic and in the absence of earlier forms we can only speculate that it, Cloch Law, and Hodyclach Burn GR 986080 are named from a stone, perhaps now disappeared: Gaelic 'Clach', genitive 'Cloiche', stone.

Clochrat Law GR 151135, **Clochridgestone**, a settlement, now deserted, GR 146134. The 1860 OS Name Book says that the settlement takes its name from the recumbent standing stone near the farmyard.

Earlier forms: 1593-4 'Clothrie stane' (read 'Clochrie'?), 1599 'Clochriestane', 1617 'Clochrastoun', 1752 'Clochrig', 1775 'Clockret Stone', 1781 'Clochrigstain', 1783 'Clochretstone', 1788-1829 'Clochridgestain' & 'Clockridgestone', 1812 'Clochret Stone', 1855 'Clochridgestone', 1860 & 1901 'Clochridgestane', 1894 'Clochrat Law', 1906 'Clochrat Farm', 'Clochrat Law'.

Derivation: The post-1700 forms quoted opt fairly equally for 'Clochridge' & 'Clochrat'. The latter makes sense as a form of Scots 'Clocharet' &c, the wheatear, the stonechat, late 18th to 19th centuries. Haliburton and Jack (see Bibliography), whose detailed local knowledge should no doubt be trusted as regards the name in their own time, give 'Clochrat' adding that 'Clochridge' was given "erroneously" on OS

Cloan House, Drawing by Ken Laing.

maps. I suspect the stone had a Gaelic name, and 'Clach Ruidhe', hillside stone, would fit the situation. The Scots translation 'Stane' was added after the Gaelic period, then the second syllable was reinterpreted as Scots 'Rig' &c, a ridge, a hillcrest, by the mid 18th century. In addition 'Clochrig' appears to have been reinterpreted by some as the bird name 'Clochret'. A local pronunciation I have heard is 'Clockartston'.

Cloon, a hill, GR 036046, **Cloon Burn** GR 040048.

In 1615 the hill was part of the lands of Carnbo OS square 0503.

Earlier forms: 1615 'mons de (ie hill of) Clwne', c1796 'Cloon', 'Cloon Burn'.

Derivation: Gaelic 'Cluan', meadow, pasture. The hill stands at 346 metres but it is fairly flat-topped, and commentators throughout the centuries have praised the excellence of the grazing on the Ochil heights.

Cloven Craigs GR 121132.

***Cloverknows**. On record in 1761 as 'Cloverknows of Glenquoy' (ie Glen Quey OS squares 9803 &c).

The Cloves GR 877001, a hill.

Easter Clow GR 057113, **Wester Clow** GR 057112, **Clow Hill** GR 060118, **Clow Bridge** GR 058109, **Easter Clow Wood** GR 064115, ***Walk-Mill of Clow**, on record from 1719 to 1820, approximate OS square 0511.

The demolition of the small but splendid Clow Bridge in 1993, seemingly to suit commercial interests, is greatly to be lamented. I am told that Clow was abandoned as an independent holding c1914-15. An intriguing fact about Easter Clow is that it is almost exactly due *North* of Wester Clow. Watson & Allan (see Bibliography) point out that in Deeside 'Wester' and 'Easter' in settlement names sometimes translate an earlier Gaelic 'Suas' and 'Sìos', upper and lower, respectively, and WFH Nicolaisen (see Bibliography) quotes, from Highland Perthshire, 'Labhar Shuas' & 'Shìos' becoming 'Wester' & 'Easter Lawers' respectively. At first sight it seemed that something similar might have happened here. However Easter Clow is in fact some 5 to 10 metres *higher* than Wester Clow so another explanation was needed. Mr G Ritchie says that as the holdings were usually approached from the east, the first one reached became known as Easter Clow.

Earlier forms: 1443 'Clow', 1719 'Walk-Mill of Clow', c1750 'The Hill of Clow', 1785 'Wester Clow', 1792 'Easter or Shadow half of Clow', 1820 'Wakmill of Clow', 1860 'Clow Wood', 'Easter Clow Wood', 'Clow Bridge'. Earliest surname form from Black (see Bibliography): 1547 'Clow'.

Derivation: Conceivably Scots 'Clow' &c, claw, from some perceived shape in the terrain?

Wester Clunie GR 211173, **Easter Clunie** GR 221175, **Clunie Field** GR 221176, ***Middle Clunie**, on record from 1750 to 1792, all settlements, **Clunie Wood**, recorded in 1860, ***Clunie Muir**, recorded from 1828 to 1855.

Earlier references: 1592 'Cluny', 1595 'W Cluny', 'E Cluny', 1855 'Clunie Bleachfield' (now Clunie Field), 1860 'Clunie Field'.

Derivation: Gaelic 'Cluanach', locative 'Cluanaigh', at meadow place.

Coalcraigy Hill GR 041076. Earlier: c1796 'Coal cragie', 1860 'Coalcraigy Hill'.

Derivation: Perhaps Gaelic 'Cùil Creagaigh', nook at craggy place.

Cock Law GR 032102, on record since 1860.

Derivation: 'Cock' can sometimes represent P-Celtic 'Coch', red, but this hill may simply be named for the male grouse. Scots 'Law', a rounded hill, in placenames 12th century on.

Cockersfauld, a settlement, GR 026109, **Cockersfauld Hill** GR 022110.

Earlier: 1783 'Cockersfold', 1818 'Cuchiesfold', 1860 'Cockersfauld Hill'. Derivation: Unless the 1818 form quoted represents something old and obscure, this seems likely to be simply from the surname 'Cocker'?

Cockplea GR 860053, a settlement.

Earlier forms: 1600 'Cokplay', 1654 'Cockpla', c1723 'Cockplay', 1855 'Cockpla', 1860 'Cockplay'.

Derivation: *The Concise Scots Dictionary* dates 'Cock' from the late 14th century. 'Pla' was a Scots variant spelling for English 'Play', late 14th century on. 'Play' in its turn was a Scots variant spelling for 'Plea', quarrel, strife, discord, 16th century on, so the allusion here may be to either the display or the combat of male game birds.

Cock's Burn GR 800987, **Cocksburn Reservoir**, GR 808986, **Cocksburn Wood** GR 816988.

Earlier: 1723 'Kocksburn', 1848 'Coxburn', 1860 'Cox Burn'.

Derivation: Quite possibly from the male of one of the species of game bird.

Cold Well, on record in 1860, GR 038105 approximately.

Cocksburn Reservoir in the middle distance. (AW)

***Coldcats**, a settlement?, on record in 1783 in OS square 8099 approximately.

Coldennook, a settlement on record between 1775 & 1906. It was at or close to the site of present Warroch House GR 069045.

Earlier forms: 1775 'Couden Nook', c1796 'Cowdennook', 1860 'Coldennook'.

Derivation: Gaelic 'Calltuinn', hazel, with later addition of Scots 'Neuk', 'Nook', nook, corner, late 15th century on.

***Coldhame**, a settlement on record in 1783 in OS square 9409 approximately.

***Cole brack Burn**. In 1774 this seems to have been the name of the burn at GR 095143. An alternative name in use at the same period, 'Crook Dich', is a secondary name from Crook of Arnbathie GR 096146 approximately.

Derivation: Gaelic 'Cùil Breac', chequered or speckled nook. 'Breac' can often refer to the visual effect of a mixture of vegetation, grass and bracken for instance. 'Dich' is Scots, referring to a gully, a dell, and by extension a burn running through such a gully.

Colin's Wood GR 235130.

***Collennoweis** was a barony in the late 16th century. A charter of 1580 refers to the lands of 'Collennowyis' as Holton, Netherton, Middleton, Plains, Clashdeuglie, Gollockmuir, Glendy Mill and Blairhill (I have given these names in their modern form).

Derivation: This seems to be 'Colin('s)' followed by Scots 'Knowes', knolls, 16th century on. The location of the lands of this barony makes it likely that it was connected with Colliston, earlier 'Colleinstoun', 'Collinstoune', 'Colenstoun' &c – see the next entry.

Colliston GR 141075 & GR 135085, ie two settlements with the same name. It seems likely that this name was connected with the 16th century barony of Collennoweis – see the previous entry.

Earlier forms: 1539 'Colestoun', c1554 'Collinstoun', 1592 'Colleinstoun', 1618 'Colenstoun', 1650 'Collingston', 1654 'Collestone', 1860 'Colliston Plantation'.

Derivation: Likely to be Scots, Colin's Toun. The most prestigious bearers of the name Colin in the Ochils area around this time would be likely to be Campbells, established at Castle Campbell from the mid 15th century. I personally have seen no evidence that they held lands in this particular spot however.

Colsnaur Hill GR 861994. Earlier: 1783 'Coalsnarr Hill'. Derivation: Gaelic 'Cùl', back of, seems likely here, with an unknown second element.

North Colzie & **South Colzie** both GR 211144, **Wester Colzie** GR 201142, **Easter Colzie** GR 232138, **Colzie Hill** GR 227145 and **Colzie Wood** GR 230144. **Colzie Smithy** stood beside Lumquhat Mill in 1860, OS square 2313. ***The Colzie Burn** GR 210141 is also known as Glassart Burn and Beggars Burn (qq.v.), and Loverspool Burn where it flows through Auchtermuchty around GR 236120.

Earlier references: 1511 'Ester Coilsy', 1517 'the two parts of Cosie', 1590 'Colsay-burne alias Auchtermuchtie-burne', 1654 'Wester Colsey', 1823 'Colzie', 1855 'South Colzie', 1860 'North Colzie'.

Derivation: Gaelic 'Coille', a wood or forest, with reinterpretation as 'z' of the Scots letter 'yogh' which represented the semi-vowel [j] but resembled a hand written 'z'. The site is in Pitmedden Forest, still a partly wooded area.

Common Burn GR 020102 is a secondary name from Common of Dunning.

Common Hill GR 940050. Earlier forms: 1587 'Commounhill', 1664 'Common-Hill of Gleneglis' (a settlement).

Commonedge Hill GR 980015.

Earlier references: 1800 'the Muir called Common Edge' & 'the Common called Common Edge', 1860 'Commonedge Hill'.

Mains of Condie GR 075123, **Path of Condie** GR 073117, settlements, **Condie Wood** GR 077135 and **Condie Hill** GR 063123. **Condie Mill** is on record from 1713 to 1860 and was a sawmill at that latter date. **Pathmill**, on record 1679 to 1860, and **Pathfoot**, on record in 1855-

Path of Condie photographed in 1909. Reproduced by permission of Perth Museum and Art Gallery.

The ruins of Condie House photographed in 1909. Reproduced by permission of Perth Museum and Art Gallery.

60, both GR 074118, and **Pathgreen** GR 073116, are all secondary names from Path of Condie. **Woodhead** GR 079129, on record between 1728 and 1860, and **Woodfoot** GR 078136, on record since 1855, both appear earlier as 'of Condie'. **Woodside** GR 077136 I also take to be a secondary name from Condie.

Robert Burns is said to have inscribed his name with a ring on a window pane at Path of Condie school after a visit to Invermay House OS square 0616.

Earlier: 1505 'Condy', 1550 'the Mains of Condy', 1659 'Path of Condie', 1679 'Path Mylne', 1713 'Condiemiln', 1728 'Woodhead of Condie', 1769 'Pathgreen', 1826 'north & south Woodheads', 1855 'Pendicle of Woodfoot of Condie', 'Pathfoot of Condie', 1860 'Condie Hill', 'Condie Wood', 'Woodside'. Earliest surname form from Black (see Bibliography): 1414 'John de Conady'.

Derivation: WFH Nicolaisen (1962 – see Bibliography) states that 'Condie' is "early Gaelic" and was originally a watercourse name, now Chapel Burn OS square 0708. If it is a watercourse name it may be related to Gaelic 'Condasach', furious. Alternatively, 'Conda', canine, surviving in Irish but now obsolete in Scottish Gaelic, could be borne in mind. Liddall (see Bibliography) derives 'Condie' from a Gaelic personal name 'Contan'. He also considers that 'Path' is for P-Celtic (Pictish) 'Pett', 'Pit', portion of land, but no early spellings I have seen support that possibility. Scots 'Peth', 'Path' &c, a steep track or road leading down into a ravine and up the other side, in placenames 12th century on, fits this site perfectly.

Conlan Hill, on record between 1796 & 1860 at GR 075058. 'Conlan' is obscure to me.

Conland GR 146111, **North Conland** GR 147112, settlements. Earlier forms: 1295 (Perhaps this site) 'Conlony' & 1323 'Condolan'; c1341 but transcribed c1554-79 as 'Condolane' & transcribed c1622-32 as 'Condland', 1507-8 'Condelane', 1515-21 'Condolane', 'Condolen' & 'Condelane', 1599 'Condland', 1647 'Condlandis', 1654 'Conland'. This name is obscure to me.

Conlin Knowe GR 086110 is on record since 1860. **Conlin Road**, mentioned by the 1860 OS Name Book, passed over Newtoft Hill and is perhaps the track at GR 085110.

Derivation: In the absence of really early forms, this may be Gaelic 'Con Linn', dog falls, from Gaelic 'Con' the plural of 'Cù', a dog, and Gaelic 'Linne', a waterfall, a pool below a waterfall. Falls are marked on the adjacent Slateford Burn and one of them may have borne this name.

***Connel's Spout** OS square 9610 is described by Haldane (1944 – see Bibliography) as a waterfall "30 to 40 ft high" named "to commemorate the man who once lived in what is now the keeper's house eking out, it is said, a hard and bare existence on the croft by illicit distilling". The "keeper's house" was Bellshill GR 963103 and John Connal, "one time tenant of Billshill (ie Bellshill) and Turfpark", is referred to in a feudal disposition of 1863. Scots 'Spout', 19th century on, is a waterfall.

Coppermine Path GR 797979, a track, near an old coppermine.

Corb, a settlement, GR 009089, **Corb Burn** GR 009090, **Corb Glen** GR 000084, **Corb Law** GR 003092, **Corb Bridge** GR 016085.

Earlier references: 1428 'Crob', 1488 'Ovir Corb', 'Nethir Corb', 1613 'South Crob', 1619 'North Corb', 1750 'Corb Hill' (ie Corb Law?), 1798 "Little Corb called North Corb', 1829 'Corb Law', 'North Corb', 'South Corb', 'Meadow Burn' (ie Corb Burn), 1860 'Corb Glen', 'Corb Burn', 'Corb Bridge'.

Derivation: For the 1428 & 1613 forms quoted

Corb Farm & Corb Law.Drawing by Ken Laing.

compare Gaelic 'Crob', later 'Crobh', a hand, a claw, possibly referring here to some perceived shape in the terrain. For instance the contours on the North side of Corb Law on OS maps trace the shape of a hand with outstretched thumb and clenched fingers, though this is not easy to make out on the ground and may be merely a tantalising coincidence. Whatever the etymology, metathesis seems to have reversed the position of 'r' and 'o' (see 1428 & 1613 forms quoted) as it did in the alternatives 'Crob' and 'Corb' for a similarly named site in Alyth parish in 1506.

Cordon Hill GR 202150, **Cordonhill**, on record in 1860, a settlement at GR 205158 approximately. Earlier: 1860 'Cordon Hill'.

These are secondary names from Cordon sq 1817.

Core Hill GR 886047. Earlier: 1654 'the Coir' & 'the Core', 1783 'Core Hill'.

Derivation: WJ Watson (see Bibliography) explains this as a part translation of Gaelic 'Còrr-Bheinn', pointed horn or peak.

Corim Hill GR 928044, **Corim Burn** GR 930043, both on record since 1860. In the absence of really early forms this name is obscure to me.

Easter Cornhill GR 978000, **Wester Cornhill** GR 977997. Both these settlements figure simply as 'Cornhill' on the 1860 OS map.

Earlier references: 1569 'the hill of Pitgober called Cornehill', 1783 'Cornhill', 1823 'the Innerhill of Pitgogar (ie Pitgober) called Cornhill', 1855 'Oxgate of Cornhill'.

Derivation: As the references imply, the land now represented by these holdings was earlier part of the arable land of Pitgober OS square 9798. No doubt this site and 'lie Gersehill', later Grasshill (q.v.) were named as a contrasting pair. An oxgate (see the 1855 reference) was a measure of land, usually taken to be in the region of 13 Scots acres, about 6.5 hectares.

Cornhill GR 280132, a settlement. This may represent the earlier corn land of some larger nearby holding, estate or barony, but I have come across no earlier references.

Corn Hill GR 952091, **Cornhill** GR 948100, a settlement, **Cornhill Cottage** GR 948103. Haldane (1944 – see Bibliography) has 'the Cornhill Burn' and 'the glen of Cornhill' for Carlownie Burn GR 950089 and the glen in which it runs. Though the hill name is virtually certain to have been the primary feature I have not found it on record before 1860, 77 years later than the farm to which it presumably gave its name. In general, natural features are much less well documented than settlements and the date of their first appearance on record often tells us little about the date when they were actually first coined.

Derivation: Like the Cornhills of the two previous entries this is likely to have been the earlier corn land of some larger nearby holding, estate or barony.

***Corra Linn**, mentioned by Jack (1906 – see Bibliography) as a "cascade" on the Dron Burn, OS square 1314.

Derivation: Gaelic 'Coire', a cauldron, a corrie,

with Gaelic 'Linne' or the Scots loanword from it, a waterfall, a pool below a waterfall. Compare the not uncommon Scots waterfall name 'Cauldron Linn'.

***Corrachie**, a holding on record from c1544 and forming part of the barony of Gleneagles. It was absorbed into the Mains of Gleneagles c1799.

Derivation: Perhaps Gaelic 'Coire Achadh' or 'Coire Achaidh', which could translate as either 'field corrie' or 'corrie field', with 'field' probably in the sense of a cleared piece of ground. If this is the case the corrie concerned may have been Corryuby GR 944074. Another possible derivation is 'Còrr Achadh', tapering 'field'.

Corrinzion GR 169106, a settlement.

Earlier: 1494 'Carrynane', 1516 'Carrynzheane', 'Carringzeane', 1654 'Caringean', 1828 'Carinzion'.

Derivation: The written forms suggest a Gaelic original such as 'Còrr an Ein' or 'Còrr nan Eun', bog or moss of the bird or birds, with 'z' and 'g' representing the semi-vowel [j] as they can often do in Scots orthography. However, one modern pronunciation I have heard accents the second syllable, which suggests that '-inzion' may be for Gaelic 'Innean', anvil, which appears to suit the shape of the hilltop at GR 167107.

Corryuby, a corrie, & **Corryuby Burn**, both GR 944074, are both on record since 1860.

Derivation: Gaelic 'Coire', a corrie, with an obscure second element.

Corse Burn GR 060066.

Earlier forms: 1752 'Corseburn', 1783 'Crossburn', c1796 'Corse Burn'.

Derivation: Scots 'Corse', cross, crossways, as in 'Corshous', a house standing crossways to others, late 16th to early 17th centuries. Corse burn runs East to West, at right angles to Warroch East Burn.

Mickle Corum GR 857025, **Little Corum** GR 860036, hills. ***Little Carim** was a settlement West of Millstone Burn in approximate OS square 8403, ***Orchals Carim** would be a Carim holding belonging to Orchill OS square 8711 & ***Green Scares of Little Carim** may be connected with 'Scares Hill' and 'Pirrack of Skershill' (q.v.), approximate OS square 8403. **Carim Lodge** GR 858052, **Carim Burn** GR 858040, **Carim Cottage** GR 858052.

Earlier references: 1551 'Coryne', 1687 'Carrin', 1736 'Mickle Carim', 'Little Carim', 'Orchals Carim', 1805 & 1821 'part of Rotearns called Carrim' (ie Rottearns OS square 8407), 1808 'part of the Barony of Ogilvy viz Carrim', 1855 'Carim' (a farm), 1860 'Carrim Lodge', 'Mickle Corum', 'Little Corum'.

WJ Watson (see Bibliography) suggests Gaelic 'Còrr-thom', taper knoll, for 'Corum', but the earlier forms of the name do not bear this out. The pronunciation I have heard is 'Crim', which implies that the stress originally fell on the second syllable. The lack of stress on the first vowel might explain the uncertainty in spelling it. The 1551 form quoted could be for Gaelic 'Coire Ighne', claw or talon corrie, from some perceived shape on the ground.

Carim Lodge , with Little Corum on the skyline. (AW)

Cottartown, a settlement on record until 1860, GR 981000 approximately, close to the site of modern Castleton.

Earlier: 1783 'Cottertown'.

Derivation: Scots 'Cottar toun', a hamlet, especially of farm cottages, 16th century on, from Scots 'Cottar', a married farmworker who has a cottage as part of his contract, 15th century on.

***Cotterknow**, a settlement on record until 1818. A cottage at GR 023141 still has this name and presumably represents the location.

Earlier forms: 1653 'Cotterknow of Pittcairns' (ie Pitcairns OS square 0214), 1661 'Cottoune', 1708 'Cottersknow', 1818 'Cotterknow of Pitcairns'.

Derivation: Scots 'Cottar', a married farmworker who has a cottage as part of his contract, 15th century on; Scots 'Knowe', knoll, 16th century on.

A house name marking the location of Cotterknow of Pitcairns, Dunning. (AW)

North Cotton, a settlement on record in 1860, GR 227163 approximately.

Derivation: Scots 'Cot Toun', a township of farmworkers' tied cottages, 16th century on.

***Cottown**, a settlement on record in 1750, approximate OS square 0615.

Derivation: Scots 'Cot Toun', a township of farmworkers' tied cottages, 16th century on.

***Cottown**, a settlement on record in 1775 in OS square 1912 or 1913, just North of Dumbarrow.

Derivation: Scots 'Cot Toun', a township of farmworkers' tied cottages, 16th century on.

***Cottowns**, on record until 1824, seemingly in the vicinity of Blairstruie OS square 1313.

Earlier: 1493 'Cotownis', 1650 'Cotoune'.

Derivation: Scots 'Cot Toun', a township of farmworkers' tied cottages, 16th century on.

Coul GR 967125, **Upper Coul** GR 974121, **Easter Coul** GR 972127, all settlements. **Heuch of Coul** runs from GR 975121 to GR 976124 approximately. **Coul Hill** GR 975104, **Coul Burn** GR 980092, **Coulshill**, a settlement, GR 979093, **Coulshill Burn** & **Glen of Coulshill** both GR 996095. ***Hill of Coul**, on record until 1829, appears to be a holding mainly in OS square 9710 centred on the modern Coul Hill. The 1860 OS Name Book describes Heuch of Coul as a "remarkable" rocky chasm carrying the Pairney Burn.

Earlier references: c1260 'Coule', 1488 'Cowlyshill', 1749 'Over Coull', 'Nether Coull', 'the hill of Coull', 1750 'Craig of Coul' (ie Castle Craig OS square 9712?), 1829 'Coul Burn', 'Glen of Couls Hill', 1846 'Easter Coul', 1855 'Overcoul', 1860 'Upper Coul', 'Coul Hill', 'Coulshill Burn'.

Derivation: Gaelic 'Cùil', nook, tucked away place.

The Heuch of Coul. (AW)

Coulsknowe GR 011053, a settlement.

Earlier: 1650 'Cowlisknow', 1808 'the fourth part of the lands of Coulsknow and Fannyhill commonly called the Infield Room of Fannyhill' (ie Inner Fannyhill approximate square 0105?).

Derivation: I know of no evidence that the lands of Coul ever extended this far (see previous entry). 'Coulsknowe' nonetheless looks likely to be from Gaelic 'Cùil', nook, tucked away place, with later addition of Scots 'Knowe', knoll.

Coupers Hill GR 068110, on record since 1860.

Derivation: The 1860 OS Name Book cites a local tradition that the name derives from 'horse dealer', Scots 'Couper' &c, a horse-dealer, late 16th century on.

Court Knowe GR 987048, on record since 1860.

Derivation: Like the Cuthil names (q.v.) this name may indicate the former meeting place of a local judicial court under hereditary jurisdiction. Gallows Hill is in the same OS square.

Court Knowe GR 206102, marked as an antiquity on the OS Landranger sheet.

Derivation: Like the Cuthil names (q.v.) this name may indicate the former meeting place of a local judicial court under hereditary jurisdiction. Demperston OS square 2211, the 'toun' of the officer of the court who pronounced sentence, is just over 2 miles away.

***Cow Burn**, on record in 1829, rises at GR 983094.

***Cow Strand**, on record in 1774, GR 108145 approximately.

Derivation: Scots 'Strand', a small stream, late 15th century.

Cowcleuch Burn 963040, on record since 1860.

Derivation: Scots 'Cleuch', a gorge, a ravine, in placenames 12th century on. The burn flows in very steep country.

Cowden, a settlement at GR 265148 on record until 1860, **Cowden Hill** GR 266153.

Earlier: 1595 (Perhaps) 'Cordon' (read 'Cowden'?), 1653 'Cowdoun of Wodmilne' (ie Woodmiln OS square 2715).

Derivation: Gaelic 'Calltuinn', hazel.

Cowiefauld GR 194096, a settlement.

Derivation: Scots 'Fauld' &c, a fold, a pen, a small field, late 14th century on.

Cows Moss GR 024102.

Earlier: 1723 'Coos Moss'. Macfarlane (1723 – see Bibliography) calls it "very serviceable to the people".

Derivation: Scots 'Moss', boggy ground, peat bog, late 14th century.

*Burn of **Cowstraw**, an unidentified burn on Sheriffmuir, on record in 1766.

***Craig Burn**, on record from 1617 until 1906, and also known as Boyak Burn (q.v.). It emerges from Clevage Loch OS square 0513 and passes to the North East of Easter Clevage OS square 0514. Earlier: 1617 & 1625 'Craigburne alias Boyakburne'.

Derivation: 'Craigis', a settlement on record in 1617, appears to have been close by and may have given its name to the burn.

Craig Head GR 949096. Earlier: 1860 'Craig Head'.

Craig Well GR 112065. Earlier: 1860 'Craig Well'.

Craigden, a settlement, GR 187150.

Derivation: The Scots loanword 'Craig', from Gaelic 'Creag', rock, crag; Scots 'Den', a narrow valley especially with trees, 16th century on.

Craigdownie, a crag, GR 223159. Earlier: On record since 1860.

Derivation: Gaelic 'Creag Dùnaigh', crag at hill place.

***Craigend**, a settlement in approximate OS square 9705, on record in 1783.

Craigendivots GR 082121, on record since 1860. The 1860 OS Name Book describes this as a number of large rocks on either side of the Water of May near its junction with Chapel Burn. It is 'Craigendirots' on some OS maps. I am told that the site is now known locally as 'The Craigs'.

Derivation. 'Craigen-' is likely to be Gaelic 'Creag', rock, crag, followed by the genitive article 'an' or 'nan', 'of the', with '-divots' as a reinterpretation of an unidentified Gaelic noun.

Craigenroe Hill GR 054139, on record since 1860. The 1860 OS Name Bk suggests 'Creagan Ruadh', little red hill, though Gaelic 'Creag an Ruaidh' or 'Creag nan Ruadh', craig of the roe deer, is equally possible. Ruglen and Roeglen Wood are nearby and their names too could refer either to a red colour in the landscape or the presence of roe deer.

Craigentaggert, a crag, GR 907052, **Craigentaggert Hill**, on record since 1860, GR 906057.

Derivation: Gaelic 'Creag an t-Sagairt', the Priest's crag. If only all Gaelic names were so well preserved!

***Craigfodd**, GR 182103, is on record between 1240 and 1771 as the name for what is now Freeland. The latter name began to be used in the early 18th century.

Earlier forms: 1240-49 'Craigfod', 1505-7 'Cragfod' & 'Cragfode'.

Derivation: Gaelic 'Creag', rock, crag, and Gaelic 'Fòd'. The sense could be 'peat crag', 'peats crag' or 'sward crag' depending on the precise grammatical form of the original.

Coulshill Billies. Hay-making at Coulshill in the late 1800s photographed by Magnus Jackson. Reproduced by permission of Perth Museum and Art Gallery.

Craighall, a settlement on record in 1860 at GR 983049.

***Craighead**, a settlement in OS square 0112 approximately, was on record between 1719 and 1783. Its alternative name 'Woodhead' has also disappeared.

Earlier: 1719 'Woodhead alias Craighead Keltie's ground' (ie Keltie OS square 0013).

Craighead Farm GR 044040. As the earlier reference shows, it was formerly part of Carnbo OS square 0503.

Earlier: 1615 'Craigheid alias Wester Carniebo'.

Craighead, a settlement, GR 087114. As the earlier reference shows it was formerly part of Pitquhanatrie, but it has outlived that older and more substantial holding.

Earlier: 1820 'the quarter of Pitwhanatry called Craighead'.

Craighorn GR 885003, a hill, ***Craighorn Burn** & ***Spout of Craighorn**, a large waterfall by which Craighorn Burn enters Alva Glen. The 'Spout' may be at GR 883987 on the burn now also known as Glenwinnel Burn and Benever Burn?

A Waterfall near Coul Photographed by Magnus Jackson in the late 1800s. Reproduced by permission of Perth Museum and Art Gallery.

Earlier: 1783 'Craigharr'.

Derivation: WJ Watson (see Bibliography) says that this is " 'myre rock', near it is Myreton Hill", deriving 'Horn' from Gaelic (Old Irish) 'Gronna', a bog, a mossy moor, with metathesis reversing the position of 'r' and 'o'. Myreton Hill though is some two miles away as the crow flies and in any case takes its name no doubt from The Myretoun OS square 8597 near Menstrie, much lower down. Gaelic 'Creag Chùirn' is not impossible as 'Còrn', genitive 'C(h)ùirn', horn, may here have the sense of spur or promontory and refer to the hill's shape. The 1783 form fits neither of these suggestions however and if reliable suggests an original along the lines of Gaelic 'Creag Chàrra', rock-shelf crag.

Craigie Cleuch GR 996997. Through it runs Back Burn.

Derivation: 'Craigie' may be the Scots adjective or be from a Gaelic locative 'Creagaigh', at craggy place.

Craigincat, on record between 1783 and 1901 as a settlement, approximate OS square 0913. I am told it was the site of a meal mill. ***Craigencat Burn** GR 099140 approximately is recorded in 1774.

Derivation: Gaelic 'Creag nan Cat', craig of the wild cats.

***Craiginfermer**, a settlement in approximate OS square 0805. Derivation: This name occurs in a 17th century transcription of a charter of c1346. If reliable it implies a hybrid name, Gaelic 'Creag nan', craig of the, plus Scots 'Fairmer' &c, farmer?

Craiginnan GR 961002. A sheepfold is marked here on the 1860 OS map, I am told that the farmhouse was last occupied in the early 19th century. **Craiginnan Hill** GR 954004 is also known as Saddle Hill. **Craiginnan Falls**, on the Burn of Care, are at GR 962994. In the late 18th century Craiginnan was famed for the quality of its mutton and wool and at that time belonged to the Duke of Argyle.

Earlier: c1680 'Craiginin', 1793 'Craiginnan Hill Farm'.

Derivation: Gaelic 'Creag', crag, rock. '-innan' could possibly be from Gaelic 'Innean', genitive 'Innein', anvil, giving 'anvil crag' from some perceived shape in the landscape. Alternatively Gaelic 'Creag Ingheann', maiden crag, would point to a possible link with nearby Maiden's Well & Maiden's Castle (qq.v) – near these sites are crags or rocky outcrops which could have given rise to the original name.

*__Craigleith__, on record in 1591. Perhaps the crags marked on the North side of Broom Hill OS square 2013.

Derivation: Gaelic 'Creag Liath', grey crag.

Craigly Burn GR 994088. Earlier references: 1783 'Craigly' (a settlement?), 1829 'Craigly Burn'.

Craigomish, GR 850972, on record since 1860. A "precipitous knoll" in the words of the 1860 OS Name Book.

Derivation: This form of the name was given to the original Ordnance Survey surveyors c1860 by three different informants and looks very likely to be Gaelic 'Creag Thòmais', Thomas's Craig. The name also occurs now as 'Craigomas' – which doesn't rule out 'Thomas' – and 'Craig o Moss', which is understood locally to be Scots, referring to the crag on the way to the peat bog. I have had 'Craigomas' from a Menstrie man and 'Craigomish' from a Tillicoultry man. 'Craig o Moss' looks like a reinterpretation, perhaps a fairly recent one.

Craigow GR 088064, **Craigowmeigle** GR 083070, **Craigomill** GR 090057, **Nether Craigow** GR 091058, all settlements, **Craigow Burn** GR 084061, ***Knock of Craigow**, on record from 1796 to 1828, a hill at GR 076076. Secondary names from the last of these are **Knock Wood** GR 076076 & ***Knock Burn**, on record c1798, which rises at GR 078081.

Earlier references: 1615 'Nether Craigow', 1616 'Over Crago', 'molendinum (ie mill) de Crago', 1626 'the Mylne of Nether Crago', 1654 'Craigo-mylne', 1750 'Upper Craigie', 'North Craigie', c1796 'Craigymeigle', 1860 'Upper Craigo' (ie modern Craigow), 'Craigo Burn', 'Craigo mill (corn)'.

Derivation: Gaelic 'Creag', rock, crag – crags are at GR 092065. '-ow', '-o', '-ie', is most likely to be from the Gaelic adjectival ending '-ach', giving 'Creagach', craggy place. '-meigle' in 'Craigowmeigle', like Meigle near Blairgowrie, WJ Watson (see Bibliography) considers to be from P-Celtic 'Mig Dol', bog meadow.

Craigowerhouse GR 241126, a hill. Earlier: On record since 1860.

Derivation: Gaelic 'Creag Ghobhar', goat crag, or 'Creag Odhar', dun-coloured crag.

Craigowny Hill GR 089142,on record since 1860.

Derivation: Gaelic 'Creag Gamhnaigh', crag at stirk place. Auchengownie & Ardgowny (qq.v.), just over a mile away, are also named from the raising or pasturing of stirks.

Craigs GR 154091, a hill, **Craigs Well** GR 158092. Earlier: 1860 'Craigs Well'.

East Craigs GR 944069, **West Craigs** GR 936066. Both are on record since 1860.

*__The Craigs__. An alternative name for Craigendivots OS square 0812.

Craigshonnochy GR 086141, a settlement. **Craigshonnochy Wood** is recorded in 1860. Earlier forms: 1860 'Craigshannochy' & 'Craigshonnochy'.

Derivation: In the absence of really early forms, perhaps Gaelic 'Creag Sheanachaidh', story-teller, historian, genealogist crag, referring to one of the traditional 'office-bearers', as it were, of Gaelic society.

Craigwell GR 075035, a settlement. Earlier: On record in 1860.

*__Cree Craig__ GR 975129. See Kay Craig.

Creich Burn GR 992060, **White Creich Hill** GR 995061, **Black Creich Hill** GR 997065, are all on record since 1860. It is not unusual for two hills or other features to have the same name and to be distinguished by 'Black' and 'White', even if they are not so coloured. Also **Easter Creich Burn** on record in 1860, GR 995056.

Derivation: Gaelic 'Allt na Crìche', 'Cnoc na Crìche', march or boundary burn, march or boundary hill, may well lie behind this name.

*__Croik Hoill__, recorded in 1574. This is seemingly on the South face of Seamab Hill OS square 9901.

Derivation: Scots 'Cruik' &c, a hook, but in toponymy referring to a bend of some kind, in placenames 13th century on; Scots 'Holl', 'Hole' &c, a hole, a hollow, late 14th century on.

Crombie Wood GR 132115.

Derivation: 'Crombie' can derive from Gaelic (Old Irish) 'Cromb', Gaelic 'Crom', P-Celtic 'Crwm', bent. Here it may well simply be from the surname however.

Cross Burn GR 030028, ***Crossburn Mill**, on record between 1775 & 1783, GR 041027 approximately where there were the ruins of a corn mill in 1860.

Earlier: 1860 'Cross Burn'. Derivation: The lie of the land takes this burn a good way eastwards before it is able to plunge South towards the Pow Burn.

*__Crossmagouge__. The reference, dated 1819, reads: 'the lands of Crossmagouge, being part of the lands & Estate of Craigpotty lying without the Parks thereof'. Craigpotty was the estate also known as Ayton, OS squares 1615 &c.

Derivation: On the face of it this name looks like Gaelic 'Crois Mo Gouge', the Cross of my Saint "Gouge". The Gaelic possessive 'mo', my, was commonly used as an affectionate prefix to saints' names and often transcribed in placenames as 'ma', as in 'Ecclesiamagirdle' OS square 1016.

Croupie Craigs GR 179156.

Derivation: Scots 'Croupie', a raven, 19th century on. The 1860 OS Name Book states that a pair of "corbies" (ie ravens) nested here for "some years".

Crow Wood GR 240154. I have no earlier forms but it could be borne in mind that 'Crow' is sometimes from Gaelic 'Crò', a sheepfold.

Crowclag GR 168151, a hill.

Derivation: The 1860 OS Name Book reports that this was a "favourite residence" of a "considerable number" of crows. For the second part, perhaps Scots 'Clag', a lump or mass of clay, mud &c, 19th century on.

Crunie Burn GR 838990. This is also known as the Fourth Inchna Burn.

Derivation: Possibilities might be Gaelic 'Allt na Cruinnich', misty burn, burn of the mist, or even 'Allt a' Chruithnich', the Pict's burn.

Culteuchar GR 082159, a settlement, **Culteuchar Burn** GR 080157, **Culteuchar Hill** GR 097152. Earlier references: 1505-11 'Ovir' & 'Nethir' 'Culcuiquhir', 'Culcuquhir', 'Colkewhyr', 'Culcuichquhir' & 'Colquhuir', 1537 'terras de Nethir Cowlequhecher, cum mansione, molendino, terras molendinariis, silva, lacu, et lie forestar-seittis earundem' (the lands of Nethir Cowlequhecher with the dwelling, the mill, the mill lands, the forest, the loch and the forester seats of the same), 1581 'Cultuquhair', 1593 'West Milne of Culteucher' (ie perhaps Westmiln OS square 1016?), 1621 'Coltcuchquhar', 1623 'Coltoqr', 1624 'Colkeuquhar', 'Mylne of Colkeuquhar', 1645 'Colcuquhar', 1650 'Cultuqher', 1658 'Cultioquhoir' & 'Cultiequhair', 1667 'Colceuquhar' 1681 'Colteuchar', 1690 'Cultcuquhair', 1720 'Culteucher', 1750 'Branders' (ie the present Culteuchar), 1774 'Halfpenny Burn' (ie the present Culteuchar Burn), 'Drumdriel' (ie the present Culteuchar Hill), 1789 & 1820 'Over Culteuchar & pendicle called Branders', 1801 'Wester Culteucher' (ie the former Branders, present Culteuchar), 'Easter Culteucher' (ie the former Over Culteuchar and Culteuchar, GR 096155), 'Halfpenny Burn', 'Drumdriel', 1860 'Culteuchar' (ie the former Branders, present Culteuchar), 'Old Culteuchar' (ie the former Culteuchar & Easter Culteucher, GR 096155), 'Culteuchar Burn', Culteuchar Hill', late 1800s 'Culteuchar', 'Old Culteuchar', 'Culteuchar Hill'.

All that remains of the earlier Culteuchar steading, near Culteuchar Hill and Castle Law. (AW)

A complicated one! 'Nether Culteuchar' of the 1537 reference quoted could have been the holding later known as Branders, the present Culteuchar. The fact that I have found no reference to 'Nether Culteuchar' after the first appearance of the name 'Branders' lends some support to this. At the same time however, 'lacu(s)' (ie loch) and 'silva' (ie forest), in the same reference, raise at least the possibility that Nether Culteuchar was on the lower ground, near the present Lochend and Woodend, both OS square 0816. From the early 19th century the references show Over Culteuchar losing importance and becoming 'Easter Culteuchar', then 'Old Culteuchar', before being abandoned. Branders however, after a time as 'Wester Culteuchar', was by 1860 'Culteuchar' and the main holding. Halfpenny Burn (q.v.), in the 1774 & 1801 references above, is still used locally for what the OS maps call Culteuchar Burn.

Derivation: The many early forms which have the second part of this name beginning in 'c' or 'k' must rule out the suggestion by WJ Watson (see Bibliography) of Gaelic 'Eochair', now obsolete in Scottish Gaelic, a bank, the edge of a river, which in any case does not describe the site of the earlier holding at GR 096155. Gaelic 'Cùil', a nook, a tucked away place, is almost certainly the first part. The only suggestion I have for a second part beginning in 'c' is Gaelic 'Cuchar', a hunter, giving 'Cùil Cuchair', hunter's nook. There certainly appears to have been significant hunting activity at Culteuchar after the Gaelic period judging from the 'forestar-seittis' mentioned in the reference quoted above from 1537: A 'Foresterseat' was land held by the forester of a hunting forest. See also Branders.

***Cunnynghoillis**, a settlement on record between 1591 & 1617, approximate OS square 2317. This is the same site as the unclear name on a late 16th century map by Timothy Pont (see List of Maps & Plans Consulted) which looks like 'Luninghals'.

Fank at Culteuchar, July 1994. (AW)

Derivation: Scots 'Cuning' &c, a rabbit, 15th century on; Scots 'Holl' &c, a hole, late 14th century on, or a howe, a hollow, 16th century on.

Cuparlaw Wood GR 805992. This appears to be a secondary use of a lost 'Cupar Law' (I have no name for the round topped hill at GR 815997).

Derivation: WJ Watson (see Bibliography) says that Cupar Fife, Cupar-maculty and Coupar-Angus "are doubtless British", ie P-Celtic. Alternatively, compare Coupers Hill OS square 0610, possibly from Scots 'Couper', a horse-dealer, late 16th century on.

***Curly Hall**, on record in 1775, is a settlement at GR 242165 approximately.

Cuthil Towers GR 153080, a settlement, representing an earlier **Cuthilgourdy**. Also **Cuthil Moor**, centred on GR 152072 approximately and on record between 1796 & 1860, and **Cuthilmoor Inn** GR 149067 approximately, on record in 1860. Sibbald (see Bibliography) mentions that the barony of Cuthilgourdy was removed from Fife & Perth in 1685 and placed in Kinross-shire.

Earlier: 1471 'terras baronie de (ie baronial lands of) Cuthilgurdy', 1577 'Cuthill Burngranys alias Burnsyde' (see Burnside OS square 1608), 1636 'Cuthill'.

Derivation: 'Gourdie' was obscure to WJ Watson (see Bibliography) and is so to me. Professor GWS Barrow (1981 – see Bibliography) suggests that Cuthil names probably derive from Gaelic 'Còmhdhail', assembly, meeting, and represent a former meeting place of a local judicial court (compare Court Knowe).

***Easter Cuthill**, a settlement in approximate OS square 0113, is on record until 1783.

Earlier: 1709 'Cuthell Keltie's ground', & 1709 & 1721 'Cuthill of Keltie' (ie Keltie OS square 0013).

Derivation: This name quite possibly represents the former meeting place of a judicial court – for further information see the previous entry. There is a Gallows Knowe nearby at GR 017143.

***Cuthliebog**, on record between 1709 & 1729, was a settlement in approximate OS square 0415.

Earlier forms: 1709-19 'Cuthliebag (& 'Cuthlieboge') Garvock's ground' (ie Garvock OS square 0314).

Derivation: This name quite possibly represents the former meeting place of a judicial court – for further information see Cuthil Towers. There is a Gallows Knowe nearby at GR 048162. The last syllable may simply be Scots 'Bog', as a later addition to the primary name – Bogtonlea is in OS square 0415.

Cutty's How GR 175149.

Derivation: Perhaps Scots 'Cutty', a hare, late 18th to 19th centuries; Scots 'Howe', a hollow, 16th century on.

D

Daiglen Burn GR 910985.

Earlier: 1845 'Daiglen', 1860 'Daiglen Burn'.

Derivation: Presumably from a lost glen name which could have been Gaelic 'Daimh Ghleann', stag or buck glen.

Dalgairn GR 135095, a settlement.

Derivation: Gaelic 'Dail na gCàrn', dale of the cairns. In the older language 'c' would be sounded 'g' in this grammatical context (eclipsis).

Dalqueich. See Queich.

***Dalry**, a settlement on record between 1612 & 1812, approximate OS square 9612, **Dalry Burn** GR 964125. Earlier references: 1612 'Dalry', 1812 'the Bridge of Dalry', 'the lands of Dalry', 1846 'Dalry Burn'.

Derivation: Perhaps Gaelic 'Dail Ruighe', the meadow near the hillslope.

Damakellis GR 909084, a settlement, **Damakellis Burn** GR 908080. Earlier references: 1624 'Dammakelleis', 1629 'Drumakelles', 1824 'town & lands of Dammakellis', 1860 'Damakellis Burn'. The Scots plural '-is' suggests that multiple holdings existed at some time.

Derivation: If weight is given to the 1629 form quoted above this could be Gaelic 'Druim na Coille', wood ridge: Drumhead, 'head or end of the ridge' is close by. The other seeming contender for '-kell', Gaelic 'Cill', church, churchyard, can probably be ruled out in our area, unless of course it was to be found in conjunction with a Saint's name or at an ancient church site. Note Professor Nicolaisen's remarks (1976 – see Bibliography): "the signs are that ... (names with Gaelic 'Cill') had ceased to be created when Gaelic speakers moved into Pictish territory proper on any appreciable scale".

The Western tip of Upper Glendevon Resorvoir. (AW)

***Damhead** OS square 1310. This was the name of the site of modern Glenfarg village until c1890. My earliest reference only goes back to 1750. A turnpike (ie toll booth) stood here in 1828.

Danny Burn GR 882060.

Earlier references: 1654 'the burne of Glenany', 1783 'Burn of Daunie', 1854 'Burn of Dannie', 1860 'Danny Burn'.

Derivation: Since the burn flows in Glen Anny, a Gaelic original consisting of 'Allt', burn, plus the original form of 'Anny' is not impossible. For the 't' of 'Allt' becoming 'd', compare 'Auldearn', near Nairn, which is in Gaelic 'Allt Eire' or 'Allt Eireann'. Suggestions for 'Anny' might be Gaelic 'Abhnaig', little river, or 'Anaich', (burn of) cleansing or of anger.

Darn Cleuch, described by the 1860 OS Name Book as a small hollow near Ben Shee, **Darn Stripe**, a small stream, both GR 950035. Earlier: Both are on record since 1860.

Derivation: Scots 'Darn', secret, hidden; Scots 'Cleuch', a gorge, a ravine, in placenames late 12th century on; Scots 'Stripe', a small stream, 15th century on.

Darn Road GR 787995, a track.

Derivation: Perhaps Scots 'Darn' or 'Dern', secret, hidden, late 14th century on, or desolate, late 18th century on.

***Davidson**, a settlement on record in 1813, OS

square 8407. This was an alternative name for Middle Rottearns.

Dawson's House, on record in 1901 in approximate OS square 0814.

***Dead Man's Grave**, recorded in 1774. This was in the vicinity of the South East corner of OS square 1014.

Deaf Knowe GR 882093.

Derivation: Probably Scots 'Deaf', barren, unproductive, late 18th century on; Scots 'Knowe', a knoll.

Deaf Knowes GR 015078, described by the 1860 OS Name Book as a small heathery knowe.

Derivation: Probably Scots 'Deaf', barren, unproductive, late 18th century on; Scots 'Knowe', a knoll.

***Dean's Moss**. On record in 1769 and seemingly centred on OS square 8902.

***Deich Burn**. See The Dich.

***The Deil's Bucket**. This is a pool in Wharry Burn, South of Sherrifmuir.

***Deil's Cradle**. This is South of Wizard's Stone GR 966990 near Kelty Burn. It is said to be where witches rock Satan to sleep on Halloween.

Demperston GR 223115, a settlement, **Demperston Hill** GR 212125.

Earlier references: 1450 'Dempstartoune', 1517 'Demperstoun with Layng's Land', 1529 'Layngisland vocat. (ie called) Warde de Dempstertoun', 1626 'Wester Dempstertoun', 1654 'Easter Demperstoun', 1828 'Demperston Hill'. Earliest surname form from Black (see Bibliography): 1395 'Dempsterton'. Macfarlane (1727 – see Bibliography) calls this site a village. In 1828 there was a Toll Bar South of Demperston at GR 224112.

Derivation: Scots, the 'toun' or holding of the Dempster, the officer of the court who pronounced sentence, late 14th century on. Court Knowe 206102, the likely site of the meeting place of a local judicial court, is just over 2 miles away

The Den GR 193159.

Derivation: Scots 'Den', a narrow valley especially one with trees, 16th century on.

Den Burn GR 276140, **Denhead**, a settlement on record in 1860, GR 271142. These sites are named from Collessie Den, through which the burn flows.

Derivation: Scots 'Den', a narrow valley especially one with trees, 16th century on.

The ruins of Denmylne Castle. Drawing by Ken Laing.

Denmylne Castle, ruins, GR 249175. Sibbald (1705 – see Bibliography) says Denmiln existed in the 14th year of the reign of Jas II (ie 1451) and belonged "anciently" to the Earls of Fife. Snoddy (1966 – see Bibliography) talks of "Glenburnie or Denmiln" (the Glenburnie of 1860 was at GR 252171) and says that the castle was presumed built c1560.

Earlier references: 1541 & 1567 'Dene-mylne or Wod-mylne' (ie Woodmiln OS square 2715), 1595 'Dane milne', 1598 'Dene milne', 1616 'Deanemylne', 1695 'Den myln', 1860 'Denmill', 'Denmill Castle' ("in ruins"), 'Den Burn'.

Derivation: The early spellings point to Scots 'Dane', 'Dene' &c, a Dean, perhaps referring to some ecclesiastical dignitary from Lindores? This seems to have been followed in the 17th century by a reinterpretation as Scots 'Den', a narrow valley, especially one with trees, 16th century on, perhaps influenced by the Den of Lindores, OS square 2517.

***Den-Shade** is on record in 1801. It is a stretch of the North bank of the Halfpenny (or Culteuchar) Burn centred on GR 083156.

Derivation: Scots 'Den', a narrow valley, especially one with trees, 16th century on; Scots 'Shed', Shade' &c, a strip of land, now chiefly in placenames, late 15th century on.

Wester Deuglie GR 108119, **Deuglie Cottage** GR 118109, **Abbot's Deuglie** GR 118108, **Middle Deuglie** GR 121109, **Glendeuglie** GR 129106, ***Clash Douglie** (on record between c1400 & 1827), all settlements. Also **Easter Abbotsdeuglie** OS square 1211, **Wester Abbotsdeuglie** OS square 1211, **Easterton** GR 125113, all settlements last found on record by me in 1860. **Eastertown Hill**, found in 1860 only, & **Eastertown March Burn** GR 130118, are secondary names from Easterton. Candy OS square 1109 appears as 'Candydeuglie' &c in the 18th century.

Earlier references: 1196 'Douglie' & 'Duglyn', c1400 (transcribed c1622-32) 'Casdughly', 1505-7 'Glasduglie' & 'Clasduglie', 1510 'Claschedeugly', 1628 'Abbotes Deuglie', 1650 'Westertowne of Abbots Douglie', 'Midletowne of Abbots Douglie', 'Eastertown of Abbots Douglie', 'the Mylne of Abbots Douglie', 1667 'mylne of Deuglie', 1673 'Denhead of Easter Douglie', 1742-4 'Easter Deuglie', 'Wester Deuglie', 1781 'part of Wester Duglie called Abbot's Duglie', 1828 'part of the lands of Abbots Deuglie called the Knowhead', 1829 'the lands of Easter Deuglie called Eastertown', 1855-6 'WesterDeuglie', 'Middle Deuglie', 'Deuglie', 'Hill of Deuglie'.

Derivation: The specific could be 'Black Glen' in either P-Celtic or Gaelic. 'Clashdouglie', 'Glasduglie' &c contain either Gaelic 'Glais', stream, or Gaelic 'Clais', a narrow shallow valley, often interchanged in transcriptions of placenames.

*The **Devil's Loch** or Lochan. This is a 'crater' on Dumyat OS square 8397.

Devil's Well (site of) GR 194148. According to the 1860 OS Name Book this was so named because the mark of a cloven hoof was to be seen on a nearby rock.

Glen Devon c1913, from a postcard. Reproduced by courtesy of Perth and Kinross District Libraries.

River Devon & **Glen Devon** both GR 980050 &c, **Glendevon**, a settlement, GR 991045, **Glendevon House** GR 978048. **Upper Glendevon Reservoir** OS square 9004 &c (completed in 1952), **Lower Glendevon Reservoir** OS square 9304 &c (completed in 1924). ***Dundovane**, on record in the 14th & 15th centuries, may have taken its name from the fort on Down Hill OS square 0003, as fort (Gaelic 'Dùn') of Devon. Glendevon village was 'Downhill' in 1860 and the site of a marketplace and a 'Market Inn'.

Earlier references: c1173 'aquam de (ie water of) Douane', 1271 'Glendofona', 1333-4 'lie Woidland de Glendouan', 1358 'dundovan', 'ly bordland de Glendovan' (ie Borland OS square 9804), 1443 'Dundovane-Bordland', 'Dundovane-Glencoy' (ie Glenquey OS squares 9803 &c), 1510 'Glendovene-Lindesay', 1612 'the Mylne of Glendevon', 1662 'Newmylne', c1680 'Kirk of Glendevon', 1786 'half of the Miln of Glendovan called New Miln', 1860 'Glendevon Castle', 'Glendevon House'.

Derivation: 'Devon' is probably P-Celtic in origin. WJ Watson (see Bibliography) says: "Probably for an early British 'Dubona' or 'Dobona'; compare the River Doubs in France, and its other form 'Dova' (for 'Doba'), black one. This is a goddess name". Professor WFH Nicolaisen (see Bibliography) agrees with the derivation but is doubtful about the divine status.

The River Devon and the dam of the Castlehill Reservoir. (AW)

*The **Dich**, the den at GR 102155, on record since 1790 and still a locally used name. Also ***Little Digh**, on record in 1801 and seemingly the burn at GR 097156. **Deich Burn** rises at GR 102154. Jack (see Bibliography) explains the term 'Dich', 'Deich' &c as meaning a hill-burn. The Minister of Forgandenny in material submitted for the Old Statistical Account but not printed derives 'Dich' from an unspecified Gaelic word meaning chasm or gully – the only remotely similar Gaelic word I know of is 'Dìg', a ditch. *The Scottish National Dictionary* has Scots 'Deigh' &c, a gully, cleft, dell, and does not give it a Gaelic origin.

Flanked by pylons and conifers the Dich descends from the foot of Castle Law above Forgandenny. (AW)

***Dirlie Muir**, recorded in 1783-88, centred on GR 078040 approximately. This name is now represented by **Dirley Moor Plantation** GR 082040. Earlier: 1783 'Dirly Muir Common', 1860 'Dirley Moor Plantation'.

Derivation: Perhaps Scots 'Dirl' in the sense 'gust of wind', though *The Concise Scots Dictionary* gives this as from the 20th century only.

***Dirt Pot Burn**, the burn at GR 935010; ***Dirt Pot Moss** lies between Dirt Pot Burn, Priest Goat Burn (ie the first stretch of Burn of Sorrow) and Cairnmorris Hill GR 934017; ***Dirt Pot Green** is the third of Dirt Pot Moss lying to the West of Dirt Pot Burn. These are all on record in 1779. They no doubt are secondary names from a particularly clarty pot-hole or pool in the burn or the moss.

Dochrie, a settlement on record between c1796 & 1891 at GR 086073 approximately, **Dochrie Hill** GR 082083.

Earlier: c1796 'Dochrie Hill', 'Dochriehall', 1828 'Dochrie'.

Derivation: 'Doch' can derive from Gaelic 'Dabhach', a measure of land perhaps ultimately of Pictish origin. Given the position of the settlement 'Dabhach Ruighe', hillslope davoch, would be a possibility.

***Doghillock** approximate GR 923011, on record between 1779 & 1822. Earlier: 1779 'Doghillock Carn' (ie 'Cairn', presumably marking the hilltop).

Dollar Burn & **Dollar Glen** both GR 962990, ***Haughs of Dollar** a farm on the Harviestoun estate, **Banks of Dollar** GR 949992, a hillside. Earlier: 1580 'lie (ie 'the') Bank de Dollar'. These are secondary names from Dollar, OS square 9698 &c, which is 'Dolair' in the Pictish Chronicle, derived by WJ Watson from P-Celtic 'Dol', dale, valley, "with 'ar' extension". See also under Burn of *Care*.

Doo Craigs GR 189152. This appears to be the same feature as 'Pigeon Craigs' on the 1860 OS map.

Derivation: Scots 'Doo', a dove, late 14th century on.

Douranside GR 098068, a hill. This appears to have been a settlement name in the 18th century.

Earlier forms: 1771 'Duringside at Siggie' (ie Seggie OS square 0907), c1796 'Douranside'.

Derivation: Gaelic 'Dobhran', streamlet, with subsequent addition of Scots 'Side', perhaps here with the sense of a sloping piece of ground, a hillside, late 17th century on.

***Dovecoathills**, a settlement on record in 1783, approximate OS square 0013.

Dovens Den GR 213164. Obscure to me.

Dow Burn & **Glen Dow** both GR 920050, both on record since 1860.

Derivation: Gaelic 'Gleann Dubh', black glen, is likely here.

Dow Linn, on record between 1796 & 1860, GR 072086 approximately.

Derivation: Gaelic 'Dubh Linne', black pool or waterfall.

***Dowglas-fawldis**, found in 1616. This was a pendicle or subsidiary holding of Ledlation OS square 0605.

Derivation: Probably from the surname, plus Scots 'Fauld', a small field, late 15th to 17th centuries.

Dowmyre Wood GR 065152.

Earlier: 1625 'the pendicle (ie subsidiary holding) now called Dowymyre'.

Derivation: Scots 'Dowie', 'Dow' (the latter probably shortened from 'Dowie'), sad, dismal, late 15th century on; Scots 'Myre', a bog or peat-bog, late 14th century on.

Down Hill GR 001036, also known as 'Castle Hill', **Easter Downhill**, a settlement, GR 999033.

Downhill GR 993044, the earlier name for the present Glendevon village, is described by the 1860 OS Name Book as "a hamlet". **Wester Downhill**, described by the 1860 OS Name Book as "ruins", was in approximate OS square 9904. Downhill & Wester Downhill are on record until 1860.

Earlier references: 1542 'Donehill', 1545 'terras de duobus (ie lands of the two) Dounhillis', 1650 'easter Downehill', 'wester Downehill', 1673 'Easter Dunhill', early1800s 'Downhill' (the settlement), 'Downhill Wood', 1860 'Down Hill', 'Easter Dunhill' & 'Easter Downhill'.

Derivation: Very probably named from the fort, Gaelic 'Dùn', on the hill's summit, with the reinterpretation 'Down' long co-existing as a doublet. Dundovan (see under Glen *Devon*) seems to have taken its name from the same fort. The alternative name 'Castle Hill' also refers to the fort (see remarks under Castle Craig GR 976127).

Downeri GR 047041, a hill. In 1615 this was part of the lands of Carnbo OS square 0503.

Earlier forms: 1615 'mons (ie hill) de Downraw', 1620 'Dunraw', c1796 & 1828 'Downdraw Hill', 1860 'Downeri'.

Derivation: Gaelic 'Dùn Ràth', here meaning something like 'hill settlement', 'hill dwelling'.

Downhill, a settlement in ruins recorded in 1860 at GR 102115 approximately. This area is now under Glenfarg Reservoir.

Dron Burn GR 120140, **Dron Hill** GR 126144, **West Dron Hill**, also known as Mundie Hill, GR 115150, ***Path of Drone**, on record in 1750, a 'den' in OS square 1314.

Earlier reference: 1530 'Wester Drone & Hildrone'.

Derivation: These are secondary names from Dron OS square 1415, Gaelic 'Dronn', a ridge.

***Dronachy**, a hillside, on record in 1796, **Dronachy Wood** GR 057170. The Old Statistical Account for Forteviot (see Bibliography) 1796-7 says that upon a rising ground called Dronachy a stone cross lay broken over at the pedestal, on which were "many emblematical figures".

Derivation: Gaelic 'Dronn' and 'Achadh', which could mean either field ridge, or ridge field, depending on the exact grammatical form of the original. 'Field' here probably means a piece of ground cleared for grazing or cultivation.

***Drum Driel**, on record until 1801. This was a former name for modern Culteuchar Hill GR 097152.

Earlier references: 1774 'Drumdriel hill', 1860 'Culteuchar Hill'.

Derivation: Gaelic 'Druim', a ridge, with an obscure second element.

Drumbrae GR 802978, a settlement.

Derivation: In theory Gaelic 'Druim a' Bhràighe', ridge of the upper part or upland, but the earliest reference I have seen to it is on a map of Aithrey Estate AD1885 and it may be an 'off the peg' name. It is on a ridge.

***Drumbu**, a settlement on record c1796, GR 108063 approximately.

Derivation: The name is not fully legible. Perhaps for 'Drumbuy' which would be from Gaelic 'Druim Buidhe', yellow ridge.

Drumcairn GR 880078, a settlement.

Earlier: 1650 'Eister & Wester Drumcairnes', 1855-6 'Easter Drumcairn', 'Wester Drumcairn'.

Derivation: Gaelic 'Druim Càirn', cairn ridge.

Drumcairn GR 177147, a settlement, **Drumcairn Glen** GR 180144. ***Drumcairn Hill**, perhaps GR 174145 or 174143?, had a standing cairn in 1897 according to Butler (see Bibliography).

Earlier forms: 1602 'Drumcarne', 1617 'Drumcairne'.

Derivation: Gaelic 'Druim Càirn', cairn ridge.

***Drumcairn**, on record in 1800. It was part of the lands of Ballieliesk OS square 0001.

Derivation: Gaelic 'Druim Càirn', cairn ridge.

Drumdruills GR 791991, a settlement.

Earlier forms: 1442 'Drumdowlis', 1650 'Drumdulles', c1680 'Drumduils', 1699-1701 'Drumdrulls'. The earlier forms indicate that the second 'r' is intrusive.

Derivation: Gaelic 'Druim', a ridge, an unknown second element, and the Scots plural '-is', '-es', probably implying that the holding was once multiple.

Drumfad, a settlement, GR 916093.

Earlier forms: 1650 'Drumfad', 1668 'Drumfauld', 1679 'Drumfald'.

Derivation: Gaelic 'Druim Fada', long ridge. The later 17th century forms look like a short-lived reinterpretation.

Drumfinn Hill GR 083162.

Earlier: 1774 'Tarfine Hill', 1860 'Drumfinn Hill'.

Derivation: Gaelic 'Druim Fionn', white or fine ridge, or just possibly Gaelic 'Druim Fhionn', Finn (Mac Cumhail)'s ridge. 1774 'Tarfine' is Gaelic 'Tàrr F(h)ionn', white &c bulging hill.

Relating the contours to the sense of the names, it seems quite likely that 'Drumfinn' applied to the whole ridge from GR 082160 to GR 083165 approximately, and 'Tarfine' to the summit at GR 083162, until that name fell out of use sometime between 1774 & 1860. The small eminence at GR 083164 appears to have been 'Garbhlach', later 'Garb Law' (q.v.).

***Drumfork**, a settlement on record until c1796 at GR 097052 approximately.

Earlier forms: 1750 'Drumforth', 1775 'Drumfork'.

Derivation: The word order implies a Gaelic etymology. Scots 'f' can represent a Gaelic 'ch' so the 1750 form quoted (if reliable) may represent Gaelic 'Druim a' Choirthe', pillar or standing stone ridge. 'Drumfork' suggests 'Druim a' Choirce', oats ridge.

Drumgarland GR 059047, a hill, **Drumgarland**, a settlement, GR 062046.

Earlier references: 1370 'Drumgarlet', 1389 'Drumgarlot', 1500 'the town of Drumgarland', 1616 'Drumgerlat vulgo (commonly called) Drumgarland'.

Derivation: Gaelic 'Druim a' Ghearrleathaid', ridge of the severe or short slope. Drumgarland is close to two other 'Leathad' names, Ledlation and Ledlanet (qq.v.).

Drumhead GR 905085, a settlement on record since 1721.

Derivation: Scots 'Drumheid' &c, the head of a ridge, early 17th century. 'Drum' is here the Scots loanword from Gaelic 'Druim'.

Drumlochy GR 915099, a settlement on record since 1666.

Derivation: Gaelic 'Druim Locha', loch ridge, or 'Druim Lochaigh', ridge at loch place. Lochans are marked nearby now, and the area is likely to have been much less well drained in the Gaelic period.

Drummond's Fold GR 951105, a settlement on record since 1785.

Earlier: 1821 'Drummonsfold now called the Easter Third of Technad' (ie Technad OS square 9508). See next entry.

Drummond's Top 008115, a hill.

Derivation: From the surname, a common enough one in the area. There were for example seats of the Drummonds at Drummond Castle OS square 8418 and at Balhaldie OS square 8205.

***Drumness**, on record until 1793, was the older name for Glenbank GR 812058.

Earlier: 1545 'Drumnes alias Glenbank'.

Derivation: Gaelic 'Druim', a ridge. The at first sight obvious Gaelic 'Neas', a promontory, came into Gaelic placenames from Norse in the areas where Scandinavians had settled and it is highly unlikely to be found in our area. In the absence of really early forms Gaelic 'Druim an Fhais', ridge of the stance or station, might be suggested, supposing later influence of the Scots placename element 'Ness' (also from Norse in many cases). Compare Alanais, Easter Ross, of which the last element is also Gaelic 'Fhais' and which becomes in Scots/English 'Alness'.

***Drumsheen Knowe**, on record in 1771. This was close to West Blair, perhaps at GR 111101.

Derivation: Gaelic 'Druim Sithein', round hill ridge or fairy hill ridge.

***Drumstoun**, a settlement recorded in 1654, approximate OS square 2415. A toun named for a lost 'Drum', from Gaelic 'Druim', a ridge, or the Scots loanword therefrom.

Drunzie GR 142086, **Drunzie Feus** GR 138087, **Drunziehill**, on record until 1901 but in ruins by 1860, GR 135078 approximately, ***Meickle Drungie**, on record in 1750, all settlements.

Earlier forms: c1554 'Drongy', 1649 'Dronzie', 1860 'Drunzie Feus'.

Derivation: Gaelic 'Droighneach', thorny, locative 'Droighnigh', at thorny place, with 'z' replacing the letters 'yogh' (resembling a hand-written 'z') & 'g', both of which could represent the semi-vowel [j] in older Scots orthography.

***Dry Burn** joins Knock Burn at GR 074084 approximately, on record c1796. ***Dryburn Well** is mentioned by Morris (see Bibliography) as being near Cairnavain OS square 0608. Morris quotes the following traditional rhyme:

"In the Dryburn Well, beneath a stane,
Ye'll find the key of Cairnavain,
That'll mak a' Scotland rich, ane by ane."

Dry Knowes GR 021077. Earlier: 1860 'Dry Knowe'.

Duchally GR 937097, **Milton of Duchally** GR 932098, **Duchally Mill** (corn), on record until 1860, OS square 9309, **Loanhead of Duchally** GR 940097, all settlements.

Earlier references: 1553-8 (Perhaps this site) 'Ducaly', 1632 'Duchalie', 1683 'Overduchallie', 1793 'the Mill of Kincardine or Duchally' (ie Kincardine OS square 9411).

Derivation: Possibly Gaelic 'Dubh Choille', black wood.

***Dug Linn**. A pool in Menstrie Burn above

Duchally House and Glen c1933, from a postcard. Reproduced by courtesy of Perth and Kinross District Libraries.

Dumyat from the West. (AW)

Washing Linn OS square 8497? Derivation: Possibly Gaelic 'Dubh Linne', black pool, or perhaps more likely, Scots 'Dog Pool'.

Dumbarrow Hill GR 195134, **Dumbarrow**, a settlement, GR 197127.

Earlier forms: 1331 'Dunberauch', 1511 'Drumbarrow', 1586 'Dumbarro', 1598 'Drumbarroch', 1860 'Dumbarrow Hill'.

Derivation: Gaelic 'Dùn', hill or fort, or possibly Gaelic 'Druim', a ridge (see the 1511 & 1598 forms quoted). '-barrow' may well be from Gaelic 'Barrach', high-topped, eminent, overlooking. There are no hills behind Dumbarrow Hill that are more than about 5-10 metres higher than it, so seen from the lower ground to the South it would appear to dominate.

Dumyat GR 835977, a hill, **Dumyat Farm** OS square 8497.

Earlier forms: 1783 'Demyat', 1790 'Dunmyatt', 1855 'Dumyat' (ie the Farm).

Derivation: This name is accepted by for example WJ Watson (see Bibliography) and Professor John McQueen (Scottish Studies Vol 84 1980 pp1-21) as being 'Fort of the Maeatae'

Dumyat seen from Menstrie. Drawing by Ken Laing.

from the Southern Pictish confederation mentioned by Dio Cassius in the early 3rd century AD. There is a brief account in WJ Watson (from p56) though MacQueen differs in placing the Maeatae North of the Antonine Wall. Watson says the anglicised form of the hill's name seems to reflect a "Welsh" (ie P-Celtic) rather than a Gaelic form.

Dun Moss GR 969021, **Dunmoss Burn** GR 970023. Earlier: Both on record in 1860.

Derivation: Scots, dun coloured moorland or peat bog.

***Dun Moss**. An unidentified site on Sheriffmuir recorded in 1766.

Derivation: Scots, dun coloured moorland or peat bog.

Dun Muir GR 982083.

Earlier: On record in 1860.

Derivation: Scots, dun coloured moorland.

***Dunaheidis**, recorded in 1592 as a pendicle (subsidiary holding) of Lumquhat OS square 2413.

Duncan's Hill, on record in 1860. According to the 1860 OS Name Book this is a distinct elevation close to and to the South of Corb Law. Perhaps the spur at GR 002089.

***Duncreesk Moor**, on record in 1654 in approximate OS square 1106.

Derivation: Gaelic 'Dùn Creisg', crossing hill or crossing fort.

Duncrievie GR 136092, **Hilton of Duncrievie** GR 131096, settlements. **Hilton Hill** GR 129097 is a secondary name from the latter.

Earlier: 1606 'Hiltoun of Drumtrivie' (read 'Drumcrivie'?), 1654 'Drumcrivey', 1750 'Hillton Burn' (ie Glendy Burn?), 'Crievie', 1775 'Crevie', 1790 'Crivie', 1836 'Plantation Crivie', 1860 'Duncrievie Cottage', 'Hillton Hill', 1901 'Hilton of Crevie'.

Derivation: Gaelic 'Druim Craobhaigh', ridge at tree place, or 'Druim Craoibhe', tree ridge. The 'Crievie' &c forms (ie those without 'Dun-' or 'Drum-') may imply that that was the primary name, unless it developed later as an abbreviation or nickname.

Dundie Burn GR 052040. An alternative name for Golland Burn on record in 1860. Possibly Gaelic 'Dùn Dhè', God's fort or hill?

***Dunimax**, mentioned by Snoddy (see Bibliography), is the western summit of Pitlour Hill GR 205127.

Derivation: Possibly Gaelic 'Dùn nam Mac', fort or hill of the sons, with the Scots plural. Such a Scots plural sometimes developed due to an awareness that a plural had been present in the earlier Gaelic name.

Dunning Burn GR 024136, **Common of Dunning** OS squares 0109 &c (see below). **Common Burn** GR 020102 is a secondary name from the latter. ***Edendunning**, on record until 1686, was a barony taking in the Common of Dunning and called 'Thainsland' (q.v.) by the late 16th century and 'Glendunning' by the end of the 18th century.

These are secondary names from Dunning OS square 0214. According to Wilson (see Bibliography) the Common of Dunning in the late 17th century comprised the lands of Pitmeadow, Blaeberry Hill and Fairney Knowe, ie the hillslopes to the West of Dunning Burn in OS squares 0109, 0110, 0210, 0111, 0211, 0112 & 0212 approximately.

Earlier references: c1320 'the common of Edendunning', 1380 'pratum (ie meadow, grazing) de Duny', 1530 'Commoun-donyng', 1801 'part of the Thainsland or Glendunning formerly called the Common of Dunning and now Greenhill' (ie Greenhill OS square 0209).

Derivation: 'Dunning' is likely to derive from Gaelic 'Dùn', hill or fort, though as far as I know no-one has managed to explain the precise development of the name. 'Edendunning' is Gaelic 'Aodann', hillslope, hillface (of Dunning), which suits its apparent location.

Dykedale GR 797014, a settlement, **Dykedale Wood** GR 793011.

Earlier reference: 1755 'Dykedale of Kippendavie' (ie Kippendavie OS square 7902).

Derivation: Scots 'Dyke', a wall, 15th century on.

Duncrievie, from an old postcard. Reproduced by courtesy of Perth and Kinross District Libraries.

E

Glen Eagles GR 935080, **Gleneagles Castle** (remains of) GR 929092, **Gleneagles House** GR 930087, **Gleneagles Chapel** GR 930089 (the 1860 OS map has "disused since 1745"), **Gleneagles Old Toll House** GR 940075 (this is 'Gleneagles TP' ie 'Turnpike' on the 1860 OS map). **East Mains** GR 934088 & **West Mains** GR 927085 also belong here, as do **North Mains of Gleneagles**, last on record in 1860, GR 928090 approximately, & ***Egeis Water** (on Pont's map of c1595). Common sense would suggest that 'Egeis Water' is the Ruthven Water, since that river flows in Glen Eagles, but the location on Pont's map seems to be further West.

Earlier references: 1336 (Perhaps) 'Ard Glenelgi', 1463-1513 'Glennegas', 1539-47 'Glenegess', 1555-8 'Glenagaiss', 1587 'lie Manys of Glennegyis', 1653 'Glenegeis', 1664 'Gleneglis', 1685 'Glenegills', 1695 'Glenegles', 1731 & 1746 'Gleneagles', 1799 'the barony of Gleneagles comprising Mains of Gleneagles & Mill, Cairnquarter, Buchthill', Wallhill, Carselounie (ie Carlownie?), Eastside, Willenbuss & Glen, all now comprised under the names of East & West Mains & House Park of Gleneagles', 1855 'North Mains'. It will be seen from the above forms that the 'l' of '-eagles' does not appear until the 17th century. Robertson (see Bibliography) writing in 1869 says Glen Eagles "was always, until comparatively modern times, written and called 'Gleneagis', and is so still by the lower orders".

Gleneagles House and Avenue, from an old postcard. Reproduced by courtesy of Perth and Kinross District Libraries.

Derivation: From a Gaelic form 'Gleann Eagais' or 'Eigis' of which the second part may be Gaelic 'Eigeas', genitive 'Eigis', a learned man, a poet. The name is now popularly thought to be from Gaelic 'Gleann na h- Eaglaise', glen of the church, or 'Gleann Eaglaise', church glen, and the 17th century forms in '-eglis' & '-egles' could in theory represent a reinterpretation to that form in the process of taking place, perhaps in the speech of Gaelic speakers such as the drovers who used the glen extensively throughout this period. In that case however one would expect to find the final 'sh' of the Gaelic pronunciation reproduced in some at least of the spellings, so it is possible that what we are really seeing in these 17th century forms is already the reinterpretation to Scots 'Egill', 'Egle', an eagle. 1366 'Ard Glenelgi' (see earlier forms) is mentioned in conjunction with 'Ochturather' (ie Auchterarder) but even if it is Gleneagles the form seems too far out of step with other early references to be given too much weight on its own.

***Earls Seat**, on record between 1769 & 1836, a hill. This appears to be the spur of hill at GR 899041.

***Earlsmuir**, on record between 1528 & 1829, a settlement. This was an alternative name for Turflundie OS square 1914.

Earlier: 1528 'Erllismure'.

Derivation: Macduff's Cross is only 2.5 miles away so there could in theory be a connection here with the Earls of Fife.

***Earlyhead**, a settlement on record in 1783, approximate OS square 8297.

Derivation: Perhaps Scots 'Heid', the top of a brae, late 15th century on.

A print of Gleneagles dated c1840. Reproduced by courtesy of Perth and Kinross District Libraries.

Earnside GR 016053, a settlement, was '**Upper Airnside**' in 1783 and '**North Earniside**' in 1812. ***South Earniside** approximate OS square 0104, on record in 1812, was in 1783 '**Nether Airnside**'. **Nether Town Hill** GR 025049 is a secondary name from the latter holding. Also **Earnieside Cottage** GR 015055. In 1615 Earnieside was part of the lands of Carnbo OS square 0503.

Earlier references: 1615 'Erniesyde' 1618 'Over Erniesyde', 1620 'Ernesydis', 1666 'South et North Earnsydes', 1860 'Nether Town Hill'.

Derivation: For 'Earn-', perhaps Gaelic 'Earrann', a division or portion of land. Alternatively a number of names with 'Earn' &c are thought to contain a reference to Ireland, Gaelic 'Eirinn' (eg Rottearns OS square 8407). '-side' here could imply that the first element was the old name of the adjacent stream or it could be Scots 'Side', a sloping piece of ground, a hillside, late 17th century on.

Eastbow Hill GR 947080, on record since 1860.

***Eastburn**, on record between 1783 & 1808 in approximate OS square 9799, ***Westburn**, on record in 1848, GR 976998, both settlements. Eastburn was a pendicle of Wester Pitgober.

***Easterrough Burn**, diverted to fill Airthrey Loch OS square 8096 in the late 18th century, & ***Westerrough Burn**. The burns descend into Airthrey Estate OS squares 8096 &c.

Easterton OS square 1211. On record since 1650 as part of the Deuglie lands.

Eastfield GR 093131, a settlement. Earlier: 1860 & 1901 'Eastfields'.

Eastplace Burn GR 983060, **Westplace Burn** GR 974060. Earlier: Both on record since 1860.

Derivation: Scots 'Place', a holding of land, an estate, farm or croft, late 14th century on.

Eastrig Burn. A secondary name from The Rig GR 960075.

***Eastside**. A settlement forming part of the barony of Gleneagles, absorbed into the Mains c1799. Earlier: 1587 'Eistsyde', 1633 'East-side of Glennaglis'. Derivation: Perhaps Scots 'Side', a sloping piece of ground, a hillside, late 17th century on.

Eastside, a settlement at GR 047047 forming part of the lands of Carnbo OS square 0503, was in ruins in 1860.

Earlier: 1615 'Eistsyidis', 1683 'Eastsyde of Carnbo'.

Derivation: Perhaps Scots 'Side', a sloping piece of ground, a hillside, late 17th century on.

***The Ebenezer Stone** stands between Easter Gatherleys & Wester Gatherleys OS square 0411. It is a small grey stone marked 'EBENEZER' erected by James Lawson of Auchterarder (1747-88) to commemorate a religious experience he had at this spot.

***Ecclesiamagirdle Muir** is recorded in 1801 South East of Drum Driel (ie the present Culteuchar Hill), approximate OS squares 1014,

1015. This may be the same as AD1750 **'Exmgairdle Hill'** in the region of OS squares 0915, 1015, 1115, & AD1600 **'Cuthkin Eklismagirgill'**.

Derivation: These are secondary names from Ecclesiamagirdle OS square 1016, which was in AD1211 'Eglesmagrill' and in 1618 'Eglismagirdill', from Gaelic 'Eaglais mo', 'Church of my', followed by a saint's name. WJ Watson (see Bibliography) says "It is 'my Grill's church'; Grillán, the diminutive of Grill, was one of the twelve who accompanied Columba from Ireland". 'Cuthkin' in the AD1600 reference quoted is from Gaelic 'Coitchionn', common land.

***Eclmurghuall** approximate OS square 1709.

Derivation: I have come across no reference to this site other than on James Gordon's map of Fife of 1642. If it is a reliable name the first syllable no doubt represents Gaelic 'Eaglais', church, and the second syllable is probably the affectionate 'mo' commonly prefixed to saints' names (compare 'Ecclesiamagirdle' OS square 1016). A form along the lines of 'Eaglais mo Reguil' might be possible. WJ Watson (see Bibliography) quotes 'Reguil' as a Gaelic genitive form of the name of St Regulus whose cult was apparently associated with St Andrews. I am in no way competent to discuss early religious history, though it may be relevant that this part of the Ochils area formed part of the diocese of St Andrews from at least 1274. It may also be relevant that our site is close to Bannaty (q.v.), 'blessed place'.

River Eden GR 170082. The Old Statistical Account for Strathmiglo, 1790, says this river was also known as 'Water of Miglo'. Earlier: 1173 'fluvii (ie river) Hedene', 1654 'Miglo fluvius' (in approximate OS square 1608). Skene (see Bibliography) identifies Ptolemy's river Tina with the Eden.

Derivation: WFH Nicolaisen (1976 – see Bibliography) gives 'Eden' as a "water word", ie meaning river, stream, flowing water.

Edmund's Grave GR 147145, site of a cairn. According to the 1860 OS Name Book it was said to be the burial place of one of Agricola's generals.

Ben Effray GR 981115, ***Boonafrie** a settlement on record in 1783 in OS square 9711, on the North West slopes of the hill.

Earlier form: 1860 'Ben Effrey'. Haldane (1944 – see Bibliography) has Ben 'Affray', still a local pronunciation, and mentions its "Pictish encampment".

Derivation: 'Ben', from Gaelic 'Beinn', a hill, a mountain, does not seem to have been productive in Scots and so implies a Gaelic original. Possibly Gaelic 'Beinn an Aifrinn', mountain of the Mass, 'Aifreann', being the

Ben Effray. (AW)

etymon of the second half of 'Inchaffray' – in 1190 'Incheffren' and in Latin 'Insula Missarum', Isle of the Masses. If this suggestion were to prove correct, the relevant sense at our site might be 'land belonging to, or gifted to, the Church', and Inchaffray itself could be the religious house concerned as by 1219 the churches of Dunning, Aberuthven and Auchterarder had been granted to it "with their lands and pastures". 'Boonafrie' makes good sense as Gaelic 'Bonn' or 'Bun', foot, plus the hill name – (steading at) the foot of Affray, though Gaelic 'Both an Aifrinn', cottage, dwelling of the Mass, is also possible. 'Tarneybackle' OS square 8607 is another name which seems to reflect earlier tenure by the Church.

Ruins near the site of Boonafrie on the NW slopes of Ben Effray. (AW)

Eind, a settlement, GR 959108. ***Over** or **Easter Eind**, a settlement on record until 1808, was also known as Foswellbank from at least 1790, and is now Foswell GR 962107.

Earlier references: 1789 'Over or Easter Eind', 'Wester or Nether Einds' (ie the present Eind), 1790 'Fosswal Bank', 1793 'Eind Meadow', 1800 'Eindshaugh' (ie Eind's Meadowland), 'Nether Eind', 1860 'West Eind'.

***Eistertown Glen** on record in 1819 & 1836 & ***Eastertown Burn** recorded in 1769, are the present Harviestoun Glen & Burn. They are secondary names from Eastertown of Tillicoultry, which was also known as Elistoun (q.v.).

Eldritch Hill GR 014106.

Derivation: Scots 'Eldritch', 'Elrage' &c, weird, ghostly, strange, unearthly, 16th century on, is at first sight the obvious candidate, but in an area where practical names vastly outnumber emotional ones 'Eldritch' may well be a reinterpretation of Gaelic 'Eileirg', a deer trap, which can give 'Elrick', 'Eldrig' &c elsewhere in Scotland. The deer trapping consisted of driving them into a narrow glen where they were encircled and slaughtered. The approach from the North here, culminating in the narrow glen of Thorter Burn, may well have been suitable.

Elistoun GR 931979, a settlement, had the alternative name of Easter Tillycultry or Eastertown of Tillicultry until at least 1783. Also **East Elistoun Wood** GR 931981, **West Elistoun Wood** GR 929981, **Elistoun Hill** GR 926992. Bernard (1986 – see Bibliography) has ***the Ellistoun Crags** for GR 921985 to GR 926983.

Earlier: 1613 'Ellistone of Tillicultre', 1617 'Easter-toune of Tullicultrie', 1667 'Elistoune', 1678 'Eister Tilliecultrie nuncupata (ie called) Eliestoun', 1769 'Elliestoun', 'Pirrat' (ie the present Elistoun Hill), 1769 'Law Head' (ie Elistoun Hill), 1819 'Ellieston Hill'.

Derivation: WFH Nicolaisen gives Elliston, Roxburghshire, as from the Scandinavian personal name 'Isleifr', possibly borne by an Angle. I do not know if our name is old enough for a similar explanation to be feasible here. 1769 'Pirrat', quoted above, is perhaps for Scots 'Pirrack' &c, a mound or pinnacle – see further under Pirrich.

Ben Ever GR 893001, a hill. **Benever Burn** GR 890011, on record in 1860, is marked as 'Glenwinnel' & 'Glenwinny' burn on recent OS maps.

Derivation: 'Ben' implies a Gaelic original. Gaelic 'Beinn Eibhir', granite hill, has been suggested, though I do not know whether the hill is in fact granite.

Ewe Lairs GR 830972. The 1860 OS Name Book describes this as a rugged face of rock.

Derivation: Scots 'lair', a place where animals lie down, a fold or enclosure, 16th century on, frequent in placenames.

***Ewlairfolds** approximate OS square 9702. This appears to be a settlement and is recorded in 1783. For derivation see previous entry.

F

***Faery Well**. See Hielanman's Well for which this is an alternative name.

***Fairneyhole**, a settlement on record between 1680 & 1783, seemingly on Harviestoun Burn above Elistoun OS square 9397.

Earlier: 1680 'Farniehall'.

Derivation: 'Farnie', 'Fairney' &c is from Scots 'Farn', 'Fern' &c, fern, late 15th century on, bracken, 18th century on.

***Fairneyknows** a settlement on record until 1795, approximate OS square 0210. It was part of or closely associated with Blaeberryhill OS square 0210 and formed part of the Common of Dunning.

Earlier: 1574 'terras de (ie lands of) Blaberryhill et Fairny-Knowis', 1792 'pendicle of Fairneyknowls now called Shadow half of Blaeberryhill', 1794 'the pendicle of Fairneyknows on the north & west side of the burn of Knows'.

Derivation: 'Farnie', 'Fairney' &c is from Scots 'Farn', 'Fern' &c, fern late 15th century on, bracken 18th century on; Scots 'Know', a knoll, 16th century on.

Fairy Knowe GR 796982.

***Fallow Bog**. An unidentified site on Sheriffmuir on record in 1766.

Fank Wood GR 973054. Derivation: Scots 'Fank', a sheepfold or pen, 19th century on, a loanword from Gaelic 'Fang'.

Fanks Burn GR 976032. Earlier: On record since 1860.

Derivation: Scots 'Fank', a sheepfold or pen, 19th century on, a loanword from Gaelic 'Fang'. A sheepfold is marked on the 1860 OS map near this burn's junction with the Glenquey Burn.

Fanny Hill GR 004068, **Fanny Burn** GR 010064, **Fannyhill Burn** GR 010057. Fannyhill lands seem to have comprised ***Inner** or **Nether Fannyhill** perhaps at GR 011056 approximately, & ***Outer** or **Upper Fannyhill**, not so far located by me, perhaps in OS square 0006?

Earlier: 1542 'Fawnehill', 1545 'Fawnyhill', 1650 'Fanihill', 1750 'Upper Fannyhill', 1783 'Inner Fannyhill', c1796 'Nether Fannyhill', 'Upper Fannyhill', 1808 'the fourth part of the lands of Coulsknow & Fannyhill commonly called the Infield Room of Fannyhill' (ie Inner Fannyhill?), & 'lands of Outer Fannyhill commonly called Nivensfold', 1829 'Fanny Burn', 1855 & 1860 'Fernyhill' (= Inner Fannyhill?), 1860 'Fanny Hill Burn'. The 16th century forms quoted seem to solve this name, puzzling in its later guise. The woman's name 'Fanny', very popular in the 18th century if not earlier, may have influenced the reinterpretation.

Glenfarg in 1935, from a postcard. Reproduced by courtesy of Perth and Kinross District Libraries.

River Farg & **Glen Farg** both GR 143120, **Glenfarg** (ie the village) OS square 1310, **Glenfarg Cottage** GR 143121, **Glenfarg Reservoir** OS square 1011 &c, **Craigfarg**, a settlement, GR 102107. **Glenfarg House** is on the 1860 OS map at GR 160131 approximately. The present

Glenfarg House is at GR 162153. Glenfarg village was until c1890 known as 'Damhead'.

Earlier: WJ Watson (see Bibliography) quotes a very early undated form "Apurfeirt (? read 'feirc')", 1629 'the mill of Farg', c1720 'Farg Water', 1750 'Water of Farg', 1855 'Glenfarg', 'Farg's Mill', 1860 & 1901 'Low Plains' (ie modern Craigfarg).

Derivation: WJ Watson (see Bibliography) says that 'Farg' may well be from the same Celtic root as Gaelic 'fearg', wrath, and older Gaelic 'ferg', a warrior.

Old Fargie GR 157114, **Old Fargie Cottage** GR 165114, **New Fargie House** GR 158127, **New Fargie Cottages** GR 163124, **New Fargie Farm** GR 156125, all settlements. Fourgie or Forgy, later Fargie, was a feudal barony.

Earlier: 1281 'Fourgie', 1282 'dominus de (ie lord of) Forgy', 1324 'Fourgy', 1507 & 1522 'Forgy' 1551 'Ald-Fargye of Arngask' (ie Arngask OS square 1310), 1599 'New-Fargy', 1650 'Fargie's Mylne'. The earlier forms suggest that 'Fargie' is not related to Glen & River 'Farg' though it is not unlikely that analogy with 'Farg' names contributed to the name's evolution.

***Farnyhall** a settlement in approximate OS square 0810, on record between 1567 & 1783. Earlier forms: 1567 'Fernyhollis', 1610 'Fairnyhoillis'.

Derivation: 'Farnie', 'Fairney' &c is from Scots 'Farn', 'Fern' &c, fern late 15th century on, bracken 18th century on.

***Fawns Hill** (also given as 'Fawn Hill') GR 097145 approximately, ***Fawns Burn** GR 100143 approximately. Both are on record in 1774.

Fawncleuch Burn GR 967068, **Fawncleuch Hill** GR 965069. Earlier: Both on record in 1860.

Derivation: Scots 'Cleuch', a gorge, a ravine, in placenames late 12th century on.

***Ferniemack Burn** on record between 1769 & 1819, GR 933990.

Earlier: 1769 'Farnie Mack Burn' & 'Fairnie Mack Burn'.

Derivation: Gaelic 'Fearann nam Mac', the sons' land, is possible.

Ferny Braes, a steep hillside in OS squares 0208 & 0209, on record in 1860.

Derivation: 'Farnie', 'Fairney' &c is from Scots 'Farn', 'Fern' &c, fern late 15th century on, bracken 18th century on; Scots 'Brae', steeply rising ground, a hillside, late 14th century on.

A quarry in Glenfarg photographed by Magnus Jackson in the late 1800s. Reproduced by permission of Perth Museum and Art Gallery.

Ferny Knowe GR 188148.

Earlier: 1801 'the Fairneyknow'.

Derivation: 'Farnie', 'Fairney' &c is from Scots 'Farn', 'Fern' &c, fern late 15th century on, bracken 18th century on; Scots 'Know', a knoll, 16th century on.

Fiddle Plantation GR 067041 is, on the 1860 OS map, vaguely fiddle-shaped.

Little Fildie GR 143138, a settlement with a sheepfold, **Fildie Burn** GR 145130, **Meikle Fildie** GR 149129, a settlement. Also ***'Feldie Bridge'**, on record in 1848, GR 149125?

Earlier forms: 1516 (Perhaps our site) 'Feldeis', 1648 'Fildie', 1649 'Mekill Fildie', 1775 'Littlefildie', 1795-1825 'Rudry (& Rudrie) or Little Fildie', 1827 'Littlefieldie', 'Micklefieldie'. Earliest surname form from Black (see Bibliography): 1585 'Fildie'.

Derivation: Obscure to me. The earliest spellings do not really support this being a Scots diminutive of 'Field', though it may at times have been reinterpreted as such. There is a slight possibility that 1795-1825 'Rudry' may be a much older name, from the Gaelic personal name 'Ruaidhri'.

Fin Glen & **Finglen Burn** both GR 882027. Earlier: Both on record since 1860.

Derivation: Gaelic 'Fionn Ghleann', white or fine glen.

Fincraig GR 231169, crags, on record since 1860.

Derivation: Gaelic 'Fionn Chreag', white or fine crag.

Finderlie GR 093050, a settlement.

Earlier forms: 1620 'Findlarie', 1630 'Finlarie'. The earlier forms seem convincing as Gaelic 'Fionn (earlier 'Find') Làrach', white or fine site or dwellingplace.

Findony Farm, a settlement, GR 019140.

Earlier: 1380 'Fyndony', 1622 'the Mill of Findony', 1671 'Ovir & Nathir Findonies', 1784 'Wester Rooms (ie holdings) of Findony', 1800 'Wester Findony', 1855 'Meal Mill of Findony', 'Wool Mill of Findony'.

Derivation: Gaelic 'Fionn', white or fine. The second part may well, like nearby 'Dunning', be from a derivative of Gaelic 'Dùn', hill or fort.

Fir Knowe GR 989042. Earlier: On record since 1860.

The Firs, a settlement, GR 793003.

Fochy Burn GR 107050, on record since 1654.

Derivation: Obscure to me.

Foggyleas GR 247148, a hillside.

Derivation: Scots 'Foggie', mossy, 18th century on; Scots 'Lea', grassland of various kinds, 16th century on.

***Fold Burn** is on record in 1769. It joined the River Devon from the South at GR 907045 approximately but is now under Upper Glendevon Reservoir.

Fordel GR 131122, **Easter Fordel** GR 142126, **Wester Fordel** GR 130123, **Fordel Croft** GR 133122, settlements, **Fordel Wood** GR 130122, **Fordel Hill** GR 127135, **Fordel Cottage**, on record in 1860, GR 140117 approximately. Part of Fordel was known as 'Paris' from the early 17th century at least, until the early 20th century (for further information see Paris).

Earlier: 1449 & 1480 'Fordale', 1493 'Estir Fordale', 1505-6 'Meklfordale', 'Littilfordale', 1512 'Le Estertoun de Fordell nuncupat (ie called) Mekle Fordell', 1523 'the mill of Fordale', 1616 'Paris', 1855 'Nether Fordel', 'Upper Fordel'. Earliest surname forms from Black (see Bibliography): 1296 'Richard de Furdale' & 1305 'Gregory de Fordale'.

Derivation: This is not likely to be straightforward 'Fore Dale', dale at the front, as the first recorded use of 'Fore' in this sense in the OED is later than the earliest references to our site. Gaelic 'Fordhail', upper, or big, or perhaps fine, meadow or dale.

Fore Bank GR 901974. The ***Fore-Hills** of **Easter** & **Wester Tillicoultry** in 1769 stretched from the northern half of OS square 9197 to the western half of OS square 9498, approximately, so ***Fore-hill Farm**, on record in 1792, is likely to have been in that vicinity.

Derivation: At the 'front' or South side of Tillicoultry parish. The Old Statistical Account contrasts Fore-hill Farm and the Back Hills (q.v.).

Forecraig Wood GR 171099.

Foresterseat GR 156115, a settlement.

Earlier: 1620 'Forrester-sait', 1645 'Fostersait', 1654 'Froster seat', 1691 & 1717 'Fosterseat', 1742 'Foresterseat'.

Derivation: Scots 'Frostar' &c, a forester, late 14th to early 17th centuries. For the forms with 'Foster-' compare Scots 'Fosterschip', 16th to early 17th centuries, and 'Fostery', late 15th century, forestership, the office of forester. Gilbert (see Bibliography) says that in the 14th and 15th centuries the land which the forester held either inside or outside a hunting forest was known as the forestercroft or foresterseat.

Fordel House photographed in 1909. Reproduced by permission of Perth Museum and Art Gallery.

Forglen Burn OS square 8097. Unfortunately I have no earlier references.

Derivation: This could be either a lost Gaelic glen name 'Forghleann', upper, or big, or fine glen (compare Fordel), or Scots 'Fore Glen', glen at the front (compare Fore Bank). Its position perhaps favours the latter.

Fossaquhie, on record until 1885, GR 821974? This was a farm steading behind Craig Gullies OS square 8297, in ruins by 1860. This name appears to have had some influence on, or been confused with, the name 'Fossoway' (see the next entry) which was 'Fossoquhey' &c from the 15th century on.

Major Robert Duncanson of Fassokie (sic) was second in command of the detachment of Argyle's Regiment involved in the Massacre of Glencoe in 1692 (see for example Prebble *Glencoe* pp 216-9 &c and Hill Burton *History of Scotland* vol vii p.404). In 1650 the occupant was a 'Helen Dunkisone', perhaps the same as in the 1669 reference quoted below.

Earlier references: 1451 'Fossachy', 1635 'Fossoquhyemaner', 1669 'Helena Duncansone haeres (ie heiress of) Roberti Duncansone de Fossoquhay', 1688 'Fossoke', 1799 'Fossochie with the Manor place thereof'.

Derivation: Gaelic 'Fos', 'Fas', 'Fasadh', a stance or dwelling place, perhaps with Gaelic 'Achadh', a 'field' or piece of cleared ground: thus the sense would be 'stance field', or 'field stance', depending on the exact grammatical form of the original.

Easter Fossoway, a settlement, GR 047031, **Fossoway Lodge** GR 015020, **Fossoway Cottages** GR 019019, **Fossoway Church** (remains of) GR 015018, **Middleton Fossoway**, a settlement, GR 026021.

Earlier references: 1194-98 'Fossedmeg', c1210 'Fossadmag', 1308 'Fosuiv', 1453 'the church of Fossoquhy', 1650 'Fosoqwhie Parish', 1763 'Fossachie', 1775 'Middletown', 1798 'Fossoquhey or Fossoway', 'Westertown of Fossoquhey' 'Thorntown & Common of Fossoquhey & Mill', 1860 'Wester Fossaway', 'Fossaway Lodge'.

Derivation: WJ Watson (see Bibliography) suggests Gaelic 'Fosadhmhagh', firm plain. The 12th century to 14th century forms would not normally develop into the 'Fossoquhy' of 1453 quoted above, but from that date there is a close similarity between spellings of Fossoway and Fossakie until they begin to diverge again in the late 18th century.

Foswell GR 962107, a settlement, **Foswell Low Wood** GR 963107, **Foswell High Wood** GR 966100. Also ***Braes of Foswell**, on record in 1800, & ***Foswell Loch** GR 961101, man-made, Mr John Haldane tells me, in 1908. The present Foswell was earlier known as 'Foswell Bank' and before that 'Easter Eind' or 'Over Eind'. 'Foswell' was occasionally confused in transcription with 'Fossoway' – for examples see under Broadgate OS square 9511 and Headdyke OS square 9510.

Earlier references: c1260 'Foscayl', 1504 'Foschwallis', early 18th century 'Fosswall', 1749 'Foswell', 1781 'Hill of Fosswall', 1790 'Fosswal Bank', 'Mill of Foswell', 1796 'the Waulkmiln (ie of Foswell) now converted into a Papermiln', 1808 'Corn Mill of Foswell now called East Mill', 1860 'Foswellbank'.

Derivation: The first syllable is likely to be Gaelic 'Fos', 'Fas', a dwelling place or 'stance', which WJ Watson (see Bibliography) glosses as "a nice level spot such as a drover would choose as a night's quarters for his charge". The second syllable is obscure to me.

Fountain Wood GR 234147, **Upper Fountain Wood** GR 228148.

Derivation: Perhaps 'Fountain' in the sense of a spring, or the source of a stream. There are springs marked in the surrounding area.

Fourstanes, a settlement on record in 1860, GR 955052.

***Fowl Hill** GR 101149 approximately. Recorded in 1774.

Frandy GR 942043, a settlement, **Frandy Moss** GR 925038, **Frandy Burn** GR 930030. ***Old Frandy Loch** is now incorporated into the **Frandy** or **Lower Glendevon** reservoir OS squares 9204 & 9304, completed in 1924.

Earlier: 1650 'Frandie', 1860 'Frandy Burn', 'Frandy Moss'.

Derivation: 'Frandy' is not clear to me, but as 'f' can sometimes represent a Gaelic 'ch' in Scots orthography, Gaelic 'Allt a' Chrainn Dhuibh', black tree burn, might be one suggestion.

Freeland GR 182103, a settlement, **Freeland Plantation** GR 180104. The earlier name for this site was 'Craigfod' (q.v.).

Earlier: 1240-1771 'Craigfod', 1711 'Freeland'.

Derivation: Scots 'Freeland', land held free of rent or services.

Frenchman's Neuk GR 126118, a hillside.

Friarsmill, on record until 1860. This was a settlement at GR 207105 approximately.

Earlier: 1240-49 'Friarmyln', 1505 'Freirmyll'.

Forts: Clearly visible fortifications on Castle Law Forgandenny (top); less clear traces on Ben Effray (left) photographed from Beld Hill and on Rossie Law (right) taken from Craig Rossie. (AW)

G

Gallows Hill GR 889981. See The Gowls.

Gallows Knowe GR 981048. Earlier: On record since 1860. Hunter (see Bibliography) says that here were hanged "some of the last Highland reivers". Court Knowe, the site of the meeting place of a judicial court, is nearby at GR 987048.

Gallows Knowe GR 017143. East Cuthill, a site whose name probably marks the meeting place of a judicial court, was nearby.

Gallow Knowe GR 071128.

Earlier: c1750 'Gallow Bank', 1860 'Gallow Knowe'.

In the foreground, Gallow Knowe near Lumbennie, complete with modern 'gallows' (AW).

***Gallow Hill**, on record in 1790 at GR 134104 approximately. Here, says the Old Statistical Account for Arngask, "it is said stood a gallows on which persons belonging to the barony of Balvaird were executed during the feudal system".

Gallow Knowe GR 238165.

Gannel Burn GR 915990.

Earlier: 1769 'Cannel's Burn' & 'Cannell's Burn', 1848 'Gannel Burn'. See Andrew Gannel Burn and Gloomingside Burn.

Ganner Dub GR 123132, a pond or lochan.

Derivation: Scots 'Ganner' &c, a gander, 15th century on; Scots 'Dub' &c, a pond, late 15th century on. Compare Scots 'Guse Dub', a goose pond, late 16th century on, frequent in placenames.

Gap Moss. A level tongue of ground between steep sides, centred on GR 992112.

Earlier: On record since 1860.

***Garb Law**, recorded in 1774, GR 083164 approximately, & **Garblie Wood** GR 077165.

Earlier: 1774 'Garb Law' & 'The Garblaw'.

Derivation: The wood name appears to have kept closer to the original and points to Gaelic 'Garbhlach', a shortened form of 'Garbh Thulach', rough knoll, rough hillock, with '-lach' later reinterpreted or translated as Scots 'Law', a rounded hill, in placenames 12th century on.

Garchel Burn GR 970017. This may be the burn Gibson (see Bibliography) refers to as the 'Garthland'.

Earlier: On record since 1860.

Gardener's Well GR 183156.

Derivation: According to the 1860 OS Name Book this was named for a man who lived nearby.

***Gardenook**, a settlement in approximate OS square 9605, on record in 1783.

Derivation: 'Garden' &c can sometimes represent P-Celtic 'Cardden', a thicket, but I have no evidence that our name is old enough for this.

Little Garret GR 194126, **Big Garret** GR 195122, hills.

***Garter Hill**. On record in 1774 at GR 101141 approximately.

Garvock GR 037148, a settlement, **Garvock Burn** GR 040147, **Nethergarvock Burn** GR 030143. **Garvock Glen**, on record in 1860, presumably carries the Garvock Burn?

Earlier: 1444 'Garvok', 1508 'Nether Garvok', 1539-47 'Drumgarock', 1563 'Garrock', 1664 'the Milne of Garvock', 1686 'Drumgorake', 1788 'Leatherhill of Garvock', 1801 'lands & Barony of Garvock comprising Upper & Nether Garvock, Shaws, Outsetts & pendicles of the same called Wellhill & Drum', 1802 'Latherhill of Garvock'.

Derivation: This name is very possibly related to Gaelic 'Garbh', rough, like The Garioch in Aberdeenshire which is Gaelic 'Gairbheach', place of roughness. The early forms without 'v' quoted above are perpetuated by a local pronunciation to this day. Gaelic '-ach' appears to have become '-o(c)k' quite early in this name.

Gateside, on record until 1860, a settlement at GR 023123 approximately.

Earlier: 1671 'Gaitsyde'.

Derivation: Scots 'Gate' &c, a way, a road, a path, late 14th century on.

***Gateside**, approximate OS square 1413, on record between 1732 & 1750. Derivation: Scots 'Gate' &c, a way, a road, a path, late 14th century on.

Gateside GR 183091, a settlement on record since c1240. According to Wilkie (see Bibliography) a chapel dedicated to the Virgin Mary was founded here post 1249. Jack (see Bibliography) says that Gateside was known "of old" as 'the Chapel Town of the Virgin'.

Derivation: Scots 'Gate' &c, a way, a road, a path, late 14th century on.

Gathering Stone GR 811022. This is reputed to be the gathering point of Mar's army before the battle of Sheriffmuir. On it the Highlanders were said to have whetted their blades.

Easter Gatherleys GR 052121, **Wester Gatherleys** GR 042119, settlements. I am told that Wester Gatherleys was abandoned as an independent holding c1890-1900 and Easter Gatherleys c1930.

Earlier: 1649 'Gatherlees', 1788 'Wester Gatherleys', 1800 'Easter Gatherleys', 1810 'Easter Gatherlees being part of the Barony of Pitcairns' (ie Pitcairns OS square 0214).

Derivation: Perhaps straightforwardly, the grassland on which stock was gathered.

Gattaway GR 193162, a settlement, **Hill of Gattaway** GR 197157. ***Gattaway Burn** mentioned by Morris (see Bibliography) is perhaps the burn joining the Nethy Burn at GR 193159? The older name for the settlement 'Petindy', 'Pittindy' &c, now represented only by Pittendie Hill OS square 2016, co-existed with 'Gattaway' until 1827 at least.

Earlier: 1528 'Gawtowy et Petindy', 1620 'Gatovie', 1699 'Gatway', 1742-4 'Gattaway', 1860 'Hill of Gattaway'.

Derivation: 'Gattaway' is not clear to me. The earliest forms quoted imply that '-way' is the result of a reinterpretation.

Cairn Geddes GR 119131. Jack (see Bibliography) writes that in 1906 only the base of the cairn remained, the stone having been removed at the beginning of the 19th century for filling drains and building dykes, at which time a "rude stone coffin" was found.

Derivation: From the surname? Certainly the word order appears Gaelic. The Gaelic form of the surname is 'Geadais' but I do not know whether it existed early enough in Gaelic to be a possibility here. 'Geadais' as a noun gives the not very likely sense of 'Coquetry Cairn'!

Geordie's Burn GR 823060. Earlier: 1860 'Geordie's Burn'. It appears to have been known as 'Green Burn' in 1736.

Derivation: Scots 'Geordie', a pet form of 'George', also a yokel, a rustic, 19th century on.

Gillies Burn GR 223173.

Earlier: On record since 1860.

This burn rises from, or very close to, Nine Wells (q.v.), and given the traditional religious connections of that location it is tempting to consider 'Gillies' here as Gaelic 'Gille Iosa', servant of Jesus. It may well simply be from the surname however, which of course itself comes ultimately from the same Gaelic words.

***Glashgarie Burn** on record in 1774, GR 110138 approximately. At that time it was also known as Turfhill Burn, a later Scots name from Turf Muir (q. v.) where the burn ran.

Derivation: Gaelic 'Glais Gàrraidh', wall or enclosure burn.

The gathering Stone,from an old postcard. Reproduced by courtesy of Perth and Kinross District Libraries.

Glassart Burn GR 230133, also known as Beggar's Burn & Colzie Burn. **Glassart Den** runs South East from GR 226136, ***Glassart Steps**, on record in 1823, were at GR 232132 approximately.

Earlier: 1860 'Glassart Burn', 'Glassart Den'.

Derivation: Gaelic 'Glais Ard', high stream, or Gaelic 'Glas Airde', green height or promontory, are possible here.

Glassingall GR 799045, ***Burn of Glassingal**, a settlement recorded between 1783 & 1837 in approximate OS square 7903, **Glassingalbeg Burn** GR 813060. ***Glassingalbeg**, a settlement on record until 1855, approximate OS square 8104, appears to have become part of Balhaldie OS square 8105 in the 19th century.

Earlier: 1442 'Classingalbeg', 1485 'Classingallis', 1493 'Glassingallis', 1536 'Classingall-more', 1538 'Classingall-Wester', 1539-47 'Classingall', 1611-1674 'Glassingall Sterline', 1612 'Gaitsyde of Glassingall' (ie Gateside sq 7904), 1632 'Glassingall-Drummond', 1650 'the Mylne of Glassingall', 1662 'Classingallmore', 'Classingall Wester', 1674 'Glesingall-Stirling', 1720 'Loanhead of Glassingall', c1723 'the Burn of Glenbank' (which appears to be the present Glassingalbeg Burn), 1766 'Burn of Glassengalbeg', 1837 'Glassingalbeg of Balhaldies', 1855 'Inn, Pendicle & Nether Part of Glassingalbeg'. 'Drummond' and 'Stirling' appended to the names in the 1611, 1632 &c forms quoted, no doubt refer to the then holders of the parts of the lands concerned.

Derivation: Confusion between Gaelic 'Clais', a shallow valley, and Gaelic 'Glais', a stream, is not uncommon in early transcriptions of placenames. The pre-17th century forms I have favour the former which would give Gaelic 'Clais nan Gall', shallow valley of the strangers. 'Gall' was often applied to non-Gaels and here it perhaps indicates the early presence of Normans or Angles, as does 'Ballingall' OS square 1004. These are names given by the surrounding population which survived whatever name the occupants themselves may have coined.

It is also interesting to note that 'Clais nan Gall' was already seen as an indivisible name-unit by the time, still in the Gaelic period, when the 'Big' and 'Little' component parts of the holding were named. Otherwise grammar would require 'Clais Mhòr nan Gall', 'Clais Bheag nan Gall'.

Gled's Nose GR 969042, a spur of hill.

Earlier: On record since 1860.

Derivation: Scots 'Gled' &c, a hawk, in placenames 13th century on. The New Statistical Account for Tillicoultry (1845) says "the glede, once an everyday object, is never seen in this part of the country".

***Glen**. An unidentified settlement, part of the barony of Gleneagles and absorbed into the Mains c1799.

Earlier references: 1587 'Over et Nether Glennes de Glenneges', 1685 'Glen'.

Derivation: 'Glen' in this and the following six names is a good example of a productive loanword, that is, a borrowing from Gaelic subsequently used freely to create new Scots names.

***Glen Burn** OS square 0304. This was an alternative name for Golland Burn, or possibly for its upper reaches only, on record in 1828.

Glen Burn GR 894060 flows in the Glen of Kinpauch. Earlier: On record since 1860.

Glen Burn GR 999100.

Earlier: On record since 1860.

Glen Cottage GR 878085.

Glen Wood GR 936081 &c extends from the Mains of Gleneagles to Gleneagles Old Toll House approximately.

Glen Wood GR 185135, **Glen Cottage** GR 188133.

Glenach Burn & ***Glen Egh**, a form on record until 1836, both GR 915010. ***Spout of Glen Egh** GR 920013 I have found on record between 1819 & 1836.

Earlier references: 1769 'Glen Egh', 1819 'Spout of Glen Egh', 1860 Glenach Burn'.

Derivation: The earlier forms quoted suggest Gaelic 'Gleann Eich', horse glen.

Glenbank GR 812058, **Glenbank Cottage** GR 814055, settlements. ***The Burn of Glenbank**' recorded c1723 seems to be Glassingalbeg Burn GR 813060. 'Drumness' (q.v.) was used as an alternative name for Glenbank until the late 18th century at least.

Earlier: 1545 'Drumnes alias Glenbank', 1654 'Glenbank'.

Glenbow OS square 2216. See Bow Burn.

Glenburnie, a settlement, GR 252171. The name was used until the early 20th century at least. Snoddy (see Bibliography) talks of "Glenburnie or Denmiln" (ie Denmiln sq 2417).

Derivation: Gaelic 'Gleann', glen; '-burnie', '-birnie' can derive from 'Brénnain' (ie St Brendan) and from Gaelic 'Braonach', locative 'Braonaigh', at moist place.

Glenburnie photographed in 1903. Reproduced by permission of Perth Museum and Art Gallery.

Glencairn Bridge GR 961992. ***Glencairn**, also 'Glencairny' &c, was an area, earlier a feudal landholding, seemingly centred on the glen of the Burn of Sorrow OS square 9599 and perhaps 9400 & 9300. The last reference I have seen to this name dates from 1791.

Earlier: 1579 'Glencairny', 1580 'terras de Glencarny jacen post lie Bank de Dolour' (ie 'lands of Glencarny lying behind the Bank of Dollar'), 1605 'the lands of Glencairne', 1695 'Glencairnie'.

Derivation: Gaelic 'Gleann Càrnaigh', glen at cairn place. It may be no coincidence that Innercairn (q.v.), Mid Cairn, Outer Cairn and Cairnmorris Hill all overlook Glencairn. See further under Burn of *Care*.

Glencloch Burn GR 976080. See Cloch Law.

Glendeuglie. See Wester *Deuglie*.

Glendevon. See River *Devon*.

Glendey Burn GR 007040.

Earlier: On record since 1860.

Derivation: This seems to be a lost glen name, Gaelic 'Gleann', glen, plus an unknown second element; the suggestion put forward for Glendy Burn OS square 1210 might apply here also: Gaelic 'Allt a' Ghlinne Dhuibh', burn of the black glen.

***Glendowaly**, on record in 1595, appears to be the glen that carries Carlownie Burn GR 945100.

Glendy Burn GR 126100, **Glendy Mill** GR 124098. This site may be the 'Glenduy' on Gordon's mid-17th century map of The West Part of Fife. Glendy Burn appears to be 'Hillton Burn' (ie from Hilton of Duncrievie OS square 1309) on Roy's map of 1750.

Earlier references: 1580 'Glendy-mylne', 1790 'the mill lands of Barleymill of Glendy', 1828 'the Mill Dam called the Clatteringdam erected on the lands of Glendymiln', 1860 'Glendy Burn'.

Derivation: Perhaps Gaelic 'Allt a' Ghlinne Dhuibh', burn of the black glen.

Gleneagles. See Glen *Eagles*.

The ruins of Glenearnhill, above Forgandenny. (AW)

Glenearn Hill GR 106155, **Glenearnhill**, a settlement, GR 101153. Secondary names from Glenearn OS square 1016.

Glenfarg. See River *Farg.*

***Glenfaulds Burn** on record between 1790 & 1822. It joins the Burn of Sorrow from the North at GR 945003, where copper and lead mines are marked on a plan of 1819.

Earlier: 1790 'Glenfauld Burn'.

Derivation: Scots 'Fauld', a fold, a pen, late 14th century on.

Glenfoot, a settlement, GR 989049. Earlier: On record since 1860.

Glenfoot, a settlement, GR 181157.

Earlier reference: 1790 'Glenfoot of Abernethy'.

Glenhead Farm GR 951053. It earlier formed part of Gleneagles barony.

Earlier references: 1587 '8 marcatas de Glenheid nuncupat. (ie called) Wester Glenkeattie' (ie Glenkeattie – see next entry), 1636 'Glenhead of Glenhegeis'. A 'marcata' (see 1587 form quoted) was perhaps a 'merkland', a Scots term for a measure of land originally valued at one merk, 15th century on.

***Glenkeattie** OS square 9605, lands on record until 1828. The 1587 form quoted below seems to imply that the respective parts of this holding lay West and East of the present Hillkitty Burn GR 962060, so 'Glenkeattie' is presumably the glen carrying that burn.

Earlier: 1587 '8 marcatas de Glenheid nuncupat. (ie called) Wester Glenkeattie, 8 marcatas de Eister Glenkattie nuncupat. Holkattie' (now Hillkitty), 1629 'Eister Glencattis in baronia de Glennegeyis (ie in the barony of Gleneagles)', 1828 'Glenkeattie or Hollkeattie'.

Derivation: Perhaps Gaelic 'Gleann Cait', wild cat glen. See also Hillkitty.

Glenmacduff. See Glen *Macduff.*

Glenquey. See Glen *Quey.*

Glenross Burn GR 015060, on record since 1860.

Derivation: Gaelic 'Gleann Rois', wood or promontory glen.

Glensherup. See Glen *Sherup.*

Glenside GR 877083, a settlement. Earlier: On record since 1855.

Glentarkie GR 192119, a settlement, **Glentarkie Hill** GR 190133.

Earlier: 1539 'Glentarky', 1699-1701 'Glentarkie'.

Derivation: Perhaps Gaelic 'Gleann Torcaigh', glen at boar place?

Glentye. See Glen *Tye.*

***Glentyre**, which I have found on record between 1811 & 1822, was presumably at or close to Rashiehill GR 042092. This seems to have been a new name imported by a new owner, which didn't last. Dunning Parish Historical Society have a plate bearing the name, taken from a pew in the parish church.

Earlier reference: 1811 'the half of the town and lands of Easter Lategreen or Rashiehill now called Glentyre'.

***Glenvye**. This is unidentified, but seemingly within half a mile of Cockplea OS square 8505. My only reference comes from material dating from somewhere between the late 16th century and the mid 17th.

Glenwinnel Burn GR 888000. Another lost glen name? It is '**Glenwinney Burn**' further downstream around OS square 8899 on some OS maps. On the 1860 OS map it appears to be called 'Benever Burn' (from Ben Ever OS square 8900), at least in its upper reaches.

Derivation: In the absence of earlier forms this name is not clear to me. The second part may be, or may have been reinterpreted as, Scots 'Windle', 'Winle' &c, a bundle of straw, 16th century on.

Gloom Hill GR 963992, **Gloomhill**, a settlement, GR 966992. ***Castle Gloom** was the earlier name of Castle *Campbell* (q.v.).

Earlier references: 1497 'terras ecclesiasticas de Campbel, alias Dolare seu Gloum nuncupatus' (ie the church lands of Campbell otherwise called Dollar or Gloom), 1654 'Gloum Hill', 1860 'Gloomhill'.

Derivation: 'Gloom' could very well be Gaelic

'Glòm', a chasm, applied to the spectacular Dollar Glen at the foot of the hill.

***Gloomingside Burn**, on record between 1792 & 1845, was an earlier name for Gannel Burn GR 915990. A plan dated 1769 marks ***Glooming** approximately in the South West corner of OS square 9198 and ***Gloomingsides**, seemingly an area of ground, as stretching approximately from GR 914988 to GR 918992.

Earlier references: 1769 'Glooming', 'Gloomingsides', 'Cannell's Burn' (ie modern Gannel Burn), 1792 'Gloomingside Burn' (ie modern Gannel Burn), 1848 'Gannel Burn'.

Derivation: 'Glooming' and 'Gloomingsides' are perhaps related to Scots 'Gloaming' &c, twilight, 15th century on? The lie of the land would presumably keep these locations out of the sun for a significant part of the day. A contrasting name would be 'Sunnyside', common in placenames for part of a holding receiving most sun. See further under Andrew Gannel Hill.

The Goat GR 957059, described by the 1860 OS Name Book as a small rocky ravine. From it flows Wanangoat Burn (q.v.).

Derivation: Scots 'Goat', 'Gote' &c, a trench, ditch or watercourse, 1568, first used for a natural watercourse c1627.

West Goat, on record to 1860, appears to be the burn at GR 900012. Earlier: 1769 'West Gott'.

Derivation: Scots 'Goat', 'Gote' &c, a trench, ditch or watercourse, 1568, first used for a natural watercourse c1627.

Golden Hill GR 253158.

Earlier: On record since 1860. If this turns out to be an old name it could well be from Gaelic 'Calltainn', hazel, with later reinterpretation. Cowden Hill, likely to be from the same Gaelic word, is in the adjacent OS square 2615.

Golland, a settlement, GR 055041, **Golland Linns** OS square 0504 (on Warroch West Burn). **Golland Burn** GR 050042, had the alternative names 'Dundie Burn' and 'Glen Burn' (qq.v). ***Golland Burn Haugh**, recorded in 1788, lies along the burn and is centred on GR 060041. From North to South the Golland Linns are Hadagain Linn, Black Linn & Washing Linn.

Earlier references: 1491 'Golyne', 1511 'Gowlam', 1615 'Gollane' & 'Golland', 1788 'Golland Burn', 1860 'Dundie Burn' (ie Golland Burn), 'Golland Linns'.

Derivation: Liddall (see Bibliography) feasibly suggests Gaelic 'Gabhal' with the Gaelic diminutive ending '-an', giving 'little fork', here referring to a triangular piece of land between two watercourses, Golland Burn & Warroch West Burn.

***Golloch**, a settlement on record in 1828, GR 118088 approximately, **Golloch Hill** GR 103088, ***Gollockmuir** recorded to 1771, ***Gollochsnow** (ie 'Knowe'), on record in c1796, GR 120093 approximately.

Earlier forms: 1580 'Gowlokmure', 1584 'Gawlokmure'.

Derivation: Gaelic 'Gòbhlach', forked place, referring here to a tapering piece of land between two burns .

***The Gornoch**, recorded in 1771. This was a part of Candy Hill centred on GR 119103 where "Feals" were cut (ie Scots 'Fail', turf).

Derivation: Gaelic 'Gronnach', boggy, as in the second part of Pitgorno OS square 1910.

Gornogrove GR 203103, a settlement. Compare the previous entry & see Pitgorno, of which 'Gornogrove' is a secondary name.

***Gott**, on record in 1769. This appears to be the burn at GR 910043.

Derivation: Scots 'Goat', 'Gote' &c, a trench, ditch or watercourse, 1568, first used for a natural watercourse c1627.

***Gowenyhall**, on record between 1666 & 1783, appears to be Auchengownie OS square 0912, with that name reinterpreted by analogy with Scots 'Goweny', covered with daisies, 18th century on. Mr G Ritchie, Dunning, knows the hill at GR 096124 as 'Gownie Hill'.

Earlier: 1666 'Gowane-hill'.

Gowk Hill & **Gowk Wood** both GR 232145.

Earlier: 1860 'Gowk Hill'.

Derivation: Scots 'Gowk', a cuckoo, late 15th century on.

The Gowls (also 'Ghoulls') GR 889981, a hill. This is also known as 'Gallows Hill', though this seems a high and remote site to have carried 'official' regularly used gallows?

Derivation: Perhaps from Gaelic 'Gobhal', fork, with Scots plural?

***Grains**, an area centred on GR 930996 on record in 1819 and called 'the Grains Hill' by Gibson (see Bibliography), also ***Burn Grains**, on record between 1769 & 1819 which appears to be the burn at GR 931994.

Earlier: 1769 'Burn Grains' & 'The Burn Grains of King's Seat'.

Derivation: Scots 'Grain', a place where two burns converge and by extension the spur of ground between them, in placenames late 15th century on.

***Graneburne**, on record between 1569 & 1613. This is an unidentified burn somewhere between Glenquey OS square 9702 and Auchlinsky OS square 9904.

Earlier: 1569 'lie Graneburne'.

Derivation: Scots 'Grain', 'Grane', a place where two burns converge and by extension the spur of ground between them, in placenames late 15th century on.

***Grange**. See Grange of *Lindores*.

Grasshill, on record until 1822, was the 'Outerhill' of Pitgober OS square 9798. It was presumably on the North side of Cornhill OS square 9700 which was the 'Innerhill of Pitgober'.

Earlier references: 1569 'Grisehill' & 'lie owttir hill de Pitgober seu lie gersehill nuncupatus' (ie otherwise called lie gersehill), 1822 'Outerhill of Pitgober or Grasshill'.

Derivation: Scots 'Gers', 'Girse' &c, grass, late 14th century on. The holding was no doubt named in contrast to Cornhill.

The Gray Stone GR 022118. Earlier: On record since 1860. The OS maps describe it as the 'Supposed Memorial of Dubdon Maormor of Atholl 964'.

***Graystone**, on record in 1766, an unidentified site on Sheriffmuir.

***Green**, a settlement recorded in 1783 in approximate OS square 9404.

Green Burn GR 836050. **Greenhill** GR 843057 & ***Greendike**, on record in 1783 in approximate OS square 8405, are quite possibly related names. Earlier references: 1736 'Green Burne', 'Easter Green Burne', 1783 'Greenhill'.

Green Burn GR 946020. On record since 1860.

***Green Gote.** An unidentified watercourse on Sheriffmuir on record in 1766. Derivation: Scots 'Goat', 'Gote' &c, a trench or ditch, 1568, first recorded for a natural watercourse 1627.

Green Hill GR 989123. Earlier: On record since 1860.

Green Hill GR 016100, **Greenhill**, a settlement, GR 020095, **Greenhill Woods** GR 018097.

Earlier references: 1798 'the lands of the Common of Dunning now called Greenhill', 1860 'Green Hill'.

Green Knowes GR 971072, on record since 1860.

Green Law GR 994075, on record since 1829.

Green Moss GR 998115. Earlier: 1860 'Green Moss'.

Derivation: Scots 'Green' was commonly applied to areas where grass grew well, but where 'Green' occurs in steep hilly country intersected by burns, as here, it is possible that it may be for Scots 'Grain', 'Grane', a place where two burns converge and by extension the spur of ground between them, in placenames late 15th century on; Scots 'Moss', moorland, peat bog, late 14th century on.

Greenforet Hill GR 862018, **Greenforet**, on record until 1901, an area stretching from GR 860034 approximately to the vicinity of Blairdenon Hill, GR 870015 approximately.

Earlier references: 1654 'green forret', 1860 'Greenforet Hill'.

Derivation: Perhaps 'Forest', in the sense of a tract of empty country, with 'Green' contrasting the vegetation here with nearby 'Rashie' (ie 'Rushie') Forrat approximate OS square 8603.

***Green-hill** on record in 1801 at GR 093152 approximately.

Greenhorn Burn GR 896040. Earlier forms: 1769 'Glengreenhorn Burn', 1848 'Greenhorn Burn'.

The Gray Stone, "Supposed Memorial of Dubdon Maormor of Atholl 964". Drawing by Ken Laing.

***Greennock** a pendicle or subsidiary holding of Myrehaugh OS square 0105, on record between 1663 & 1825. It appears to have been in the North East corner of OS square 0002 approximately.

Earlier references: 1663 'Greinnuik', 1825 'town & lands of Marhaugh with the Pendicle thereof called Greennook'

Derivation: Probably Scots 'Green Knock', green hill, or 'Green Neuk', green nook.

Green's Burn GR 980118. Earlier: On record since 1860.

Green's Falls GR 980076, a hillside (?). Earlier: On record since 1860.

Greens Well on record in 1860 GR 799029 approximately, ***Greens**, a settlement, on record in 1766 in approximate OS square 7902.

Easter Greenside GR 208169, **Wester Greenside** GR 203169, settlements, **Greenside Den** GR 204166.

Until the early 16th century this site was called 'Pitgrunzie' (q.v.), and this survived as an alternative name until about the early 18th century.

Earlier: 1516 'two parts of Greneside', 1662 'Easter Greensyde', 1691 'Gruinside', early 1700s 'which lands of Easter & Wester Pitgrunzies are otherwise and now called Over & Nether Greensides', 1752 'Wester Greenside', 1860 'Greenside Wood', 1977 'Upper Greenside' (ie the former Easter Greenside).

The Grey Mare. A large stone near Boghall farm, GR 045134. Earlier: On record in 1860.

Grey's Burn. The name given to modern Stank Burn GR 085041 on the 1860 OS map.

Grodwell Burn GR 912020, **Grodwell Hill** GR 915019 ('Crodwell' on the 1954 OS 1" map). Wells or springs are marked in the vicinity on the 1860 OS map.

Earlier: 1769 'Grodwell' (ie the hill), 'Grodwell Burn'.

Derivation: It is possible that this is from a lost well name from Gaelic 'Grod', putrid, stinking. Sulphurous wells, for instance, were sometimes given uncomplimentary names – WJ Watson (see Bibliography) gives the example of a 'Tobar Loibhte', stinking well, in Sleat.

Guilds Wood GR 033132.

Derivation: Perhaps Scots 'Guild', the corn marigold, 15th century on.

Craig Gullies GR 822971. "A large rugged rock" according to the 1860 OS Name Book. This suggests that 'Craig' is the generic and 'Gullies' the specific, an order which implies a Gaelic original, perhaps along the lines of 'Creag Ghòbhlaigh', crag at fork place, with later reinterpretation and the addition of the Scots plural.

Gun Wood GR 002130.

***Gutcher's Gote**. An unidentified watercourse on Sheriffmuir on record in 1766.

Derivation: Scots 'Gutcher', a grandfather, 16th century on; Scots 'Goat', 'Gote' &c, a trench or ditch, 1568, first recorded for a natural watercourse 1627.

H

Ha' Tower GR 044145. An earlier dwelling belonging to the barony of Garvock. Macfarlane (see Bibliography) relates that "Herein dwelt of old Widd (ie Wild) Willie Graeme being so called by reason of his resolution and boldness where by he struck a terror on the countrey about and by the strength of this fort defied all attacks of enemies".

Hadagain Linn GR 053045, on record since c1796. One of the Golland (q.v.) Linns.

Derivation: '-again' looks like the kind of Gaelic diminutive ending found in stream names, so one possible suggestion here might be 'Linne a' Chathagain', pool or waterfall of the little warlike one, from Gaelic 'Cath', battle, strife.

Hadydarn Burn GR 977090. Earlier: On record since 1829. This name is discussed with Hoodiemart Burn (q.v.).

***Haggiemoss**, a settlement in approximate OS square 8197, on record in 1783.

Derivation: Scots 'Hag', a hollow of marshy ground in a moor, eg where channels have been made or peats cut, 16th century on.

Haldrick GR 874063, a settlement. Earlier forms: 1783 'Haldridge', 1824 'Haldrick'.

Derivation: Scots 'Hold', 'Hald' &c, a holding, habitation, dwelling place, late 14th century on, perhaps with Scots 'Rig', 'Ridge' &c, a ridge of high ground, in placenames late 12th century on.

***Halfpenny Burn**, an older name for Culteuchar Burn GR 080157. I have seen the name in written records only up to 1801 but the burn is still referred to locally as 'the Haapenny'.

Earlier: 1774 'Half penny Burn', 1860 'Culteuchar Burn'.

Derivation: No doubt named from a Halfpennyland through which the burn ran: Scots, a piece of land valued at a half penny rental, late 15th century on.

Hall Burn rises at GR 997051. Earlier: 19th century 'Haw Burn', 1860 'Hall Burn'.

Derivation: Scots 'Hall' tended to refer to a more substantial dwelling house, in this case probably one in Glendevon village, earlier 'Downhill', past which the burn flowed.

Hallhill GR 058033, a settlement. Earlier: On record since 1775. Scots 'Hall' usually referred to a substantial dwelling house, grander than a cottage.

***Hardrigs**, on record between 1775 & 1827, a settlement in approximate OS square 1413.

Derivation: Scots 'Rig' here probably refers to the holding's arable ground, making a wry comment on the land and the living to be gained from it.

Hare Craigs GR 028112. Earlier: On record since 1860. The 1860 OS Name Book describes this as a few scattered rocks.

***Hare Stones**, recorded in 1769 on the South West face of Bencleuch OS square 9000.

Derivation: Perhaps Scots 'Harestane' &c, a conspicuously-fixed stone used as a boundary mark, in place names 14th century on.

***Hare-evirn**. This name appears on Stobie's map of Perth & Clackmannan of 1783 but it is not clear what kind of feature it represents. It may be an area of ground. It lies North of Greenforet Hill, seemingly close to Little Corum OS square 8603. The name makes little real sense to me in any language!

***Harestanes Hill** is on record in 1800 at GR 965097 approximately.

Derivation: Scots 'Harestane' &c, a conspicuously-fixed stone used as a boundary mark, in place names 14th century on.

Harperstone GR 841043, a settlement on record since 1783. After a possessive 's' '-ton', 'toun' can easily be reinterpreted as '-stone' and it is possible that earlier this name was 'Harperstoun', either from the surname, or representing 'the harper's toun'. Leases of land were made to musicians and other officials and 'professionals' in Gaelic society, but without earlier forms it is impossible to say whether this name is old enough to be a translation of an earlier Gaelic one.

***Hart Hill** was on record in 1736, perhaps at GR 862018.

Harviestoun Glen & **Harviestoun Burn** both GR 932980. ***Harviestoun Hill** referred to by Gibson (see Bibliography) and others is possibly the hill at GR 940988. These are secondary names from Harviestoun OS square 9397.

Earlier: 1616 (Perhaps compare?) 'Hervisdavok' (in Tillicoultry barony), 1688 'Harviestoune of Tillicultrie', 1769 'Eastertown Burn' (ie Harviestoun Burn), 1819 'Harviestoun Hill', 1836 'Eistertown Glen' (ie Harviestoun Glen), 1848 'Harvieston Burn', 1860 'Harviestoun Glen'. For further information see Elistoun GR 931979.

***Hatton**, on record until 1828 approximate OS square 2614?, **Halton Hill** GR 245162, both settlements.

Earlier: 1567 'Haltounhill', 1627 'the Stannie Haltoun', 1640 'Hattonhill', 1709 'Hatton'.

Derivation: Scots 'Hall Toun' with assimilation of 'l' to 't' from the 17th century on. Recent OS series have restored the 'l'. Scots 'Hall' implied a dwelling grander than a cottage. 'Stannie' in the 1627 reference quoted could imply either stony ground, or perhaps here a dwelling built of (dressed) stone.

Hattonburn GR 128054. See Holeton.

Haugh GR 054030, a settlement.

Derivation: Scots 'Haugh', river-meadow land, late 12th century on.

***Haughhead**, on record until 1829, a settlement in approximate OS square 7999. Earlier: 1792 'Hanghead'.

Derivation: Scots 'Haugh', river-meadow land, late 12th century on. If 1792 'Hanghead' quoted above is not an error, it no doubt implies a wry comment on the hardship of working the holding.

Hawk's Craig GR 943073, **Hawkescraig Burn** GR 934070.

Earlier: Both on record since 1860.

Hawkhill Plantation GR 060150.

Hayfield, on record until 1901, seemingly on the site of modern Glendeuglie GR 128105, **North Hayfield** recorded in 1860 GR 119109 approximately, both settlements. Also **Hayfield Mill** on the River Farg at GR 131104 approximately.

Earlier references: 1800 'Hayfield', 1855 'Parks, Mill & Land at Hayfield'.

Hayfield commemorated by a Glenfarg street name. (AW)

***Hays Mill**, on record until 1860, on the River Farg at GR 136110 approximately. It was also known as 'Mill of Arngask', and burnt down in 1864.

Earlier references: 1647 'Richard Hay at the Myln of Arngask', 1742 'Arngask Miln', 1750 'Hays Mill', 1761 'lands of Haysmiln be west the water of Farg being originally a part of Abottsduglie', 1795 'William Hay of Mill of Arngosk, as heir to his grandfather, seised in the Mill of Arngosk'.

Derivation: The mill was presumably renamed for the 17th & 18th century occupants (see 1647 & 1795 references quoted above), though 'Miln of Arngask' persisted as the 'official' name.

***Headdike**, a settlement on record between 1665 & 1783, approximate OS square 8001.

Earlier references: 1665 'Head-dyke of Langrig' (ie Landrick OS square 7902), 1752 'Head dykes of Kippendavie', 1766 'Head Dykes', 'Burn of Head Dykes'.

Derivation: Scots 'Heid-dyke' &c, the outer wall of a field or holding, the boundary wall, 15th century on.

***Headdyke**, a settlement on record between 1635 & 1860, GR 958103 approximately. It was also known as Bowie's Hole.

Earlier: 1635 & 1664 'Headdykes of Fossaway' (ie Foswell), 1783 'Headdikes', 1801 'Head-Dyke of Fosswell'.

Derivation: Scots 'Heid-dyke' &c, the outer wall of a field or holding, the boundary wall, 15th century on.

Head-dykes, a settlement on record since 1860, GR 836047, named for its proximity to the head-dyke of Balhaldie.

Derivation: Scots 'Heid-dyke' &c, the outer wall of a field or holding, the boundary wall, 15th century on.

Head-dykes of Balhaldie. (AW)

Heads Hill GR 052079. Earlier: c1796 'Heads', 1860 'Heads Hill'. This name may well be related to Rintoul Head Moss and Ledlanet Head Moss which were nearby.

Heart Plantation, on record between 1796 & 1860 at GR 992066. Named from its shape.

Heatherie Knowe GR 019081. Earlier: On record since 1860.

Heatherieleys GR 100125, a settlement.

Earlier forms: 1650 'Hedrie Leyes', 1742 'Hethery Leys'.

Derivation: Scots 'Lea' &c, grassland of various kinds, 16th century on.

***Helen's Muir** centred on GR 923992 approximately. The name is still well known locally, though I haven't seen it on recent maps.

Earlier: 1769 'Helens Moor' & 'Helens Muir'.

Herald Law GR 236124. Earlier: On record since 1860.

***Herd's Mailing**, recorded in 1808, was part of the Common of Pitgober. There was common pasturage on the Outerhill of Pitgober, to the North of Cornhill OS square 9700, so this holding may have been there.

Derivation: Scots 'Herd', a cowherd or more frequently a shepherd, late 14th century on; Scots 'Mailing', a rented holding, from 'Mail', rent, late 14th century on.

Hermitage Wood GR 811970. According to Menzies Fergusson (see Bibliography) there was a hermitage at approximate GR 807970, now in ruins, built by Richard Haldane owner of Aithrey Estate in the late 18th century.

***Upper Hethrefold** & ***Nether Hethrefold** are both on record in 1766. They are unidentified settlements on Sheriffmuir.

***Heughend**, on record between 1796 & 1860, a settlement at GR 141076 approximately.

Derivation: Scots 'Heugh', a steep bank overhanging a river, 15th century on.

***The Hieland Steps** GR 922010. A stile on the track from Tillicoultry to Blackford.

***Hielanman's Well**, also known as Faery Well. On the Sheriffmuir road near Drumbrae Farm OS square 8097. It was at one time reputed to be a curative or holy well. The name may refer to the Highland presence at the battle of Sheriffmuir or perhaps more likely to the use of the well by Highland drovers: Sheriff Muir and Gleneagles-Glendevon were much-used routes for cattle droving.

***Highame**, on record until 1654, a settlement in approximate OS square 1510. Earlier forms: 1507-8 'Heicham', 1620 'Hicham'. Derivation: Scots 'Heich' &c, high; Scots 'Hame', home. This name formed a contrasting pair with Letham GR 153120.

Hill End GR 981098. Earlier: 1783 'Hillend'.

Hillfoot House GR 969994, a settlement, **Hillfoot Hill** GR 969006. Earlier references: c1680 'Hillfit', 1860 'Hillfoot House', 'Hillfoot Hill'.

***Hillhead**, on record in 1800. This was a holding making up one sixth of Ballieliesk OS square 0001.

Hillhead, a settlement on record between 1796 & 1860, GR 072034.

Hillkitty GR 965059, a hill, **Hillkitty Burn** GR 962060. The holding that bore this name was to the East of Hillkitty Burn.

Earlier: 1587 '8 marcatas de Eister Glenkattie nuncupat. Holkattie' (ie 8 merklands? of Eister Glenkattie called Holkattie), 1799-1828 'Glenkeattie or Hollkeattie', 1860 'Hillkitty', 'Hillkitty Burn'.

Derivation:The name is a Scots-Gaelic hybrid: Scots 'Holl', 'Howe' &c, a hollow, 16th century on, later reinterpreted as 'hill', plus the second part of 'Glenkeattie' (q.v.), perhaps Gaelic 'Gleann Cait', wild cat glen. The Gaelic word order of 'Glenkeattie' influenced the word order of the hybrid derived from it.

Hillpark Cottage, a settlement on record in 1860, GR 233165.

Hillside, a settlement, GR 066034.
Earlier: On record since 1860.

Hilton, a settlement, GR 108045.
Earlier: 1524 'le Hiltoun', 1654 'Hilton of Binnaga' (ie Ballingall OS square 1004), 1687 'Hiltoun of Balnagall'.

Hodyclach Burn GR 986080.
Earlier: 1829 'Hody-clach Burn'. This name is discussed under Cloch Law and Hoodiemart Burn (qq.v.).

Hog Rigg GR 038059, a hill. In 1615 this was part of the lands of Carnbo OS square 0503.
Earlier: 1615 'Hogrig'.
Derivation: Scots 'Rig', a ridge, a long narrow hill, a hill-crest, late 14th century on.

Hogan's Prop GR 035106, a hill, on record since 1860. According to the 1860 OS Name Book this name was on an estate map of c1760.
Derivation: The surname?, plus Scots 'Prap', 'Prop', a boundary mark, late 15th century on.

Hog's Wood GR 053155.

***Hole**, a settlement on record in 1783, approximate OS square 7999.
Derivation: Scots 'Howe', 'Holl' &c, a depression, a hollow, or a low-lying piece of ground, 16th century on.

Hole Burn GR 993992, **Holeburn**, a settlement, GR 992993.
Earlier: 1783 'Holeburn'.
Derivation: Scots 'Howe', 'Holl' &c, a depression, a hollow, or a low-lying piece of ground, 16th century on, though in a watercourse name, as here, the reference could be to a pool or pothole.

Hole Grain, described as a ridge by the 1860 OS Name Book, & **Holegrain Burn**, both GR 965073 approximately.
Earlier: Both on record in 1860.
Derivation: Scots 'Howe', 'Holl' &c, a depression, a hollow, or a low-lying piece of ground, 16th century on; Scots 'Grain', a branch of a stream, or the promontory of hill where burns converge, in place-names late 15th century on.

Hole Mill, on record between 1828 & 1860, GR 169098.
Derivation: Scots 'Howe', 'Holl' &c, a depression, a hollow, or a low-lying piece of ground, 16th century on.

Holeton GR 114065, **Holetonburn** GR 121063, settlements, **Holeton Hill** GR 109081, **Hattonburn**, a settlement, GR 127056, **Hatton Burn** GR 128060.
A distillery was at Hattonburn from c1780 to 1828. The author of the Old Statistical Account for Orwell tells us that the product was "rather better than what is found in many places in Scotland". Moss and Hume however (see Bibliography) report that Hattonburn distillery "was reputed to make the worst whisky in Scotland"!
Earlier forms: 1580 'Holtoun', 1648 'Haltoun', 1654 'Haltone','Haltoun', 'Hulton', 1656 'the Hultounburn' (ie Holetonburn the settlement), 1765 'Holtown', 1775 'Halton Burn', c1796 'Holetown Burn' (ie Holetonburn the settlement), 'Hatton Burn' (ie Hattonburn the settlement), 1860 'Holton Hill'. On the evidence of the forms quoted the original name was 'Hol(e)toun', later differentiated as 'Hal(l)toun' in the case of the burn and one of the settlements. Then the 'l' of 'Haltoun' became assimilated to the 't' to give 'Hatton'. The interchanging of 'Hole' & 'Hall' is not at all uncommon in Scots placenames.
Derivation: Scots 'Hall', a dwelling more substantial than a cottage; Scots 'Holl', 'Howe' &c, a depression, a hollow, 16th century on. It may be no coincidence that Tillyrie (q.v.), adjacent to Holtown and Holtonburn, appears to derive its name from Gaelic 'Toll', a hole, a hollow.

***Holm**, a settlement on record in 1783, approximate OS square 8000.
Derivation: Scots 'Holm' &c, a stretch of low-lying land beside a river, in placenames late 13th century on.

Hologrogin GR 982125. The 1860 OS Name Book describes this as a hollow on Craig Rossie, half way up on the North side.
Earlier: On record since 1860.
Derivation: This name has long been a puzzle. 'Hol-' could represent either Scots 'Hole', or Gaelic 'T(h)oll' with similar sense, ie a hole, a hollow, and that at least matches the site. The middle 'o' could represent a genitive, ie 'of', or 'of the', in either Scots or Gaelic. I have no sensible suggestion for '-grogin' in any language, though the final '-in' could derive from a Gaelic diminutive.

***Holton**, a settlement on record between 1508 & 1850, GR 960118, **Holeton Mill**, on record in

1860-62, GR 961118 approximately.

Earlier: 1508 'le Holtoun', 1860 'Holtonmill'.

Derivation: Scots 'Holl', 'Howe' &c, a depression, a hollow, 16th century on. .

Holy Land, on record in 1860, a settlement at GR 236132.

***Holy Well**, recorded in 1790, approximate OS square 8398. The Old Statistical Account for Logie says that half a mile North of the North foot of Dumyat was a very fine well which issued from more than sixty springs, continuing: "It is called the Holy Well, and is said to have formerly been much resorted to by the Roman Catholics".

Home Farm GR 969992.

Earlier: On record since 1860.

Homehead, a settlement on record until 1860, GR 231145. In the 17th century it was part of Pitcairlie OS square 2315. **Homehead Wood** GR 231144.

Earlier: 1632 'the Holmeheid of Pitcairlie'.

Derivation: Scots 'Holm' &c, a stretch of low-lying land beside a river, in placenames late 13th century on, subsequently reinterpreted as 'Home'.

***Hoodiemart Burn**. Mentioned by Naomi Mitchison in her novel *The Bull Calves*. Mr Richard Haldane, Cloan, tells me that this is the burn, unnamed on OS maps, that runs West from Upper Cloan to join the Coul Burn at GR 964109.

Earlier: 1772 'Hoodiemart' & 'Hoddiemart'. Derivation: The name is said to refer to a gathering place (Scots 'Mart', market) of hoodie crows, but *The Concise Scots Dictionary* gives this sense in Scots from the 20th century only. The name must be much older than that as it appears on an estate plan of 1772. 'Hoddiemart' (see the 1772 forms quoted), Hodyclach Burn and Hadydarn Burn (qq.v) form an intriguing trio which all flow into the same 1.75 mile stretch

The Humble Bumble photographed in 1909. Reproduced by permission of Perth Museum and Art Gallery.

of the Coul Burn. 'Hod-' can be from Gaelic 'Coire', a corrie, a hollow on a hill, which is usually the source of a burn. The following 'y' or 'ie' in all three burn names could well represent the Gaelic genitive article (of the). Among the last elements '-mart' and '-clach' appear Gaelic, from 'Mart', a cow or a steer, and 'Clach', a stone, respectively, though 'Mart' also exists as a Scots loanword from the 15th century on, with similar sense. '-darn' on the face of it looks like Scots 'Darn', 'Dern', secret, hidden, late 14th century on. Without earlier forms for all three names this is as much light as I can throw on them.

Hopefield, a settlement, GR 094058.
Earlier: 1860 'Hope Field'.

Horse Burn GR 038118, on record since 1860.

Horsepark Wood GR 921978.

Horseshoe Wood GR 036147.

How Cleuch GR 990036, **Howcleuch Burn** on record in 1860, same GR.
Earlier: 1860 'How Cleuch'.
Derivation: Scots 'Howe', a plain bounded by hills, 16th century on, describes the site where the burn rises; Scots 'Cleuch', a ravine, in place-names late 14th century on.

The Howe, a settlement, GR 222137.
Derivation: Scots 'Howe', a depression, a hollow, a vale, 16th century on.

Howe, a settlement on record in 1901, GR 816055 approximately.
Derivation: Scots 'Howe', a depression, a hollow, a vale, 16th century on.

Humble Bumble, falls, GR 069161.
Earlier: 1792 'Hummel Bummel', 1796 'Humble Bumble'.
Derivation: An onomatopoeic name. Probably Scots 'Hummle' &c, humble, late 15th century, with influence from English 'Hum'; Scots 'Bummle' the noise of a bee, late 18th century, with influence from English 'Bumble' bee. Scots 'Bummel' &c, to boil up, bubble, tumble, no doubt played a part too. The Bike OS square 8099 is another site whose name compares the sound of a waterfall to the sound of bees.

Little Hunt Hill GR 842016, **Big Hunt Hill** GR 847014.
Earlier: 1736 'Mickle Hunt Hill', 'Little Hunt Hill', 1860 'Big Hunt Hill'.

Hunters Seat, a settlement, GR 036088 approximately, **Hunterseat Burn** on record in 1860, GR 045090?, ***Hunters Seat Hill**, recorded in 1837, GR 041082 approximately. The settlement appears to have passed out of use between 1783 and 1837 though the ruins were visible in the late 19th century.
Earlier: 1783 'Hunterseat', 1837 'Site of Hunters Seat Old Steading'.

Hunthall, a settlement, GR 962054. **Hunt Stripe**, a burn at GR 955035, may be a related name.
Earlier: Both on record since 1860.
Derivation: According to Gilbert (see Bibliography) 'Hunthall' can indicate the site of a temporary or permanent hunting lodge in the days when the area concerned was a hunting reserve or forest, though without earlier references we cannot be sure that this is the case here. Scots 'Stripe' is a small stream, 15th century on.

Huntly Hall, a settlement, GR 092056.
Earlier: On record since 1860.

***Hutchbraes** GR 133127. This was an alternative name, recorded in 1783, for Lochelbank.
Derivation: Perhaps Scots 'Hutch', a small rick or temporary stack of corn, though *The Concise Scots Dictionary* gives this as occurring from the 19th century only.

I

First Inchna Burn GR 850982, **Second Inchna Burn** GR 851990, **Third Inchna Burn** GR 843990, **Fourth Inchna Burn**, also known as Crunie Burn, GR 838990. One informant who grew up locally says he always knew these burns as 'First Burn', 'Second Burn' &c, and only learnt 'Inchna' from maps.

Derivation: Gaelic 'Innis an Ath', island of the ford, has been suggested. In Menstrie Glen the First Inchna divides leaving a flat island.

Inner Burn joins Frandy Burn at GR 942040. **Outer Burn** GR 942030.

Earlier: Both are on record since 1860.

Inner Burn GR 907000, **Outer Burn** GR 901000.

Earlier: 1860 'Inner Burn'.

***Innercairn**, on record until 1822, an alternative name for King's Seat Hill GR 934000.

Earlier reference: 1769 'Kings Seat or Inner Kairn'.

Derivation: Gaelic 'Inbhir Chàirn', confluence of the Cairn (burn), is a very tempting etymology since the confluence of three burns forms the Burn of Sorrow, once also known as the 'Cairn', at GR 934008 nearby. However references in 1769 & 1819 to a ***Mid Cairn** at GR 932002 very approximately & an ***Outer Cairn** at GR 933004 very approximately invalidate this by showing that 'Inner' is Scots. The presence of these three cairns however, together with Cairnmorris Hill GR 934017, could help to explain the origin of the names 'Cairn' (Burn) & 'Glencairn' (see further under Burn of *Care* and Glencairn Bridge).

Innerdounie Hill GR 032073. In 1615 this was part of the lands of Carnbo OS square 0503.

Earlier: 1615 'mons (ie hill) de Innerdowny'.

Derivation: 'Inner-' is likely to be from Gaelic 'Inbhir', confluence, indicating that a burn name follows, here perhaps based on Gaelic 'Dùnach', locative 'Dùnaigh', at fort or hill place.

Innerdownie GR 967032, a hill.

Earlier: 1333-4 (Perhaps) 'Donay' (in the Glendevon area), 1783 'Inderdownie Hill' (a transcription error?), 1860 'Innerdownie'.

Derivation: 'Inner-' is likely to be from Gaelic 'Inbhir', confluence, indicating that a burn name follows, here perhaps based on Gaelic 'Dùnach', locative 'Dùnaigh', at fort or hill place; compare the 1333-4 form quoted.

J

Jackschairs, a settlement, GR 069169, **Jackschairs Wood** GR 070170. At some time since 1860 the settlement became known as Nethertholm.

Earlier: 1774 'Jacks chairs', 1860 'Jackchairs', 'Jackschairs Wood'.

Derivation: If this is not from the personal name it may be Scots 'Jack' &c, the jackdaw, though the date given by *The Concise Scots Dictionary*, the late 19th century on, is late.

Jamie's Grain, a spur at GR 975075, **Jamie's Grain Burn** GR 958076, ***Well of Jamie's Green**, on record in 1800, GR 955078 approximately?

Derivation: The 1860 OS Name Book describes Jamie's Grain as a small ridge between two streams, ie from Scots 'Grain', a branch of a stream, and by extension the spur or ridge of land where burns converge, in place-names late 15th century on. I suspect that confusion is not unusual in hilly country between this item and 'Green', as in Well of Jamie's 'Green' here.

***Jenny's Baking Stone**. A flat stone at the Washing Linn OS square 0504.

Jerah, a settlement, GR 839992.

Earlier: 1589 'Jargrayis', 1635 'Terris de (ie lands of) Eister et Wester Gargreiss', 1664 'Park of Jarvay', 1684 'Little Jervey', 1754 'Wester Jerray', 1783 'Mickle Girra', 1788-1822 'Easter & Wester Gergriesses or Jervasses comprising Meikle & Little Jervass & a farm called the Park', 1848 'Jera'.

Derivation: This is a confusing variety of early forms! It looks as if 'Jargrayis', 'Gargreiss' &c may have been a developing reinterpretation based on Scots 'Greis', grass. 'Jarvay' &c probably remains closer to an original Gaelic name. Gaelic 'Dearg', red, seems likely for the first syllable. Red Brae (q.v.) is some 650 yds away and our site may share the same geological character? Gaelic 'Dearg Mhagh', red plain, may explain 'Jarvay' if we understand 'plain' here as a small level site. If on the other hand the final 's' or 'ss' of some earlier forms is part of the original Gaelic name and does not derive from a Scots plural, 'Jervass' may be Gaelic 'Dearg Fhas', with a similar meaning, red stance or level site. Some have believed this name to be biblical as 'Jerah' appears as a personal name in Genesis 10, 26 and 1 Chron 1, 20. This coincidence may well explain the adoption of the spelling 'Jera(h) from the mid 19th century on. 'Park' in the earlier references quoted may now be represented by Park Cottage OS square 8201, though the lie of the intervening land makes this uncertain.

Jocksbrae, a settlement on record in 1860, GR 932080 approximately.

John's Hill GR 001081.

Earlier: On record since 1829.

Jubilee Belt GR 936983, woodland. See the next entry.

Jubilee Plantation GR 116091.

Perhaps planted to commemorate some (royal?) anniversary?

K

Kaimknowe Farm GR 958053.

Earlier forms: 1685 'Combknow', 1783 'Kaimknow', 1828 'Combknow', 1855 'Kaimknowe'.

Derivation: 'Comb-' in the earlier forms quoted looks like a case of hyper-correction of Scots 'Kame', 'Came' &c, a long narrow steep-sided ridge, the crest of a hill or ridge, late 18th century on. Though this usage is ultimately an extension of the idea 'comb' based on the appearance of certain types of hill formation, the Scots word 'Kame' in its topographical sense no longer corresponded to English 'Comb'. 1685 seems an early date for such sensitivity about Scots forms?

The Kaims, on record in 1860, OS square 9812. These are described by the 1860 OS Name Book as two small ridges with ledges of rock on Craig Rossie.

Derivation: Scots 'Kame' &c, a long narrow steep-sided ridge, the crest of a hill or ridge, late 18th century on.

Kames GR 947993. A rugged rocky ridge, according to the 1860 OS Name Book.

Earlier: On record since 1860.

Derivation: Scots 'Kame' &c, a long narrow steep-sided ridge, the crest of a hill or ridge, late 18th century on.

Kalesquy Linn GR 038034, a waterfall on the South Queich on record since 1860.

Derivation: Gaelic 'Caolas Chuaich', narrow place of Queich.

***Karling Stone**. An unidentified site on Sheriffmuir on record in 1766, perhaps South of the battlefield OS square 8201.

Derivation: Scots 'Kerlying', 'Carling' &c, an old woman, a witch, late 14th century on.

Katie Thirsty Well GR 194129.

Earlier: On record since 1860.

Derivation: Obscure. This is just possibly a well dedicated to St Catherine and/or St Drustan or Drostan. According to WJ Watson (see Bibliography) Drostan may be connected with St Andrews to which diocese Abernethy parish belonged from the 13th century at least. He is commemorated on Loch Earnside by 'Ard Trostáin', Drostan's height and he is attested in Forfarshire as 'Droustie'. For metathesis of 'r' & 'u' compare 'Skirdurstan', Aberlour, 'Drostan's parish'.

Kay Craig GR 975129, on record since 1860. This is also known as 'Cree Craig', explained locally as 'Crow' Craig.

Derivation: Scots 'Kae' &c, a jackdaw, 16th century on.

***Kee Crag**. This is near the Bein Kist OS square 9912 (see Banekist Burn).

Derivation: 'Kee' is a local form of Scots 'Kae', a jackdaw.

Keerie Glen GR 037041. Earlier: On record since 1860.

Derivation: Perhaps Gaelic 'Ciaradh', genitive 'Ciaraidh', dusk, could refer here to a site often in shadow because of the lie of the land?

Kelly Burn GR 969990, **Kellybank**, a settlement earlier called 'the Whangs', GR 968984.

Earlier: c1680 'Kelly Burn', 1821-29 'the Whangs now (called) Kellybank'.

Derivation: Gaelic 'Coille', a wood, a forest. See also The Whangs.

Keltie Castle, marked as an antiquity on OS maps, GR 006133, **Wester Keltie** GR 004135, **Keltie Burn** GR 006138, **Keltie Loch** GR 003138, **Keltie Wood** GR 008130. ***Knock Kelty** recorded in 1750 appears to be Rossie Law GR 998124.

Earlier: 1443 'Kelty', 1855 'Wester Kelty', 1860 'Keltie Wood'.

Derivation: WJ Watson (see Bibliography) thinks this is probably Gaelic 'Cailtidh' from a

At Keltie Castle. Photographed by Magnus Jackson in the late 1800s. Reproduced by permission of Perth Museums and Art Gallery.

Celtic root 'Caleto', hard. WFH Nicolaisen (see Bibliography) concurs, attributing the hardness to the stream bed. If these authorities are right the burn name, not the settlement, will be the primary name.

Kelty Burn GR 100134. This is likely to have a similar derivation to Keltie OS square 0013. See previous entry.

Kemp's Score GR 961992.

Earlier: On record since 1793. This is a cleft in the rockface South of Castle Campbell running to the Dollar Burn below, said to have been cut by the giant robber Kemp who was supposedly caught and killed here after stealing the King's dinner from Dunfermline Castle (see Burn of *Care*). Alternatively Gaelic 'Ceum Sgoir', rock crevice step, has been ingeniously suggested as various writers have thought that this feature may have been a way cut to give access to water in time of siege. For his part Billings (see Bibliography) reports a tradition that Kemp's Score once afforded a hiding place for John Knox. While the vast majority of place names in the Ochils are down-to-earth, the names associated with the Castle Campbell area are conspicuously romantic and dramatic!

Kennel Wood OS square 1112.

***Kerlynlyn** on record c1320 East of the Dunning Burn, perhaps in the vicinity of OS square 0212.

Derivation: Perhaps Scots 'Kerlying', 'Carling' &c, an old woman, a witch, late 14th century on. Scots 'Linn', late 15th century on, seems too late to be possible here, so the final syllable looks likely to be Gaelic 'Linne', a waterfall or a pool.

***Kevarke**. An unidentified site from Adair's map of Clackmannanshire c1680, approximate OS square 9597?

Kidlaw Hill GR 853016.

Earlier: 1736 'The Kidd Law' & 'The Kidd Law Hill'.

Derivation: Scots 'Law', a rounded, usually conical, hill, in placenames late 12th century on. The second 1736 form quoted shows that the practice of adding a superfluous 'Hill' to 'Law' names is not restricted to recent times.

***Kildinny Hill**. According to Meldrum (see Bibliography) in the 17th century this was the name of the hill at GR 072169. It is a secondary name from Kildinny OS square 0617.

Killknowe, a settlement on record in 1860, GR 194102.

Derivation: Any of Scots 'Kiln', Gaelic 'Cùil', nook, or Gaelic 'Coille', wood, could explain 'Kill-' here.

Kiln Burn on record in 1860. It rises North of Knowehead OS square 0309 and flows to the Water of May.

***Kilsprot Hill**, on record in 1836, seemingly modern Burnfoot Hill GR 901034, ***Kames of Kilsprot** on record in 1819 GR 904038 approximately.

Earlier: 1769 'Knows of Killsprott'.

Derivation: Perhaps Scots 'Sprot', a rush (ie the plant), late 16th century on. For some possible origins of 'Kil-' see the next entry.

Kiltane Farm GR 799999. WFH Nicolaisen (1976 – see Bibliography) states that 'Kil-' can come not only from Gaelic 'Cill', a church or cell (not likely in our area, see remarks under Damakellis), but also from Gaelic 'Coille', a wood, Gaelic 'Cùil' a nook, and occasionally Gaelic 'Cinn', head, end, as well as sometimes having to be regarded as unidentifiable. Scots 'Kiln' is possible too!

Kinbuck Muir GR 804051, **Firs of Kinbuck** GR 807049, both on record in 1860. These are secondary names from Kinbuck OS square 7904.

Kinburn, a settlement, GR 845075.

Derivation: Possibly Gaelic 'Allt a' Chinn' partly translated, for 'the burn at the head of' some other feature. Just as likely though is Scots 'Kiln Burn' with assimilation of 'l' to 'n'.

Kincraigie, a settlement, GR 198109, **Kincraigie Law** GR 191110.

Earlier forms: 1240-49 'Kincraigie', 1505 'Kincragze' & 'Kyncragze'. Gaelic 'Ceann Creige' or 'Cinn Creige', end or head of the crag, with 'z' in the 1505 forms quoted representing the semi-vowel [j].

King's Arm Chair GR 184153.

King's Knowe GR 128094.

King's Seat Hill GR 934000. Innercairn (q.v.) was an alternative name for the hill in the 18th century.

Earlier reference: 1769 'Kings Seat or Inner Kairn'. WJ Watson (see Bibliography) points out that 'Seat' in Scots names can sometimes represent a translation of an earlier Gaelic 'Suidhe', seat. See also Boar's Knowe.

The Kinnaker GR 928090, a settlement.

Earlier: On record since 1783.

Derivation: Possibly 'Acre End'?: Gaelic 'Cinn', end, and Scots 'Akir', late 12th century on, or Gaelic 'Acaire', acre.

Kinpauch GR 894075, a settlement, **Kinpauch Hill** GR 897062, **Kinpauch Burn** GR 903070, **Glen of Kinpauch** GR 893060.

Earlier: 1664 'Kinpauch', 1783 'Wester Kinpauch', 'Easter Kinpauch', 'Pirrick of Kinpauch' (ie Kinpauch Hill), 1855 'Kinpauch easter & wester', 1860 'Kinpauch Hill', 'Glen of Kinpauch', 'Glen Burn' (which flows in Glen of Kinpauch), 'Kinpauch Burn'.

Derivation: Gaelic 'Ceann', locative 'Cinn', end; '-pauch' is obscure to me. Scots 'Pirrick', 'Pirrack', &c, in the 1783 reference quoted, is a mound, a pinnacle, a summit – see further under Pirrich.

*__Kinrossfold__. This is an unidentified site on Sheriffmuir on record in 1766.

From the head of Glen of Kinpauch, looking NW across Strathearn. Ben Vorlich and Stuc a'Chroin are on the horizon. (AW)

Kippen House GR 018129, **Hole of Kippen**, a settlement, GR 017128, **Kippen Hill** & **Kippenhill Plantation** both GR 015131, **Black Hill of Kippen** GR 010117.

Earlier references: 1287 'Kyppen', 1621 'Holl of Kippen', 1671 'Eistir & Westir Kippenes', 1783 'W Kippen', 1860 'Kippen Hill', 'Kippen Hill Plantation', 'Black Hill of Kippen'.

Derivation: Gaelic 'Ceap', plural 'Ceapan', turf, tussock, or when a hill name, 'lump of a hill'.

Kippen House. Photographed by Magnus Jackson in the late 1800s. Reproduced by permission of Perth Museum and Art Gallery.

Kippendavie GR 793023, on record under this name to 1860 but now known as Ryland Lodge, **Kippendavie Wood** GR 791020.

Earlier references: 1482 'Kippendave' & 'Kippandavy', 1650 'Kippendavie with the mylns', 1723 'burn of Kippendavie' (ie the present Ryland Burn), 1766 'Achnbee Mill Kippendavie' (ie Auchinbie approximate OS square 7902).

Derivation: It has been suggested that '-davie' commemorates Dabius or Davius an Irish missionary said to have come to Dunblane in the mid 5th century. Perhaps as likely is Gaelic 'Ceapan Dabhaich', Davoch Kippen, or 'Ceapan Damhaigh', 'Kippen' at ox or stag place? 'Kippen' often comes from Gaelic 'Ceap', plural 'Ceapan', turf, tussock, or when a hill name, 'block', lump of a hill.

Kippenrait, a settlement, GR 797004, **Kippenrait Cottages** GR 796006, **Kippenrait Glen** GR 790995.

Earlier references: 1489 'Kippanarate', 1650 'Kipponreat Mylne', 1860 'Kippenrait Glen'. This name is not clear to me though it could be from Gaelic 'Ceapan an Rathaid', 'Kippen' of the road? 'Kippen' often come from Gaelic 'Ceap', plural 'Ceapan', turf, tussock, or when a hill name, 'block', lump of a hill.

*__Kippon__, a settlement a little North East of

Clevage OS square 0414, on record between 1650 and 1750. Derivation: Gaelic 'Ceap', plural 'Ceapan', turf, tussock, or when a hill name, 'lump of a hill'.

The Kips GR 841973.

Earlier: On record since 1860.

Derivation: In the words of the 1860 OS Name Book this is a rocky and precipitous part of the hills: Probably from Scots 'Kip' &c, a jutting or projecting point on a hill, a peak, frequent in placenames 17th century on.

Kirk Burn GR 923990, **Wester Kirk Craig** GR 918982, **Easter Kirk Craig** GR 922984.

Earlier references: 1769 'The Kirk Burn', 'Kirk Craig', 1860 'Wester Kirk Craig', 'Easter Kirk Craig', 'Kirk Burn'.

Derivation: If the burn does not take its name from a kirk it once flowed past far below the craigs, then the craigs name could well be the primary name and derive from Gaelic 'Cearc', a (grouse) hen.

***Kirkton**, a settlement on record in 1783, approximate OS square 9705.

Derivation: The 'kirk' would be Kirk of Glen Devon, recorded in 1750 &c.

***Kittlenaked**, a settlement on record between 1769 & 1819 which also occurs as 'Skirl-Naked' in 1769, GR 903046 approximately.

Derivation: Scots 'Kittle', here perhaps in the sense of 'difficult to deal with', late 16th century on, plus Scots 'Naked' &c, of land, 'bare', 'barren', 16th to 17th centuries. Scots 'Skirl' can refer to the shriek of the wind; Scots 'Skirl-naked', stark-naked, is recorded by *The Concise Scots Dictionary* only from the 19th century on.

***Knagour**, a settlement on record until 1837, GR 074095 approximately, **Knaggour Hill** GR 072090. Since c1828, towards the end of the life of the settlement, the site has also been known as Knockover (q.v.).

Earlier forms: 1615 'Knaggour', 1806 'Knagour'.

Derivation: Gaelic 'Cnac', 'Cnag' or 'Cnoc', with Gaelic 'Gobhair' or Gaelic 'Odhar', goat crevice or hill, or dun-coloured crevice or hill.

Knapie Burn on record in 1860, a small burn running East South East from Touchie OS square 0605.

Derivation: Gaelic 'Cnapach', locative 'Cnapaigh', at lumpy, hilly place. Touchie itself is explained as 'at hillocky place'.

The fairytale tower of Kippen House, with Rossie Law on the horizon. (AW)

***Knappy**. A hill behind Upper Cloan OS square 9610. Mr Richard Haldane, Cloan, tells me this is Ogle Hill GR 970115.

Derivation: An informant who lived at Cloan as a boy was told that the name came from a Gaelic word for a small hill. Gaelic 'Cnap', a lumpy hill, no doubt was meant.

***Knock**, ***Knock Burn** & **Knock Wood**. See Craigow.

***Knock Hill** on record in 1774, GR 078168 approximately.

Knockcannon, a hill on record in 1860, GR 143113 approximately.

Derivation: Gaelic 'Cnoc', hill; '-cannon' is not clear to me but the possibility that it was originally related to 'Conland', in the same OS square, is not to be ruled out.

Knockmurdo Hill GR 232153, **Knockmurdo**, a hillside, GR 233151. There was also a settlement of this name in 1775.

Derivation: Feasibly Gaelic 'Cnoc', hill, with a Gaelic personal name. Scots 'Murdo' or 'Murdoch' is thought to come from two Gaelic names, 'Muireach' and 'Murchadh', of different origin. Black (see Bibliography) says: "Both coalesce and are hopelessly confused".

Knockover, a settlement in ruins since the mid 19th century, GR 074095 approximately, **Knockover Hill** GR 072090. These are Knaggour and Knaggour Hill (q.v.). The form 'Knockover' is not known to Mr George Ritchie who used to farm nearby.

Earlier references: 1615 to 1837 'Knag(g)our', 1828 'Knockover', 1860 'Knockover (a ruin)', 'Knockover' (ie the hill).

Derivation: 'Knockover' appears to be an anglicisation of the earlier name 'Knaggour' as if it was understood to be Scots 'Knock Ower'.

***Know Dub** recorded in 1774, GR 112142 approximately?

Derivation: Scots 'Knowe' &c, knoll, 16th century on; Scots 'Dub' &c, pool, especially of muddy or stagnant water, late 15th century on.

***Know Head**, a settlement on record in 1775 at or near the present Lochieheads GR 253132.

Derivation: Scots 'Knowheid' &c, a hilltop, late 16th century on.

Knowehead, a settlement, GR 036096, formerly part of Balquhandies OS square 0311 &c.

Earlier references: 1650 'Knowhead', 1793 'Knowhead or half of Souther Balquhandies'.

Derivation: Scots 'Knowheid' &c, a hilltop, late 16th century on.

Knowehead, a settlement on record since 1783, GR 883072.

Derivation: Scots 'Knowheid' &c, a hilltop, late 16th century on.

Knowehead, a settlement on record until 1860, GR 992045.

Earlier: early 19th century 'Knowhead'.

Derivation: Scots 'Knowheid' &c, a hilltop, late 16th century on.

***Knowhead**, a settlement on record in 1783, approximate OS square 9698.

Derivation: Scots 'Knowheid' &c, a hilltop, late 16th century on.

Knowes, a settlement, GR 021115. ***The Burn of Knows**, unidentified, is on record in 1794 and seems to be a related name.

Earlier references: 1783 'Know', 1787 'Knows'.

Derivation: Scots 'Knowe' &c, a knoll, 16th century on.

***Knows**, a settlement on record in 1783, approximate OS square 9813.

Derivation: Scots 'Knowe' &c, a knoll, 16th century on.

L

***Lackerstanes**, a settlement, is recorded in Dunning Parish in 1714.

Derivation: Scots 'Leckerstane' &c, a conspicuous stone or stone-heap, traditionally associated with burials. For more information see The Licher-Stanes.

***Lady Alva's Web** (or Veil). On Ben Cleuch OS square 9000. In the words of the Old Statistical Account for Alva, 1790-95: "Snow frequently remains here far on in the summer and assumes the appearance of a fine linen web or lace work".

Lady Ann's Wood GR 926981.

Lady Loch GR 195137, **Little Lady Loch** GR 197137 approximately, both on record in 1860.

The Lady's Mount GR 790034, a hill.

Lady's Well GR 911975. It is possible that this was earlier 'Our Lady's Well'.

Ladyscroft, on record between 1824 & 1860, a settlement at GR 909083 approximately.

Earlier reference: 1824 'Ladycroft'.

Laird's Seat GR 936031.

Lairhill GR 833027, formerly part of the barony of Balhaldie OS square 8105. ***Larehill Burn'** (see the 1766 reference quoted below) could be one of the burns at GR 830029 or GR 840028.

Earlier references: 1750 'Lairhill of Ballhadie', 1766 'Larehill Burn', 1803 'Lairhill ... being part of the Barony of Balhaldies'.

Derivation: Scots 'Lair', a place where animals lie down, a fold, an enclosure, 16th century on, frequent in place-names .

Lamb Hill GR 972041. Earlier: On record since 1860.

Lamb Linn GR 013057, **Linn Hill** GR 019057, both on record since 1860.

Lamb Hill GR 008077, **Lamb Burn** GR 010071, ***Lamb Hill**, a settlement on record between 1635 & 1855 at GR 005075 approximately(?), ***Lambs Hill Pendicle**, recorded in 1829, GR 007072 approximately.

Earlier: 1635 'Lambhill' (a settlement), 1829 'Lamb Hill' (ie the hill), 1860 'Lamb Burn'.

Landrick GR 794024, a settlement.

Earlier: 1271 'Lanyrky', 1506 'Lanerkin', 1519 'Lanark', 1629 'Lanrik', 1750 'Laindrick'.

Derivation: P-Celtic 'Llanerch', a clear space, a glade.

Langbank GR 826050, a settlement on record since 1783 and formerly part of the barony of Balhaldie OS square 8105.

Earlier references: 1783 'Longbank', 1803 'Langbank being part of the Barony of Balhaldies'.

Langside GR 122088, a settlement.

Earlier forms: c1796, 1827 & 1828 'Longside', 1860 'Langside', 'Langside Plantation'. These forms illustrate a tendency among some 18th century and early 19th century mapmakers to anglicise while the 1860 OS maps often restore the Scots forms.

Derivation: Scots 'Side', a sloping piece of ground, a hillside, late 17th century on.

Latch Burn GR 012140.

Derivation: Perhaps Scots 'Latch', a small stream especially one flowing through boggy ground, frequent in placenames, 13th century on. But compare also Gaelic 'Lad', genitive 'Laid' (pronounced approximately 'Latch'), a watercourse, a puddle.

Late Green, a settlement, OS square 0308.

Earlier references: 1428 'Ladegreven', 1488 & 1513 'Laidgrene', 1594 'Easter Letgrene called Raschehill' (ie Rashiehill OS square 0409), 'Westir Letgrene', 1616 'Leitgrein', 1688 'Lategrein', 1699-1701 'Leatgreen', 1719 'Late

The Law above Tillicoultry, looking up Mill Glen with Wester and Easter Kirk Craigs to either side and Castle Craig quarry in partial sunlight (AW).

Green' & 'Leatgreen', 1724 'Leadgreen', 1811-22 'the half of the town & lands of Easter Lategreen or Rashiehill now called Glentyre', 1860 'Leet Green' & 'Lategreen', 1905 'Leadgreen'. The forms quoted show that variants of this name have long co-existed, and 'Lead Green' and 'Late Green' are both known locally today.

Derivation: The local explanation of 'Late' Green is that the site is green later in the season than other spots. It is at the foot of a long hillslope and Gaelic 'Leathad', slope, is the likely origin of 'Late' &c (Compare Ledlanet & Ledlation). The 1428 form quoted above implies that the etymon of 'Green' may have contained a 'v' sound in which case Gaelic 'Griomhan', sometimes used for temporary stacks of peat or corn, could be a possibility? See also Rashiehill and Glentyre.

*__Laverockhaugh__ on record in 1783, a settlement in approximate OS square 9804.

Derivation: Scots 'Laverock' &c, the skylark, 15th century on; Scots 'Haugh' &c, a piece of level ground on the banks of a river, river-meadow land, late 12th century on.

*__Law__, on record in 1783. This is a hill to the West of Auchtenny, perhaps the hill at GR 057098?

Derivation: Scots 'Law', a rounded hill, often conical, in placenames 12th century on.

Castle Law, Forgandenny, with Little Castle Law in front (AW).

Garb Law above Forgandenny, a lost name now represented by Garblie Wood, visible on the left (AW).

Muckle Law GR 987093, **Little Law** GR 996087, hills.
Earlier: Both on record since 1860. Little Law seems to be named 'Coul Hill' on a plan of Foswellbank dated 1829.
Derivation: Scots 'Law', a rounded hill, often conical, in placenames 12th century on.

The Law GR 910996, on record since 1860.
Derivation: Scots 'Law', a rounded hill, often conical, in placenames 12th century on.

The Law, on record in 1860, GR 955057.
Derivation: Scots 'Law', a rounded hill, often conical, in placenames 12th century on.

***Law Head**, on record in 1769, appears to be on modern Elistoun Hill OS square 9299.
Derivation: Scots 'Law', a rounded hill, often conical, in placenames 12th century on.

Lawbank, a farm on Baadhead in ruins by 1860. In the northern half of OS square 0012? Also **Lawbank Burn** GR 004130.
Earlier: 1611 (Perhaps this site) 'Lawbank', 1673 'Laubank of Keltie' (ie Keltie OS square 0013).
Derivation: The farm may well have been named from adjacent Rossie Law?

Leas Burn GR 955058, **Leas Plantation** GR 952054 approximately, both recorded in 1860.
Derivation: Perhaps Scots 'Lea' &c, untilled ground or grassland of various kinds, 16th century on.

The Lecker Stane GR 089031.
Derivation: Scots 'Leckerstane' &c, a conspicuous stone or stone-heap, traditionally associated with burials. For more information see The Licher-Stanes.

Leckiebank GR 224122, a settlement.
Earlier: 1695 'Leckiebank'.
Derivation: Perhaps from a lost name deriving from Gaelic 'Leacach', meaning either rock-slab place or slab-like hill, with the later addition of Scots 'Bank'.

Ledgerhead Plantation GR 139094, on record since 1860.

Ledlanet GR 079058, a settlement. ***Ledlanet Head Moss**, recorded in 1837, was seemingly in the vicinity of Slungie Hill OS square 0507.
Earlier forms: c1346 (transcribed c1622-32 as 'Ledlewnewle'), 1616 'Ledleinot', 1626 'Ledlemont', 1648 'Ladlemont', 1654 'Ladlennet'. The derivation of this name is discussed under Ledlation – see the next entry.

Ledlanet, looking up the slope that gave it and Ledlation the first part of their names. (AW)

Ledlation GR 062052, a settlement.
Earlier : c1346 (transcribed c1622-32 as 'Ladeglaschun'), 1616 'Ledleschioune', 1617 'Ledlaschoun', 1648 'Ledlischioun', 1654 'Ladleshin' 'Liddlation' & 'Liddilation'.
Derivation: Gaelic 'Leathad', a slope, a brae, is very probably present in this name and in 'Ledlanet', the previous entry. The two settlements are on the same long hillslope. Liddall (see Bibliography) suggests 'elm-slope' for Ledlanet from Gaelic 'Leamhan', elm. His suggestion that the second part of 'Ledlation' is Gaelic 'Glaisean', diminutive of 'Glais', a stream, fits the early forms and gives a very feasible 'Leathad a' Ghlaisein', brae of the streamlet. In that case 'Glais', now feminine in Gaelic though masculine in Welsh, was masculine in our area, possibly under P-Celtic influence.

Lee Burn GR 987100.
Earlier: On record since 1829.

Lee Burn GR 040053.
Earlier: On record since c1796.

Leemans Knowe GR 034122, on record since 1860.

Craig Leith GR 875980. On the brow of the West Hill of Alva.
Earlier: 1790-95 'Craig Leith'.
Derivation: Gaelic 'Creag Liath', grey crag, is feasible here.

Lendrick Hill GR 019037, on record since 1860.
Derivation: P-Celtic 'Llanerch', a clear space, a glade.

Letham GR 153120, a settlement, **Letham Bridge** GR 149126.
Earlier: 1507-8 'Laithame', 1511 'Letheme', 1860 'Letham Bridge'.
Derivation: Scots 'Laich Hame', low home.

Named in conjunction with Highame approximate OS square 1510 (q.v.), which is 'high home'.

***Lethen Burn** is mentioned in 'Mines & Minerals of the Ochils', Clackmannan Field Studies Society, no date. It joins Balquharn Burn which runs through OS squares 8600 to 8697.

Derivation: The name is not clear to me. The extremely steep terrain seems to rule out Gaelic 'Leathann', wide. It is perhaps worth noting that WFH Nicolaisen (1976 – see Bibliography) derives 'Leithen Water' (Peebles-shire) from P-Celtic 'Llaith', moist.

***Leydales**, a settlement on record in 1783 in approximate OS square 8099.

Derivation: Scots 'Lea', 'Ley' &c, untilled ground or grassland of various kinds, 16th century on.

Leys, a settlement on record between 1775 & 1860, approximate GR 227135.

Derivation: Scots 'Lea', 'Ley' &c, untilled ground or grassland of various kinds, 16th century on.

***Library Cottage**, mentioned in the Old Statistical Account for Dollar, 1793.

Derivation: This was at Craiginnan OS square 9600 (q.v.) and was so called because a Johnny Christie, born 1721, a shepherd on Craiginnan Hill Farm, owned some 400 volumes there.

***The Licher-Stanes** on record in 1897, 4 miles from Abernethy Parish Church. Butler (see Bibliography) mentions the ***'Lickerstanes'** "a little distance from Abdie Church" (sq 2516) which may or may not be the same site. He goes on to describe them as two upright stones, unhewn, about three feet high, "somewhat square on the sides and flat on the top". Such-named stones, Butler says, were invariably on the side of the road leading from the outskirts of the parish to the churchyard, "the corpse carried to burial was laid on them".

Derivation: Scots 'Leckerstane' &c, a conspicuous stone or stone-heap, traditionally associated with burials, 15th century on.

Grange of Lindores GR 254165, **North Grange** GR 251169, **Grangehill**, recorded in 1860, GR 247156, all settlements, **Grange Strip** GR 243156, **Grange Hill** GR 249147, **Grange Hill Wood** GR 245147. These are secondary names from Lindores sq 2616.

Earlier references: 1549 'Grange', 1591 'Grange of Lundoris', 1828 'Grangehill', 1860 'Grange Hill'.

Derivation: Scots 'Grange' can often represent a farm at one time held by an ecclesiastical establishment.

Linn Hill GR 993042. This is probably named from Black Linn, in the same OS square.

Derivation: See the next entry.

The Linn, a waterfall, GR 037090, **Linn Hill** GR 035087, **Linnhill**, a settlement on record until 1860, OS square 0308.

Earlier references: 1594 'the Lynhill & Wolbaitis falds', 1721 'Linn -hill' (ie the settlement), 1860 'The Linn'.

Derivation: In names of Gaelic origin (such as 'Conlin' OS square 0811) Scots 'Linn' can be expected to be from Gaelic 'Linne', a waterfall or the pool below a waterfall. In Scots names 'Linn' can derive from a form cognate with Old Northumbrian 'Hlynn', or be the Scots loanword from Gaelic 'Linne'.

The Linns GR 194157.

Derivation: See the previous entry.

Lipney GR 846972, a settlement.

Earlier: 1451 'Lubnach', 1489 'Lupnoch', 1503 'Harmetage de Lupnow', 1510 'Lipnoch'.

Derivation: Gaelic 'Lùbanach', place of curves or bends.

Little Loch GR 119123, on record since 1860.

***Littlefold** recorded in 1783, a settlement in approximate OS square 0710.

***Loanhead**. This was a settlement on record between 1796 & 1828 at GR 141083 approximately.

Loanhead, a settlement recorded in 1860 at GR 064039 approximately.

***Loaninghead** & ***Loaningfoot**, settlements on record in 1801 in approximate OS square 9309, seemingly the same location as 'Loanhead' on Stobie's map of 1783.

***Loch** was a pendicle forming part of the Mains of Kincardine OS square 9411, on record in 1801 in approximate OS square 9209. It is possible that this site, 'Drumlochy' OS square 9109 ('ridge at loch place'), and 'Lochside' OS square 9209, all took their names from the same feature.

Lochelbank GR 133127, a settlement, **Lochelbank Hill** GR 120133. The settlement was also known as Hutchbraes (q.v.), a name on record in 1783.

Earlier: 1855 'Lochellbank'.

Derivation: There is no loch close by now so the first syllable may represent Gaelic 'Lòch', dark, black. For '-el', perhaps compare the Gaelic placename element '-ail', spot, place, as in examples given by WJ Watson (see Bibliography) 'Ruadhail' & 'Deargail', both meaning red spot. Thus 'Lòchail' may be a lost name meaning dark spot, with later addition of Scots 'Bank' with a sense similar to '-braes'.

Lochend GR 086169, a settlement on record since 1783.

Derivation: A charter of 1537 has 'Nethir Cowlequhecher cum lacu', ie 'Nether Culteuchar with the loch', and this is likely to have been the feature that gave Lochend its name. Memory of a loch in the vicinity persists locally even though the Old Statistical Account states that there were no longer any lochs in Forgandenny parish at the end of the 18th century.

Lochie GR 957118, a settlement on record since 1655, **Lochie Cottage** GR 957116. ***Lochy Hay**, recorded in 1800 in approximate OS square 9509 was likely to be an area used by Lochie farm to produce winter fodder. ***Lochy Fold**, on record between 1800 & 1824, was a "fold of land" in approximate OS square 9510.

Derivation: 'Lochie' could obviously be Gaelic 'Lochaigh', at loch place, but there is no loch nearby now. Alternatively, various examples of 'Lochy' and 'Lochie' are derived from Gaelic 'Lòch' plus Gaelic 'Dea', black goddess, or more simply, black one, a stream name.

Lochieheads GR 253132, a settlement. Earlier: 1592 'Locheheidis', 1828 'Lochiehead'.

Derivation: There are three existing lochs or lochans within 3 miles of this site so the derivation may well be Gaelic 'Lochach', locative 'Lochaigh', at loch place. But see also remarks under Lochie, the previous entry. Scots 'Heid', 'Head' &c, the upper part of a brae, late 15th century on.

Lochmill GR 228163, a settlement, **Lochmill Loch**, a reservoir, GR 222162, **Lochmill Hill** GR 224165.

Earlier forms: 1629 'Louche-mylne', 1860 'Lochmill Loch', 'Lochmill Hill'.

Lochside GR 929093 approximately, a settlement, **Lochside Wood**, on record in 1901, OS square 9309. Earlier form: 1673 'Lochsyd'. See also Loch .

***Lochy Faulds**, on the South East side of Gloom Hill OS square 9699. According to the Dollar Chapbook (see Bibliography) this is reputed to have been a meeting place for witches.

Derivation: Probably based on a lost Gaelic primary name: various examples of 'Lochy' and 'Lochie' are derived from Gaelic 'Lòch' plus Gaelic 'Dea', black goddess, or more simply, black one, a stream name. Scots 'Fauld' &c is a pen, a small field, late 14th century on.

***Lochy Lair** on record until 1801, GR 094152 approximately.

Earlier: 1774 'Lochie Lare'.

Derivation: This is marked as a poorly drained area even on recent maps so Gaelic 'Lochach', locative 'Lochaigh', at loch place, may lie behind the first part of the name; Scots 'Lair' &c, a place where animals lie down, frequent in placenames, 16th century on.

Logie Burn GR 815970, **Logieburn Strip** GR 814973, **Blairlogie** GR 828968, a settlement, **Blairlogie Castle**, a ruin, now known as The Blair, GR 828969, **Blairlogie House** GR 837968. These are taken as secondary names from 'Logie', which is the parish name.

Earlier: 1164 'Login', 1318 'Logynathrane' (ie 'Logy of Athray', now Airthrey OS square 8196), 1328 'Logy', 1451 'Blarlogy', 1635 'baronia (ie barony) de Logyblair', 'Blair', c1680 'Logie Kirk', 1804 & 1811 'the Kirk Burn of Logie', 1811 'the Burn of Logie'.

Derivation: Gaelic 'Lagach', locative 'Lagaigh', at place of hollows. Gaelic 'Blàr' (in 'Blairlogie' &c) conceivably here has its sense of 'marsh', since the area south of the Ochils Fault would not be well drained in the Gaelic period.

Long Burn GR 015125.

Earlier: On record since 1860.

Long Craig GR 977063.

Earlier: On record since 1860.

Long Hill GR 039101, **Long Hill Burn** GR 038100.

Earlier: Both on record since 1860.

Long How GR 183155.

Derivation: Scots 'Howe', a vale, 16th century on.

Long Plantation GR 070041, on record since 1860.

Longfauld GR 879086, a settlement.

Earlier: 1830 'Longfold', 1855 & 1860 'Longfauld'.

Derivation: Scots 'Fauld', a pen, late 14th century on, a small field, late 15th to 17th centuries.

Longdrum, on record between 1783 & 1860, a settlement at GR 044128 now disappeared, **Longdrum Wood**, on record between 1860 & the late 19th century, some 220 yards South of Knock of Boghall OS square 0413.

Earlier: 1783 'Longdrum', 1829 'the Town & lands of Boghall sometime known by the names of Boghall & Longdrum', 1860 'Longdrum Wood'.

Derivation: I am told that locally the name 'Longdrum' is applied to the length of road from GR 035130 approximately to GR 052123 approximately, with the explanation that marching soldiers needed a long period of drumming to encourage them over this stretch. It's always a shame to spoil a good story but 'Drum', ridge, the loanword from Gaelic 'Druim' in Scots since the late 18th century, is more prosaic but more likely. The area concerned is on a ridge.

***Longshot** a settlement recorded in 1783, approximate OS square 8098.

Derivation: This name looks like a comment on the chancy nature of making a living on the holding but it is more likely to be from Scots 'Shot' &c, a piece of ground, especially one cropped rotationally, late 16th century on, now only in placenames.

***Lordship** a settlement recorded in 1775, GR 218133 approximately.

Derivation: Compare Scots 'Lordship', an estate or a group of estates held as a single unit by a feudal lord, an individual fief, late 14th to 17th centuries.

***The Lorg** & ***Lorgknow**, on record in 1811 in OS square 9609. ***Lurg Burn**, on record in 1800, is the upper stretch of Maller Burn OS squares 9509 & 9609 approximately.

Earlier reference: 1811 'part of the Hill of Foswell called the Lorg & Lorgknow excepting a small spot of ground on Topmain' (ie Topmain Hill approximate OS square 9608).

Derivation: Gaelic 'Lurg', a shank-shaped piece of ground, a ridge of a hill extending gradually into a plain.

Loss, **Loss Burn** &c. See Luss.

Lossley Burn GR 134090, **Lossley Bridge** GR 137091.

Earlier: Both on record since 1860.

Derivation: This may be Gaelic 'Lios', an enclosure, with later addition of Scots 'Lea' &c, grassland of various kinds, 16th century on.

The Loup GR 801997, on record since 1860.

The 1860 OS Name Book describes this as a projecting rock on either side of the Wharry Burn, at the extremity of Kippenrait Glen.

Derivation: Scots 'Loup', a leap, late 14th century on, a place where a river may be or is traditionally thought to have been crossed by leaping, late 18th century on.

***Low-banks**. This is a settlement in approximate OS square 0412, on record in 1783.

***Ludgates**, on record between 1794 & 1820, was a settlement in approximate OS square 9511.

Derivation: Perhaps 'Lodge Gates', from Scots 'Ludge' &c, a lodge, 15th century on, and English 'Gates'?? The site seems to be near Kincardine Castle.

Wester Lumbennie GR 226156, **Easter Lumbennie** GR 237162, settlements, **Lumbennie**

Easter Lumbennie, 'enclosure at hill place'. (AW)

Hill GR 220156, **Lumbennie Strip**, woodland, GR 240161. The ***Gaits of Lumbennie** mentioned by Snoddy (see Bibliography) are the tracks in the vicinity of Lumbennie & Pitcairlie Hills (compare Seven Gates OS square 2015).

Earlier: 1510 'Lumbane', 1511 'Lumbany', 'Wester Lumbenny', 1515 'Lumbenny berclay' (compare the Barclays of Fargie & see Barclayfield?), 1517 'Easter Lumbennie', 1860 'Lumbenny Hill'. Earliest surname forms from Black (see Bibliography): 1296 'Adam de Lumbyny', 1312 'Philip de Lumbeny'.

Derivation: Gaelic 'Lann Beinne', hill enclosure, or 'Lann Beinnigh', enclosure at hilly place, certainly fit the location.

Lumquhat GR 243138, a settlement, **Lumquhat Mill** GR 237137. In 1828 a Toll Bar was at GR 237141.

Earlier: c1346 (transcribed c1622-32 as 'Lumquhat'), 1590 'Lumquhattis-burne' (ie presumably modern Pitcairlie Burn), 'molendinum de (ie mill of) Lumquhat', 1615 'Conchheid of Lumquhat'.

Derivation: Gaelic 'Lann Chat', wild cat enclosure.

***Luss**, on record until 1848, a settlement in approximate OS square 8398, **Loss Hill** GR 832000, **Loss Burn** GR 834990, **Lossburn Reservoir** GR 832990.

Earlier references: 1451 'Lessyntrule', 1724 'Loss', 1784 'Ashintrule or Loss'.

Derivation: It seems that 'Lessyntrule' represents the earlier form of this name, subsequently shortened and reinterpreted, and that Ashentrool (q.v.) is a closely related site. Gaelic 'Lios an t-Sruthail', enclosure of the streamlet.

Lustylaw, a settlement, GR 135136. In the mid 18th century this was a village of some 20 families. Immediately to the West the 1860 OS map has "Lustylaw Market Place (Disused)". It is still remembered locally that markets used to be held there.

Earlier reference: 1687 'Lustilaw'.

Derivation: Jack (see Bibliography) says that some antiquarians thought that Lustylaw was named from Sallustus Lucullus, a Roman officer who succeeded Agricola. He also reports, more feasibly, that 'Lusty' appears in Gaelic placenames in Ireland meaning a kneading trough and land so shaped. Our location, he says, is a rough and probably unploughable triangle.

Lynncot GR 059038, a settlement. This seems to be on the site of former Wester Dalqueich, a name on record between 1796 & 1860.

Derivation: The present name no doubt derives from the Golland Linns (see Golland), plus Scots 'Cot', a cottage.

Lynns GR 815012, a settlement.

Earlier: 1664 'Linns'.

Derivation: Presumably named from pools or falls on the nearby Wharry Burn. In names of Gaelic origin (such as 'Conlin' OS square 0811) Scots 'Linn' can be expected to be from Gaelic 'Linne', a waterfall or the pool below a waterfall. In Scots names 'Linn' can derive from a form cognate with Old Northumbrian 'Hlynn', or be the Scots loanword from Gaelic 'Linne'.

M

Glen Macduff & **Glenmacduff Burn** both GR 888034. The burn is '**Medaff Burn**' upstream around OS square 8802.

Earlier: Both on record since 1860.

Derivation: This site is a long way from Macduff's Cross and the territory of the Earls of Fife. 'Medaff' may represent the earlier form, subsequently reinterpreted under the influence of the clan name?

***McDuff's Cairn**, recorded in 1828 in approximate OS square 2116. This is not a mistake for MacDuff's Cross as that is given too.

Macduff's Cross GR 228166, **Macduff's Cross**, a settlement recorded in 1860, GR 226168.

For some of the history of the cross see for example Butler (see Bibliography). MacKinlay (see Bibliography) says: "Ancient burial mounds once to be seen near MacDuff's Cross were popularly believed to be the graves of those slain after claiming sanctuary and not being able to claim kinship within the ninth degree to the Earl of Fife. Their shrieks were said to be heard at night". Earlier forms: 1595 'Clan MacDuff's croce', 1654 'Corss Mackduff' & 'Cross Mackduff', 1720 'Cors McDuff', 1775 'McDuffs Cross'.

The word order of forms such as 'Corss Mackduff' (see earlier forms quoted) may imply that there was a Gaelic form of the name.

***Macrae Monument Cairn** GR 815019. This was erected in 1915 by the Clan MacRae Society to commemorate their fellow clansmen who fell at the battle of Sheriffmuir 200 years earlier. The stones were taken from the Wharry Burn.

Maddy Moss GR 928010. ***Mady Burn**, recorded in 1779, is the burn at GR 930007. ***The Maddy Inn**, is a spring running from the side of Andrew Gannel Hill used by travellers for refreshment, GR 926006 approximately.

Earlier forms: 1769 'Maldie Gott' (ie probably Mady Burn), 1779 'Mady Moss'. For 'Maldie' (see the 1769 form quoted) becoming 'Maddy' compare 'Balhaldie' (q.v.), pronounced, and often in the past written, 'Balhaddie'.

Derivation: 'Maldie' is obscure to me. It might be worth noting that 'Eglismaldie', church of St Màillidh (the same saint as in 'Kilmally' Inverness-shire) occurs in Fife in the 17th century, but there seems no particular reason to link this saint to our site. Scots 'Gott' &c, (see the 1769 form quoted) is a watercourse, late 16th to 20th centuries.

Maiden (or **Maiden's**) **Castle**, on record since 1860 at GR 971015, is a small spur of hillside projecting into Glen Quey.

The *Dollar Chapbook* (see Bibliography) relates the story of a piper passing by here one night who saw a castle ablaze with light. He was invited in to play for the company then sent away well rewarded. On returning home he recognised no-one and found that 100 years had passed as he played. There is a possibility that the Gaelic original of 'Craiginnan' (q.v.) may refer to the Maiden of this legend and/or the legend of Maiden's Well (q.v.).

***Maiden Tree**. At Castle Campbell GR 961993. This is said to have been planted by the captive princess (see under Burn of *Care*) and reputed to have been used at some time as a gallows according to Haliburton (1905 – see Bibliography). The New Statistical Account for Dollar, 1845, describes it as a plane tree, 13 feet in circumference at about 8 feet from the ground.

Maiden's Well GR 970014.

Earlier: On record since 1860. According to the *Dollar Chapbook* (see Bibliography) this was supposedly inhabited by the spirit of a maiden who could be summoned up at night, but would-be lovers with the temerity to attempt this were

The Macrae Monument Cairn, erected for the bicentenary of the Battle of Sheriffmuir. Drawing by Ken Laing.

found dead beside the well in the morning. Haliburton however (1905 – see Bibliography) says the well was named after the captive princess who named the Burn of Sorrow &c (see under Burn of *Care*) as she was sometimes allowed to walk to the well to drink its water.

Mailer's Knowe GR 942025, on record since 1860.

Derivation: Perhaps Scots 'Mailer', a tenant farmer late 14th to early 16th centuries, a cottar late 14th to 19th centuries, though this is a fairly remote spot at a height of c560 metres. Gaelic 'Meall Odhar', dun-coloured round hill, with later addition of Scots 'Knowe', is not impossible. If this were to prove correct Scots 'Mailer' and the frequent occurrence of the surname 'Mailer' in the area would help to explain the reinterpretation to the present form. Finally though, the name could simply come from the surname itself, which originated in Forteviot parish according to Black (see Bibliography).

Mairsland GR 231129, a settlement, **Mairsland Hill**, recorded in 1860, GR 236131.

Earlier: 1517 'Marisland', 1688 'Mairsland of Auchtermuchtie'.

Derivation: Scots 'Mare', 'Mair', an executive officer of the law of the Crown or of a Lord of Regality, 14th to early 19th centuries.

Black Maller GR 958097, a hill, **Maller Burn**, known as 'Lurg Burn' in 1800, GR 960097, **Maller Hill** GR 965096, **Green Maller** GR 960102, a hill.

Derivation: Perhaps Scots 'Mailer', 'Malar' &c, a tenant farmer, late 14th to early 16th centuries, a cottar, late 14th to 19th centuries.

***Manduf**, a hill. Macfarlane (1723 – see Bibliography) places it South of Abernethy, seemingly close to Castle Law OS square 1815.

Derivation: MacKenzie (1931 – see Bibliography) suggests that the name derives from Gaelic 'Monadh Dubh', black moor, 'Man-' being, he continues, "an acknowledged contraction" of Gaelic 'Monadh', moor, hill ground.

Marcassie GR 021133, a settlement, **Marcassie Burn** & **Marcassie Bridge** both GR 021132.

Earlier: 1860 'Marcassie Bridge'.

Derivation: This is probably to be compared with 'Marcassie' in Moray and Glen 'Marxie' in Ross, derived by WJ Watson (see Bibliography) from Gaelic 'Marcfhasaidh', horse stance or station.

March Burn GR 980044.

Earlier: 1783 'Marchburn'.

Derivation: Scots 'March', the boundary or boundary-marker of lands &c, 15th century on.

March Burn GR 007053, on record since 1860.

Derivation: Scots 'March', the boundary or boundary-marker of lands &c, 15th century on.

March Knowe GR 026083, on record since 1860.

Derivation: Scots 'March', the boundary or boundary-marker of lands &c, 15th century on; Scots 'Knowe', a knoll, 16th century on.

***March Knowe**, seemingly at either GR 105148 or GR 106147, ***March Slack**, the hollow from GR 107148 to GR 105149. Both are recorded in 1774.

Derivation: Scots 'March', the boundary or boundary-marker of lands &c, 15th century on; Scots 'Knowe', a knoll, 16th century on; Scots 'Slack', a hollow especially between hills, frequent in placenames, late 14th century on.

The Old House of Invermay photographed by Magnus Jackson in the late 1800s. Reproduced by permission of Perth Museum and Art Gallery.

A print of Invermay dated c1840. Reproduced by courtesy of Perth and Kinross District Libraries.

Marlpark Spring GR 020125 forms a tributary of Long Burn OS square 0112. Earlier: On record since 1860.

Derivation: Presumably from a field name. Scots & English 'Marl' is a soil consisting principally of clay mixed with carbonate of lime, late 14th century on. Several contributors to the Old Statistical Account (eg for Auchterarder & Auchtermuchty) mention discovery of marl in the Ochils area and its use as a fertilizer.

***Mavies Wood**, on record between 1769 & 1836. This appears to be on the spur of hill at GR 907013.

Earlier: 1769 'Maives Wood'.

Derivation: Scots 'Mavis', the song-thrush, 15th century on.

Maw Burn GR 145061, **Maw Cottage** GR 143061.

Derivation: Gaelic 'Magh', a plain.

Mawhill GR 086034, a settlement.

Earlier forms: c1346 (transcribed c1622-32 as 'Macoiche'), 1371 'Maucuych', 1389 'Mawcuyche', 1616 'Mawcuich vulgo (ie in the vernacular) Mawhill'.

Derivation: The earlier forms indicate that this site took its earlier name from the nearby South Queich (q.v.). The name is 'plain of Queich' from Gaelic 'Magh', a plain, and Gaelic 'Cuach', genitive 'Cuaich', a bowl, referring in river names to a pool or a pothole.

Mawkins Brae GR 793029.

Derivation: Scots 'Maukin' &c, a hare, 18th century on.

Water of May GR 076150 &c. Also **Maybank** GR 075137 & **Invermay** GR 061163, settlements, **Home Farm** (ie of Invermay) GR 058155 & ***Mill o May**, recorded in 1905.

Earlier references: 1452 'Innermeth', 1464 'Innermeith', 1474 'le Greene et pomarium de Innermythe', 1595 'Inner-May', 1619 'lie Maynes de Invermay', 1720 'May Water', 1750 'Water of May'.

Derivation: Gaelic 'Inbhir' (often pronounced 'Inner'), a confluence. WJ Watson (see Bibliography) equates 'May' with Gaelic (Middle Irish) 'Mede', 'Meide', a neck, a trunk, a stump, and by extension, a ford. MacKenzie (see Bibliography) suggests P-Celtic 'Maid', Irish 'Midhe', a "boundary term".

Meadow Burn GR 950052, on record since 1860.

Derivation: Scots 'Medow' &c occurs in placenames from c1170. As well as meadowland in the modern sense it could also mean marshy grassland where the natural coarse grasses were cut for hay. This no doubt explains the use of the term at heights which might otherwise seem surprising.

Meadow Burn GR 973026,

Earlier: On record since 1860.

***Meadow Burn**, on record in 1829, is Corb Burn GR 009090.

Meadow Strip GR 236156, woodland.

Derivation: Scots 'Strip', a long narrow belt of trees, 19th century on.

Meadowbank GR 008145, a settlement.

Meadowells GR 272133, a settlement. Earlier: 1775 'Meadow wells'.

***Meadowside** on record between 1796 & 1860, a settlement, approximate OS square 0905.

***Meal Knowes** recorded in 1774, seemingly in the vicinity of GR 110143. 'Smeal Knowes' is given as an alternative name.

Derivation: Gaelic 'Meall', a rounded hill, seems an obvious candidate here, with the Scots translation 'Knowes' subsequently added. That doesn't explain the alternative name though.

Medaff Burn. See Glen *Macduff.*

Craig Meed GR 994083. The 1860 OS Name Book describes this as a few rocks.

Earlier: 1829 'Craig mead'.

Derivation: Gaelic 'Creag', a rock, a crag, perhaps with Gaelic (Middle Irish) 'Mede', 'Meide', a neck, here in the sense of rock at narrow place? The site is at the entrance to Corb Glen.

Mellock Hill GR 023061. In 1615 this was part of the lands of Carnbo OS square 0503.

Earlier forms: 1615 'mons (ie hill) de Melloch', c1796 'Mellock'. Alternation of '-och' & '-ock' is not uncommon in placenames.

Derivation: Gaelic 'Meallach', the adjective from 'Meall', a lump of anything and here a 'lump of a hill'.

Menstrie Burn & **Menstrie Glen** both GR 846980, **Menstrie Moss** GR 864009.

Craig Meed above the entrance to Corb Glen. (AW)

Earlier: 1736 'Moss of Menstrie'.

Derivation: These are secondary names from Menstrie OS square 8496, from P-Celtic 'Maes-dref', hamlet on the plain.

*__Mercate Slope__, recorded in 1766, an unidentified site on Sheriffmuir.

Derivation: Scots 'Mercat' &c, market, late 14th century on.

Merlsford GR 197095. Jack (see Bibliography) reports the tradition of a great battle fought here when the river Eden ran red for 24 hours. According to Mackay (see Bibliography), Merlsford was at one time thought to be a possible site of the battle of Mons Graupius or Grampius.

Derivation: Scots 'Merl', a blackbird, 15th century on.

Mid Burn GR 033080, on record since 1860. Quite possibly named along with Back Burn OS square 0208 in relation to a holding such as Rashiehill OS square 0409.

Middle Hall. See Ballieliesk.

Middle Hill GR 929020, on record since 1860, **Middlehill Burn**, recorded in 1860, GR 933030.

*__Middle Hill__ GR 887986 was according to Beveridge (see Bibliography) an alternative name for The Nebit (q.v.).

Earlier: 1536 (Perhaps this site) 'Nevot', 1790 'Middle Hill'. Middle Hill together with part of Wood Hill OS square 8998 had been a sheep farm for "many years" by the time of the Old Statistical Account in the early 1790s.

Middle Rigg, a settlement, GR 067088, ***Middlerigg Burn** recorded in 1828, GR 060094. In 1616 Middle Rigg was part of the lands of Auchtenny OS square 0610.

Earlier: 1616 'Midlerig', c1796 'Middle Rigg Burn'.

Derivation: Scots 'Rig' &c, a ridge of high ground, a hill-crest, in placenames late 12th century on, a strip of arable land, 16th century on.

Middlehill Cottage, recorded in 1901, approximately a quarter of a mile South West of Topfauld OS square 8708.

Middleton GR 124068, a settlement.

Earlier: 1580 'Middiltoun'. Netherton & Wester Netherton OS square 1306 were perhaps associated names.

Midge Mill OS square 0309, also known as **Mids Mill** & **Maid's Mill**.

Earlier: 1671 'Midge-milne', 1712 'Midge Miln', 1718 'Midgemill', 1783 'Mids Mill', 1860 'Maidsmill', 'Midge Mill' & 'Mids Mill', 1905 'Midge Mill'. 'Midge' is the oldest among the forms I've found and the only one to occur in the more local written sources I've come across.

Water of Miglo. See River *Eden*.

Mill Burn GR 165120, **Mill Den** & **Millden Road** both GR 166117, **Millburn Quarry**, on record in 1860, GR 175118 approximately. Earlier references: 1727 'the Mill Burn', 1860 'Mill Den', 'Millden Road'.

*__Mill Burn__ GR 062049, on record in 1796.

Mill Glen GR 912980, which carries Tillycoultry Burn, **Millglen Burn** GR 902995, on record since 1769, ***Mill-Glen Farm**, recorded between 1769 & 1792. For Millglen Burn Gibson (see Bibliography) has 'Millglen House Burn' and says that in the late 18th century it was called 'Tankley Burn'.

Millhill GR 930099, a settlement.

Millstone Burn GR 848040. On a plan of 1736 the burn is shown running by a mill, near the present Millhill OS square 8307.

Earlier forms: 1551 'lie Mylnburne', 1723 'Milston burn', 1736 'Miln Stone Burne'.

Derivation: The 1723 form supports the suspicion that the name may well have been Mill's 'Toun', Mill's steading, later reinterpreted as '-stone'.

*__Milltown__, recorded in 1783, a settlement in approximate OS square 9904. This was a secondary name from Burnfoot Mill, see Burnfoot OS square 9804.

*__Millar Hill__ OS squares 8999, 8998 and 9098. A ridge stretching from Ben Ever OS square 8900 to above Wood Hill OS square 9098.

Millers Burn, on record in 1860. This is perhaps the burn at GR 070154, in which case the miller concerned would have been the miller of Muckersie Mill.

Miln Burn GR 081090.

Earlier: On record since 1860.

Derivation: Scots 'Miln', a mill, in placenames 13th century on.

*__Marisfold__, on record between 1800 & 1855, a pendicle at GR 955100 approx?, ***Mare's Yett**, on record between 1756 & 1800, GR 957101 approx?

Earlier: 1756 'Moir's Gate of Foswell', 1800 'Mare's Fauld', 1811 'Moirsfold'.

Derivation: The earlier references suggest that these names contain the surname 'Moir', reinterpreted as 'Mare' once the individual concerned had been forgotten.

Mon, a hill, GR 205119, on record since 1828.
Derivation: Gaelic 'Monadh', moor, hill ground. WJ Watson (see Bibliography) says that in Perthshire 'Monadh' is "always" 'Mon', though I imagine he mainly had in mind Highland Perthshire where Gaelic survived much longer than in our area.

*__Moneyready__, a settlement on record in 1796, GR 107063 approximately, **Moneyready Well**, recorded in 1860, GR 110053 approximately.
Derivation: Perhaps a slightly humorous optimistic Scots name given to the holding? If it turns out to be an old name however 'Money' may very well be for Gaelic 'Monadh', a moor, hill land, with an unknown second element.

Monks Well GR 238179.

Montalt Hill GR 054130, **Montalt**, a settlement, GR 060131. An alternative name for this site was 'Montober' (see the next entry).
Earlier: 1855 'Montalt', 1860 'Montalt Hill'.
Derivation: 'stream moor' or 'stream hill' from Gaelic 'Monadh', a moor, hill land, and Gaelic 'Allt', genitive 'Uillt', a stream. WJ Watson (see Bibliography) says that in most cases 'Mont' or 'Mount' "is not a translation but an anglicisation of 'Monadh', the form assumed by the old British (ie P-Celtic) term when taken over into Gaelic".

*__Montober__ GR 054130, an earlier name for Montalt (see the previous entry).
Derivation: Gaelic 'Monadh (an) Tobair', moor or hill-land of the spring. Mr George Ritchie, who used to farm there, tells me there is a fine spring at Montalt.

Moor Burn GR 087048. 'More' Burn further upstream on recent OS 6" maps.
Earlier: 1860 'More Burn'.

*__Moor Cleuch__ GR 002076 approximately, on record in 1829.
Derivation: Scots 'Cleuch', a gorge or ravine, in placenames late 12th century on.

*__Moorhall__ & *__Moorhaugh__. See Myrehaugh.

*__Moorhead__, a settlement in approximate OS square 0105 on record in 1775.

Mortley Burn GR 987088, on record since 1829.
Derivation: Perhaps unlikely, but compare Scots 'Mort', a dead body, late 15th to early 19th centuries; Scots 'Lea' &c, untilled land or grassland of various kinds, 16th century on.

Morton Burn GR 177095.
Derivation: Perhaps from a lost settlement name 'Muirton' or 'Moorton', or from the surname?

*__Mossend__, a settlement, is on record between 1800 & 1816. *__Mossendgreen__ is on record between 1816 & 1855.
Earlier: 1800 'Mossend being a part of Bellilisk' (ie Ballieliesk OS square 0001), 1816 'Mossendgreen', 'Pitfar called the Mossend'.

*__Mossey Water__, recorded in 1654 in approximate OS square 0604.

Mount Stuart GR 003023, a settlement. On the 1860 OS map this site is named 'Wallhaugh' so the present name seems a fairly recent one.
Derivation: Professor WFH Nicolaisen (1976 – see Bibliography) states that the tradition of popularity of 'Mount X' names began in the later 18th century with the introduction to Scotland of 'Mount Vernon', the name of George Washington's estate in Virginia.

*__Mounthoulie__ on record in 1783, a settlement in approximate OS square 8306.
Derivation: Though the word order of 'Mount X' names appears Gaelic many of them come from a different tradition – see the remarks in the previous entry. In the case of 'Mounthoulie' however a Gaelic original along the lines of 'Monadh a' Chuallaich', moor of the cattle, is theoretically possible.

Mountquharry GR 185140, a settlement.
Earlier forms: 1542 'Monquhery', 1642 'Monquherrie', 1753 'Montquharie', 1786 'Mount Quherry', 1823 'Mountquharry'.
Derivation: The 17th century forms quoted are consistent with Gaelic 'Monadh a'Cheathraimh', moor or hill-land of the quarter (ie a division of a holding). The 1786 & 1823 forms have perhaps been influenced by 'Mount X' names – see the remarks under Mount Stuart.

Chapel of Muckersie GR 073157, **Muckersie Mill** GR 074156, **Linn of Muckersie** GR 074158 (called the 'Falls of Muckersie' in the Old Statistical Account), **Wester Muckersie**, a settlement, GR 069156, **Muckersie Birch Wood** GR 068150, **Muckersie Plantation** GR 065155.
Earlier : 1377 'Mukirsy', 1472 'Mukyrsy', 1473 'Mukcressy', 1619 'molendina granorum et fullonem (ie corn and waulk mills) de Mukarsie', 1860 'Linn of Muckersie'. The earliest surname reference from Black (see Bibliography) is 1655 'Muckarsie'.
Derivation: WJ Watson (see Bibliography) says

that Muckersie, formerly 'Mucrosin', was the name of an old parish now part of Forteviot parish. He compares it to 'Mucross', "a district near St Andrews", which he explains as 'the swine's wood'.

Muckle Burn GR 910038.
Earlier: 1769 'The Mickle Burn', 1819 'Muckle Burn'.

***Muddyside**, a settlement at GR 099055 approximately, on record in 1775.
Derivation: Scots 'Side', a sloping piece of ground, 17th century on.

Muir Cottage GR 149066.
Derivation: This is likely to have been named from Cuthil Moor OS square 1507 &c (see Cuthil Towers).

Muiralehouse GR 917091, a settlement. This consisted of a house and smiddy at the time of the 1860 OS Name Book.
Earlier: 1636 'Muiralehous'.

Muirfield GR 152104, a settlement.
Earlier: On record since 1860.

Muirhead, a settlement on record between 1750 & 1860 at GR 073045 approximately.
Earlier: 1750 'Muirhead', 1775 'Moorhead'.

Mundie GR 117146, a settlement, **Mundie Hill**, also known as West Dron Hill, GR 115150.
Earlier: 1601 'Mundy'.
Derivation: The Old Statistical Account for Dron offers the gloss 'Hill or Moss of God', from Gaelic 'Monadh Dhè', and suggests this may reflect a link with Lindores Abbey about eight miles away.

Saint Mungo's Chapel (restored) GR 930089, **St. Mungo's Well** GR 938072, **St. Mungo's Farm** GR 937074.
Earlier: 1855 'St Mungo's' (ie the farm), 1860 'St Mungo's Well'.

Murniepae, a settlement on the North West side of Auchtermuchty GR 235121 approximately. Snoddy (1966 – see Bibliography) refers to the "Murnipae Road from Auchtermuchty to Abernethy".
Earlier: 1654 'Mornypee', 1755 Mourny-pea'. The name is obscure to me.

***Muttonhall**, a settlement on record in 1775 just North of Drumbarrow, OS square 1912 or 1913.
Derivation: The site may have been named when sheepruns were comparatively new? Scots 'Hall' often implies a type of dwelling more substantial than a cottage.

Muttonhole, a settlement on record between 1775 & 1860, GR 242177 approximately.
Earlier: 1775 'Mutton Hall'. The alternation of 'Hall' and 'Hole' is not uncommon in placenames.
Derivation: As in the case of the previous entry this site too may have been named when sheepruns were comparatively new. Scots 'Holl', 'Howe' &c, a depression, a low-lying piece of ground, 16th century on.

Myrehaugh, a settlement, GR 013053, **Myrehaugh Hill** GR 014046.
Earlier: 1542 'Marhauch', 1668 & 1727 'Marhaugh', 1750 'Myrhaugh', c1796 'Moorhaugh', 1800 'Myrehaugh', 1818 'Muir haugh'.
Derivation: Scots 'Haugh', river-meadow land, late 12th century on. 'Mar-' in the earliest forms quoted doesn't make a lot of sense to me unless it is the surname, later reinterpreted in two different ways as 'Myre' and 'Muir. Late Green and Midge Mill are other good examples of sites for which variant names co-existed for long periods. Our ancestors seem to have been able to live with variant names for the same place but in more recent times literacy and the wide availability of maps has tended to establish map names as the standard 'correct' forms. The Ordnance Survey, to its credit, does sometimes use different variants on different series.

Myretoun House, also known as *the* **Myretoun**, GR 859972, **Myretoun Hill** GR 858982. Rennie McOwan (*Alloa Advertiser* 14/12/1984) mentions a case of second sight at Myretoun House when the sister of Mungo Park the explorer saw a vision of him there at the time of his death in Africa.
Earlier: 1609 'Myretoun'.
Derivation: Scots 'Myre', mire, late 14th century on, a peat-bog, 16th century, late 19th century on. Scots 'Toun' &c, a farm with its buildings, late 17th century on.

N

The Nebit GR 887987, a hill also known in the late 18th century, and still known locally, as Middle Hill.

Derivation: WJ Watson (see Bibliography) thinks this site may be the one on record in 1536 as 'Nevot' but feels there is not enough evidence confidently to derive it from Gaelic (Old Irish) 'Nemed', a sacred place. More straightforwardly there is Scots 'Nebbit' &c, nosed, beaked, late 16th century on, perhaps referring here to a perceived shape on the hill?

Nether Town Hill GR 025049, on record since 1860.

Derivation: The location of the former holding Nether Airnside (see under Earnieside) indicates that it was the 'toun' this hill was named for. Scots 'Nether' &c is the lower-situated of two places of the same name, late 14th century on.

Netherhall GR 104056.

Derivation: Scots 'Hall' often implies a type of dwelling more substantial than a cottage; Scots 'Nether' &c is the lower-situated of two places of the same name, late 14th century on.

Netherholm GR 069169. Until some time after 1860 this site was called Jackschairs (q.v.).

Derivation: Scots 'Holm' &c, a stretch of low-lying land beside a river, in placenames 13th century on; Scots 'Nether' &c is the lower-situated of two places of the same name, late 14th century on.

Netherton GR 870087.

Earlier: On record since 1830.

Derivation: Scots 'Nether' &c, the lower-situated of two places of the same name, late 14th century on; Scots 'Toun' &c, a farm and its buildings, late 17th century on, an area of land occupied by a number of co-tenants, late 14th century on.

Netherton GR 132061, **Wester Netherton** GR 131061, settlements. They presumably formed part of the same group of holdings as Middleton OS square 1206?

Earlier: 1580 'Nethirtoun'.

Derivation: Scots 'Nether' &c, the lower-situated of two places of the same name, late 14th century on; Scots 'Toun' &c, a farm and its buildings, late 17th century on, an area of land occupied by a number of co-tenants, late 14th century on.

Nethy Burn GR 192160. See Abernethy Glen.

Neukend. This was a ruined steading at the foot of Hare Craigs OS square 0211, on record in 1860.

Derivation: Scots 'Neuk' &c, a nook, 14th century on.

New Farm GR 236145, on record in 1860, **New Farm Strip**, woodland, GR 234144.

New Hill GR 212137, **Newhill**, a settlement, GR 214133.

Earlier: 1828 'Newhill', 1860 'New Hill'.

New Inn GR 002024, recorded in 1860.

Newbigging, once a settlement now seemingly the name of a hillside, GR 165096.

Earlier: 1654 'New Bigging'.

Derivation: Scots 'Bigging' &c, a building, 15th century on.

Newburgh Common GR 228173, **Newburgh Muir** a settlement on record in 1860 at GR 222169, now known as Nine Wells Farm. These are secondary names from Newburgh OS square 2318.

Newhill GR 118083, a settlement, **Newhill Burn** GR 120087.

Earlier: 1860 'Newhill'.

*__Newtoft__ a settlement on record in 1796, GR 113070.

Derivation: Scots 'Toft' &c, a homestead and its land late 14th century on.

Newtoft GR 087104 a settlement, earlier forming part of Pitquhanatrie OS square 0811, **Newtoft Hill** GR 088108.

Earlier: 1855 'Newtaft of Pitquhanatrie', 1860 'Newtoft Hill'.

Derivation: Scots 'Toft' &c, a homestead and its land late 14th century on.

Newton, a settlement, GR 225128.

Earlier: On record since 1769.

***Newtown**, a settlement recorded in 1775 just North of Pittendy, approximate OS square 1916.

***Nine Hole Stone** GR 110139 approximately. Recorded in 1774.

Nine Wells GR 224172, **Ninewells Farm**, until 1860 at least called 'Newburgh Muir', GR 222169.

Earlier: 1860 'Nine Wells'.

Derivation: Butler (see Bibliography) says vaguely that tradition connects the Nine Maidens with Nine Wells. The Nine Maidens were the daughters of St Donevald who spent the latter part of their lives at Abernethy. Morris (see Bibliography) mentions no such tradition but says that nine wet spots join here to form a stream and that part of the ritual involved in claiming sanctuary at Macduff's Cross (q.v.)was to wash nine times at the well.

The stump of Macduff's Cross, with Nine Wells Farm behind. (AW)

***Nivensfold**. On record in 1808 as part of the lands of Outer Fannyhill approximate OS square 0005.

Nochnarie GR 200129, a settlement.

Earlier: 1490 'Nochnary', 1505-11 'Auchinnary', 'Auchnarye', 'Auchnary', 'Nachinary', 'Nauchnary', & 'Nauchtnary', 1508 'Nachinary' & 1509-10 'Auchnary'.

Derivation: The first part seems to be Gaelic 'Achadh', a piece of ground cleared for cultivation or grazing. Indecision about initial 'N' may have arisen from incorrect division of 'i nAchadh ...', 'in or at Auchnary'. The different forms '-nary', '-innary' &c seem to me too inconclusive to prompt worthwhile suggestions for the second part of the name.

***Norland Know**. An unidentified site near Candy Hill recorded in 1771, seemingly in the South East corner of OS square 1110 or the North East corner of OS square 1109.

Derivation: Perhaps Scots 'Norland' &c, a person from the North or North East of Scotland, late 17th century on.

North Hill GR 054086.

Earlier: 1828 'North Hills'.

North Hill GR 014096.

Earlier: On record since 1860.

***Nout Lair Burn**, on record between 1769 & 1836, appears to be the burn at GR 902042.

Derivation: Scots 'Nowt' &c, cattle, late 14th century on; Scots 'Lair', a place where animals lie down, a fold or enclosure, 16th century on, frequent in placenames.

O

The Ochil Hills. The earliest known reference to the Ochils may be by the Geographer of Ravenna in the 7th century 'Ravennatis Anonymi Cosmographia'. His 'Cindocellum' has been thought by some (eg Skene – see Bibliography) to represent the contemporary Gaelic for 'the end of the Ochils'. References in various sources relating to St Serf or Servanus may also take the name ultimately back to the 7th century, the supposed time of that saint. For example a Latin account of the life of St Serf has 'mons qui dicitur Okhèl', the mountain called 'Okhèl'. WJ Watson (see Bibliography) also quotes from an Irish text detailing Serf's supposed parentage, 'sliab n-Ochel' (see below). Other references, from for example 'The Book of Leinster' compiled from c1152 onwards from material dating back perhaps to the early 10th century, include 'Sliab Nocel', 'nOicel' and 'Noithil' (information supplied by Dr Colm O Baoill).

Later forms include: 1654 'the Ochels' & 'The Ochell Hills', c1723 'the Ockle hills', 'the Ochells' & 'the Ochall Hills'. Pronunciations with '-ch-' and '-k-' mirroring these different spellings still co-exist today. In the earlier references quoted above Gaelic 'Sliab', now 'Sliabh', could be either a single hill or a range of them. Latin 'Mons', a mountain, in the phrase quoted above, may well be itself a translation of Irish 'Sliab' and so is not conclusive. At this distance in time it is probably impossible to know which was meant in this case, but if a single hill, then among the contenders as the original 'Mons Okhèl' would be sites which still bear some form of the name 'Ochil'. These are Catochil OS square 1713, Ogle OS square 8899, Ogle Hill OS square 9611, Pitogle OS square 1813 and Rossie Ochill OS square 0813 (for the connection between 'Ochil' and 'Ogle' see under Pitogle). None of these sites seems distinguished enough to have given its name to the whole range, though it should be borne in mind that names sometimes 'move'.

Derivation: 'Ochil' is generally accepted as deriving from P-Celtic 'Uchel', earlier 'Uxellos', high.

Ogilvie Castle, remains of, GR 909081, **Braes of Ogilvie** GR 892078, **Burn of Ogilvie** GR 876070.

Earlier: 1172 'Oggoueli', 1205 'Ogilvin', 1239 'Ogeluin', 1507 'Ogilwy', 1616 'Ogilby', 1650 'Ogilvie', 1808 'parts of the barony of Ogilvy, viz lands of Cockplay, Biggs & Carrim, Biggs arable farm, Heldrick, Knowhead, Whack (ie Whaick), Burnside & Wester Drumcairn', 1824 'Mill of Ogilvie', 1860 'Ogilvie Castle (Ruins)', 'Braes of Ogilvie', 'Burn of Ogilvie'.

Derivation: WJ Watson (see Bibliography) thought that the second part of this name seemed to come from Gaelic 'Magh', a plain, or its British (P-Celtic) cognate. The 13th century forms quoted seem more consistent with a compound such as P-Celtic 'Uchel' plus Gaelic 'Maighin', Old Irish 'Maigen', high spot. If this is so the castle name may be a secondary name from a higher-ground site. The 12th century form seems to fit none of these suggestions though!

Ogle GR 886992, a hill. For possible derivation see the next entry.

Ogle Hill, marked "fort" on recent OS maps and "Roman outpost, remains of" on the 1860 OS map, GR 970115. It is also known as Knappy (q.v.).

Derivation: Perhaps from P-Celtic 'Uchel', high, like the name of the Ochils themselves. See also remarks under Pitogle.

***Onitsyd**. On record c1654 this may have been a settlement. It lay about 1 mile North East of Quoigs, thus in approximate OS square 8306 or 8406.

Ormiston GR 244170, a settlement, **Ormiston**

Hill GR 235175. Earlier: 1564 'Ormestoun', 1860 'Ormiston Hill'.

Derivation: This might be expected to derive from the Norse personal name 'Ormr' as do several Ormistons in the Borders and Midlothian, though in our case it is outwith the area of Norse settlement. WFH Nicolaisen points out (1976 – see Bibliography) that Orm had become a common name in medieval England and need not imply Scandinavian race or speech. Orm, the son of Hugh the lay abbot of Abernethy (some 3.5 miles away) and member of a wealthy dynasty, was a witness to charters around 1160. Sibbald (see Bibliography) refers to Mugdrum OS square 2218, as "the estate anciently of the Orms".

Outergrain Burn GR 975070, **Innergrain Burn** GR 976068.

Derivation: Scots 'Grain', a branch of a stream, and by extension a place where streams meet and the spur of land that divides them, in placenames 15th century on.

***Oyglethe**, described as a pasture and on record in a charter of c1346 transcribed c1622-32, approximate OS square 0705?

Derivation: This is obscure to me except that reading 'c' for 't', letters not infrequently confused in transcriptions of earlier documents, the name resembles Gaelic 'Oglach', a young man, a young hero. Compare Gaelic 'Fleasgach', with similar meaning, suggested as a possible derivation for Auchlinsky OS square 9904 &c.

The line of the Ochils Fault seen from near Coalsnaughton. From right to left: The Nebit, Craig Leith, Myreton Hill and Dumyat. (AW)

P

***Paddling Greens**, on record between 1769 & 1836, GR 905015 approximately.

Derivation: Scots 'Green' could be applied to any area of ground where grass grew well. In steep hill country dissected by burns 'Green' can sometimes be a reinterpretation of Scots 'Grain', a branch of a stream, and by extension a place where streams meet and the spur of land that divides them, in placenames 15th century on.

Pairney GR 977131, a settlement, **Pairney Burn** GR 975120.

Earlier: 1268-9 'Pronny', 1488 'Pirnie', 1504-5 'Prony', 1512 'Prynny', 1595 'Perny', 'Burn of Perny', 1631 'the Laiche of Perny', 1749 'the water of Shenee or burn of Parnee', 1855-6 'Pairney'. Earliest surname form from Black (see Bibliography): 1769 'Pirnie'. Shinafoot OS square 9613 preserves the earlier alternative name for Pairney Burn (see the 1749 reference quoted above). Derivation: WFH Nicolaisen (see Bibliography) sees this as coming from P-Celtic 'Pren', a tree, with an unknown suffix.

***Panochfauld** approximate OS square 9804?. This is on record in 1801 as part of the Mill Lands of Glendevon.

Papist Knowe GR 086060.

Earlier: On record since 1860.

Pardon Hall, a settlement on record between 1828 & 1860, GR 176093. Scots 'Hall' tended to be applied to a reasonably substantial dwelling.

Paris, an alternative name for Fordel OS square 1312 &c, **Paris Cottage** GR 136117, **Paris Bridge** GR 137114 now absorbed into a bridge over the M90 motorway. On the 1860 OS map 'Paris House' appears to be the present Fordel GR 131122 and 'Paris' the present Paris Cottage.

Earlier references: 1616 'Paris', 1647 'Pareis alias Wester Fordell', 1750 'Bridge of Parish', 1781 'Wester Fordell & pendicle called Paris', 1843 'Paris House', 'Little Paris', 1848 'Paris farm', 'Paris house & farm', 1873 'Farm of Paris', 'Mansion House of Paris', 1894 'Paris'. The name Paris, then, was used of some part of Fordel estate from at least the early 17th century to at least the late 19th century, but the references are not always consistent as to which component holding in particular bore the name. Derivation: Snoddy (see Bibliography) claims that 'Paris' was a common estate name and signified 'Paradise'. The spelling 'Pareis' (see the 1647 form quoted) is found in 17th century Scots for the French capital.

***The Park**, a settlement on record between 1650 & 1822 and forming part of Jerah OS square 8399 for at least part of that period. It may have been close to Jerah but see also the next entry.

Earlier: 1650 'Park', 1664 'Park of Jarvay' (ie Jerah OS square 8399), 1788-1822 'Meikle & Little Jervass (ie Jerah) & a farm called the Park'.

Park Cottage GR 829015. It is possible that this name is a relic of the farm 'The Park' (see the previous entry), though the distance from Jerah and the lie of the intervening land make this by no means certain. See also Burniepark Burn.

Parkhead, a settlement, GR 811974.

Parkhead, on record between 1783 & 1860. This was a settlement in approximate OS square 0710.

***Parkhill**. A settlement on record in 1783 in approximate OS square 0714.

***Parsonley**. A settlement on record in 1783 in approximate OS square 8100.

Path Green & **Pathmill**. See Mains of *Condie*.

***Patrickend**. A settlement on record in 1783 in approximate OS square 0004.

A Pictish Stone from Abernethy, now at the foot of the Round Tower there. (AW)

Peat Burn GR 005047.

Earlier: On record since 1860.

Peat Hill GR 977043.

Earlier: On record since 1860.

Peat Hill GR 064064, on record between 1796 & 1860.

***Peatford**. In 1801 this was part of the Mill Lands of Glendevon approximate OS square 9804.

Pendreich GR 802990, also **Pendreich Mill** & **Pendreichmuir**, both on record in 1860, all settlements. ***Hill of Pendrick**, recorded in 1783, approximate OS square 8100.

Earlier: 1288 'Petendreich', c1323 (transcribed c1554-79 'Pettindreiche' & c1622-32 'Pendreche'), 1650 'Pendrich', 1736 'Hole of Pendreich', 1792 'the pendicle or half ploughgang of land called Hillhead of Pendreich', 1848 'Pendreich Mill'.

Derivation: WJ Watson (see Bibliography) explains this as 'Peit an Dreacha', portion of the sunny aspect or hill-face. Sunnylaw is in OS square 7998. For details of 'Pett-', 'Peit-', 'Pit-' &c, see the remarks under Pitcairlie.

***Pepperhall** a settlement on record in 1796, GR 090061 approximately.

***Glen Perk**, a name recorded in 1829 for the western part of Corb Glen around GR 000084.

Perk Hill, according to the 1860 OS Name Book, is nearly half a mile South of Corb Law, close to Duncan's Hill, forming the North side of a steep glen, presumably GR 001087. It was also known as 'Shore Heads' (q.v.) in the early 19th century.

Derivation: The word order of the glen name raises the possibility of a Gaelic original, though I have no Gaelic suggestion for 'Perk'. If the hill name is the primary name Scots 'Perk' &c, a perch, late 14th to early 19th centuries, would be a feasible derivation.

Peterhead GR 923093, a settlement. This has been on record since 1801 when it was a pendicle forming part of the Mains of Kincardine OS square 9411.

Pigeon Craigs on record in 1860, OS square 1815 on the North slopes of Castle Law. Probably the same as 'Doo Craigs' GR 189152 on recent OS maps.

Piper's Craig GR 063162. The 1860 OS Name Book calls this a steep rocky precipice.

***Pipersknow**, on record in 1783 in approximate OS square 0313.

Piperstones Hill GR 997117, on record since 1860.

It is possible that 'Piperstones Hill' was earlier 'Piperstoun's Hill', from a lost holding. A similar reinterpretation seems to have taken place with 'Millstone' Burn and may have done so with 'Harperstone', both in OS square 8404.

***The Pirrack** also known as **Pirrack Top**.

This is a name for Wester Kirk Craig OS square 9198 that as far as I know has never found its way onto maps.

For derivation see the next entry.

***Pirrich**, on record in 1819 in approximate OS square 9200. It may be the summit of Andrew Gannel Hill.

The five examples I have of hill names with 'Pirrich' &c all lie West of a line from the foot of Glen Eagles to the eastern edge of Tillicoultry and are at heights of between 340 and 670 metres approximately.

Derivation: Scots 'Pirrack', 'Pirrich', 'Pirrick' &c, a mound or pinnacle. The only dictionary entry I have seen for this item is from the *Scottish National Dictionary* which has only one example, from a late 19th century written source from Perthshire, and gives the sense: 'a little mound or knoll of earth'. Gaelic 'Biorach', pointed, could lie behind this word – initial Gaelic 'b' is quite similar in sound to Scots or English 'p'.

*__The Pirrick__ OS square 9599, possibly the summit of Bank Hill?

It had a cairn dating back "many years" according to the *Dollar Chapbook* (see Bibliography). The mention of the cairn is significant as it adds yet another to the series of cairns which appear to have given Glencairn and the Cairn Burn their names (see under Burn of *Care*).

For the derivation of 'Pirrick' &c see the previous entry.

Pitcairlie House GR 238150, **Pitcairlie Farm** GR 235148, **Pitcairlie Burn** GR 238140, **Pitcairlie Hill** GR 212161. **Pitcairlie Turnpike** GR 237142, on record since 1860 and now known as **Pitcairlie Toll**, also served as an inn according to Snoddy (see Bibliography).

Earlier: 1507 'Petcarly', 1517 'Pitcairlie', 1598 'Pitcairlys Easter and Wester', 1607 'Boghall of Pitcairlie' (ie Boghall OS square 2315), 1616 'the Cottartoun of Pitcairlie', 1632 'the Holmeheid of Pitcairlie' (now Homehead OS square 2314), 1828 'New Pitcairly', 1860 'Pitcairly House', 'Pitcairly Hill', 'Pitcairly Wood'.

Derivation: In this and the following 17 names the first syllable is probably from P-Celtic 'Pett', 'Peit', taken into Gaelic probably from Pictish, and having the sense 'portion of land'. It appears to have become a productive loanword in Gaelic, perhaps because the Gaelic incomers adopted the Pictish system of land tenure for a time, perhaps also because the Picts themselves continued to use the term after becoming Gaelicised. '-cairlie' is obscure to me.

Pitcairlie old Turnpike or Toll House. (AW)

Pitcairns GR 027142, **Newton of Pitcairns** GR 023142, **Mains of Pitcairns** GR 028136, settlements, **Pitcairn Glen** GR 026125. The Scots plural in the modern settlement names is a relic of the earlier division of the lands into multiple holdings.

Earlier references: 1247 'Peticarne', 1283 'Petikarn', 'Peticarn' & 'Petcarn', 1451 'le West-thrid-parte terrarum de (ie of the lands of) Petcarne', 1482 'Myddilpetcarne' (presumably the present Middle Third OS square 0313), 1526 'Ester-thrid de Petcarne', 1598 'Mains of Pitcairnis', 1606 'Holl of Pitcairnis', 1650 'Pitcairns & Mylne', 1653 'Cotterknow of Pittcairns' (ie Cotterknow OS square 0214), 1740 'West Third', 1757 'Walkmill of Pitcairns', 1774 'Middle-third of Pitcairns', 1794 'East Third (ie of Pitcairns) called Boghall' (ie Boghall OS square 0413), 'Hole of Pitcairns', 1855 'Pitcairns Saw-Mill', 1860 'Pitcairn Glen'.

Derivation: The 'i' in three of the 13th century forms quoted above probably represents the Gaelic genitive article 'of the', giving Gaelic 'Peit a' Chàirn' or 'Peit nan Càrn', portion of the cairn or cairns.

Pitgober GR 978982, **Wester Pitgober** GR 972979, **Thorn of Pitgober**, also known as Thorn Farm, GR 981986, all settlements.

Earlier: 1569 'Hill of Pitgober called Cornehill' (ie Cornhill OS square 9700), 'lie owtter hill de Pitgober seu lie gersehill nuncupatum' (ie 'otherwise called the gersehill' – later Grasshill q.v.), 1593 'Pitgoberis Eister et Wester', 1695 'Middle Pitgogar', 1794 'Law of Pitgobar', 1798 'the Drum of Westertoun of Pitgobar', 1800 'Hilltown of Pitgober' (perhaps the modern Cornhill?), 1808-17 'the outer Hill of Pitgober called Shouliergerhill' (probably a misreading of earlier Latin 'seu lie gersehill'), 1823 'the Innerhill of Pitgogar called Cornhill & common pasturage on the Outerhill of Pitgogar or Grasshill', 1855 'Farm of Thorn', 'Greenhead of Pitgober'.

Derivation: Gaelic 'Peit Gobhair', goat portion.

Pitgorno GR 193102, a settlement, ***Pitgorno Hill**, on record in 1828, approximate OS square 1810. **Gornogrove**, a settlement, GR 203103, is no doubt to be regarded as a secondary name from this site.

Earlier: 1331 'Pitgornoch', 1505 'Petgorno', 1645 'Pitgornoche' & 'Pitgorno', 1828 'Pittgorno Hill', 'Gorno Grove'.

Derivation: WJ Watson (see Bibliography) derives this from Gaelic 'Peit Ghronnach', boggy portion, with metathesis (the reversal of the position of 'r' and 'o') and the common development of '-ach' to '-o'. The Gornoch OS square 1110 has the same derivation.

*__Pitgrunzie__, a name in use, in documents at least, until c1822. This is now Upper & Wester Greenside OS square 2016.

Earlier: 1611 'Pitgrugnie', 1616 'Pitgrugnyis',

1628 'Pitgrengneis', 1699-1701 'Pitgrunzies' & 'Greenside', 1795 'Easter & Wester Pitgrunzie now called Over & Nether Greensides'.

Though the first reference I have to Greenside predates my first reference to Pitgrunzie the latter is certain to be the older name. Derivation: Perhaps Gaelic 'Peit Grèine', sunny portion.

Pitillock GR 144099, a settlement.

Earlier: 1507 'Pettilloche', 1617 'Pitullock', 1626 'Pitillok', 1662 'Pitilloch'. Earliest surname form from Black (see Bibliography): 1305 'Adam de Pethilloch'.

Derivation: Gaelic 'Peit Thulaich', hillock portion.

Pitkeathly Loch GR 100147, **Pitkeathly Hill** GR 110150. These are secondary names from Pitkeathly OS square 1116, explained by WFH Nicolaisen (see Bibliography) as containing a Gaelic personal name: Cathalan's portion.

Earlier: 1504 'Petcaithly', 1511 'Petcathly', 1636 'Pitcaithlie', 1774 'Pitkeathly Loch'.

Pitlair Cottage GR 237121.

Earlier: 1478 'Petlair', 1593 'Pitlair'.

Derivation: Perhaps Gaelic 'Peit Làir', which could mean either mare portion or low ground portion.

Pitlochie, formerly 'Nether Pitlochie', GR 180095, **Westfield of Pitlochie** GR 167093, **Upper Pitlochie** GR 173097, all settlements.

Earlier: 1452 'Pethlochy', 1775 'Nether Pitlochy', 'Upper Pitlochy', 1828 'West Pitlochie' (ie modern Westfield of Pitlochie), 'East Pitlochie' (ie modern Upper Pitlochie), 'Nether Pitlochie'.

Derivation: There are no lochs in the vicinity now but WJ Watson suggests that Pitlochie and other nearby names such as Pitgorno, 'boggy portion', and Strathmiglo, 'strath of bog-loch', testify to the wetness of the area in earlier times. Thus Gaelic 'Peit Lochaigh', portion at loch place.

Pitlour House GR 209112, **Wester Pitlour** GR 207113, **Pitlour Farm** GR 210113, **West Lodge** GR 205109, all settlements, **Pitlour Hill** GR 205127, **Pitlour Wood** GR 205128, **Pitlour Park** GR 210110, ***Nether Pitlour**, recorded in 1828, a settlement. According to Snoddy (see Bibliography) the western summit of Pitlour Hill was earlier known as Dunimax (q.v.).

Earlier: 1189 'Petinlouer', 1442 'Petlour', 1490 'Wester Petlour', 1509 'Estir Pitlour', 1827 'Pitlour House', 1860 'Pitlour Wood', 'Pitlour Hill'.

Derivation: Without the 1189 form quoted we would not know whether the Gaelic genitive article occurred in this name, but the middle syllable '-in' suggests that it did. Gaelic 'Peit an Lobhair' or 'Peit nan Lobhar', portion of the leper or the lepers, is possible here.

Pitmeadow GR 025128, a settlement.

Earlier references: c1360 'Petmady', 1568 'Petmaddy', 1574 'Pitmedy', 1612 'the Lynhead of Pitmedie', 1686 'Pitmedie cum monte vocato (ie with the hill called) Bleaberriehill' (ie Blaeberry Hill OS square 0210), 1727 'Trees of Pittmeadie', 1738 'Kilts of Pittmeadie' (ie Quilts OS square 0212), 1855 'Pitmeadow'. 'Lynhead' in the 1612 reference quoted may have been at the head of the 'Kerlynlyn' (q.v.), seemingly near Pitmeadow.

Derivation: Gaelic 'Peit Mhadaidh', dog, wolf, or fox portion. Alternatively compare Polmadie near Glasgow, in 1179 'Polmacde', where '-macde' is perhaps for 'the sons of Dith', a Gaelic personal name.

Pitmedden GR 225141, a settlement, **Pitmedden Wood** GR 220150.

Earlier forms: 1577 'Petmedden', 1632 'Pitmedan', 1650 'Pitmedeine'.

Derivation: This is likely to be from Gaelic 'Peit Mheadhain', middle portion.

Pitmenzies GR 217137, a settlement.

Earlier: 1615 'Pitmunzeis', 1616 'Pitmungzies', 1621 'Pitmungeis', 1635 'Pitmungizeis', 1783 'Pitmenzies'.

Derivation: According to Black (see Bibliography) the name 'de Meyners', the origin of 'Menzies', is first recorded in Scotland in 1224. Not only does that seem late for a 'Pit' name to be coined but the 'u' of the 17th century forms quoted also makes '-menzies' less likely. Perhaps Gaelic 'Peit na Muine', portion of the mountain, or thorn, with the addition of the Scots plural and subsequent interpretation as the well-known surname.

***Pitogle**, on record in 1783, approximate OS square 1813. Note that it could conceivably be an error for Catochil OS square 1713.

Derivation: 'Cat-' and 'Pit-', as far as we know, from different P-Celtic languages or dialects, appear to have been broadly equivalent in sense. As for '-ogle', WJ Watson (see Bibliography) quotes c1200-1450 'Okelfas', 'Ogelfas', 'Ogleface', & 'Ogilface', "possibly for 'Uchelfaes', high-field". It is possible then that '-ogle' and '-ochil' are both from P-Celtic 'Uchel' and that 'Pitogle' and 'Catochil' thus confer the same description, 'high portion', on two neighbouring sites.

Pitquhanatrie GR 087114, the site of the present Craighead, ***New Pitquanitrie** recorded in 1783 approximate OS square 0811. ***Pitquhanatrie Burn** is identified by Meldrum (see Bibliography) with Slateford Burn OS square 0811. According to the OS Name Book Pitquhanatrie was "dilapidated" in 1860. The name appeared on OS maps up to 1901 at least and is still known locally, at least to some.

Earlier references: 1392 'Petwhonardy', 1463 'Petquhonordy', 1625 'Pitquhannertie', 1650 'Pitquhanartrie', 1699-1701 'Pitquhanatrie', 1742 'Pitwhanatree', 1750 'Pittwanety', 1820 'the quarter of Pitwhanatry called Craighead'.

Derivation: WJ Watson mentions 'Kilquhanatie', Kirkcudbrightshire, which may contain the saint's name 'Connaith'. This is the closest I can get to a suggested etymology but it doesn't take account of the 'r' in our name. Although the early forms quoted above vary the position of 'r', they are almost unanimous in including it! Tullyquhanatrie Knowe OS square 0209 presents the same problem.

Craig of Pittenbrog Quarry, disused, GR 190133.

Earlier: 1577 'Pettinbrog', 1650 & 1667 'Pittinbroige' (a settlement), 1722 'Craig of Petinbroge' (a hamlet). Earliest surname forms from Black (see Bibliography): 1550 'Pittinbrog', 1650 'John Pittinbroige'.

Derivation: Gaelic 'Peit na Bròige', portion of the shoe. According to Grant (see Bibliography) in Highland Gaelic society the shoemaker seems to have been rare until the 18th century, but if the suggested derivation is correct it may indicate the presence of one here soon after the assimilation of the Picts by the Gaels.

***Pittendie**, a settlement on record between 1528 & 1827, at or near the site of the present Gattaway GR 194162, Pittendie Hill GR 202163.

Earlier: 1528 'Gawtowy (now Gattaway) et Petindy', 1611 'Pittindie', 1775 'Pittendie', 1860 'Pitendie Hill'.

Derivation: Pictish & Gaelic 'Peit', a portion of land; '-en' may well represent the Gaelic genitive article 'of the', but '-die' is not clear to me here.

Pittuncarty 190115, a settlement.

Earlier: 1517 'Pittuncarlie', 1581 (Perhaps this site) 'Pittoncardie', 1616 'Pituncartie'.

Derivation: Unless the 1517 form is reliable this name probably derives from Gaelic 'Peit na Cèardaich', portion, holding, of the forge or smithy.

Plains GR 100102, a settlement, **Plains Burn** GR 104097. **Low Plains**, a settlement on record between 1860 & 1901, was on the site of the present Craigfarg GR 102107.

Earlier: 1580 'Planis', 1654 'Plains', 1860 'Low Plains', 'Plains Burn'.

Derivation: Scots 'Plain', a small or limited piece of level ground, late 15th to early 16th

The ruins of Pottie Mill at the entrance to Glen Farg. Drawing by Ken Laing.

century.

Pleasance GR 234128, a settlement, **Pleasance Cottage**, GR 233130.

Earlier: 1860 'Pleasance'.

Derivation: Scots 'Pleasance' &c, a pleasure ground or park 16th century on, a source of pleasure late 14th to 15th centuries; a loanword from French.

***Pliverburn**, a settlement on record between 1752 & 1783, approximate OS square 8199.

Earlier: 1752 'Ploverburn'.

Derivation: Scots 'Pluvar', 'Pliver' &c, the plover, 15th century on.

Pothill GR 961113, a settlement.

Earlier references: 1498 'Pothill', 1713 'Pothill of Foswall' (ie Foswell OS square 9610).

Derivation: Scots 'Pot' &c, a pit or hole in the ground whether natural or man-made, in placenames 13th century on, a deep hole in a river, a pool, in placenames late 15th century on.

Pottiehill GR 159139, a settlement, **Pottiehill Clump** GR 156134, a hill, **Pottiehill Wood** GR 155145, ***Pottie Mill**, on record between 1614 & 1855, & **Pottie House** (South of the mill) both GR 164152. By 1781 'Pottie' had been replaced by 'Ayton' as the name of the main residence of the estate, GR 167153. The influence of English senses of 'Pot', such as chamberpot, recorded from 1705 (OED), may have had something to do with this.

Earlier: 1528 'Cragpoty', 1583 'Knychtis Potie' (ie modern Newbigging OS square 1515), 1614 'Poty milne', 1618 'Kirk potie', 1682 'Calysyde of Craigpotie', 1688 'Newtoun of Potie', 1720 'West Potte', 'East Potte', 1758 'Parkhead of Pottie', 1783 'Pottie Hill', 1792-1820 'parts of Kirkpottie called Wright's Pottie, Greenend & Moreshade', 1797 'Pottie called Kirkpottie', 1800 'Mr Murray of Ayton for Potty', 1819 'Crossmagouge being part of Craigpotty', 1855 'Pottiehill', 'Lands of Wright's Pottie'.

Derivation: Scots 'Pot' &c, a pit or hole in the ground whether natural or man-made, in placenames 13th century on, a deep hole in a river, a pool, in placenames late 15th century on.

Pow Burn GR 050028.

Derivation: Scots 'Pow', a slow-moving stream, in placenames late 15th century on.

Preaching How GR 186154. The 1860 OS Name Book found "no reliable local tradition" concerning this name.

Derivation: Scots 'How', a hollow or vale, 16th century on.

***Priest Goat Burn** on record between 1779 & 1836. This is the first stretch of the Burn of Sorrow (see under Burn of *Care*), OS squares 9301 & 9300.

Derivation: At least as likely as the quadruped here is Scots 'Goat' &c, a watercourse, early 17th century, with addition of 'Burn' as the sense of 'Goat' was forgotten.

Priest Knowe GR 010104, on record since 1860.

Priests Burn GR 262162. Snoddy (see Bibliography) mentions a tradition that this burn never freezes.

Prins Pendicle GR 166112, a settlement.

Derivation: Perhaps Scots 'Preen', 'Prin', a pin, late 14th century on, but if 'Prins' should turn out to be a very old name a possibility would be P-Celtic 'Pren', a tree, which not uncommonly becomes 'Prin'. Scots 'Pendicle' is a piece of land regarded as subsidiary to a main estate, 15th to 19th centuries, a small piece of ground let to a sub-tenant, late 18th century on.

Purie's Knowe GR 206156, on record since 1860.

Derivation: This name invites comparison with 1632 'Tullipureis', 1814 'Tullypuries', in Logierait parish, as 'knowe at pasture place'. Our version of the name, used longer in a Scots-speaking environment, has seen more reinterpretation and part-translation. From Gaelic 'Tulach', a knowe, and 'Pòraigh', the locative of 'Pòrach', at seed or crops or pasture place.

Purliehall, a settlement on record between 1775 & 1860, GR 237163.

Earlier forms: 1775 'Curly Hall', 1828 'Purliehill'. 'Purlie' is not clear to me. Scots 'Hall' was used of a dwelling more substantial than a cottage.

***The Pykstane**, on record in 1591. This was a stone, seemingly in the vicinity of Glentarkie Hill OS square 1913, marking the boundary of Auchtermuchty Common.

Derivation: It was probably a pointed or spiked stone from Scots 'Pike' &c, a pointed tip or end, a spike, late 15th century on.

Q

Quarrel Knowe GR 187155.

Derivation: This looks likely to be Scots 'Quarrel' &c, a stone-quarry, 16th century on, especially as Bogle's Quarry is in the same OS square and an "old quarry" is marked on the 1957 OS 1" map in square 1915. Nonetheless the 1860 OS Name Book relates traditions that the Picts "celebrated their military games" here and that Abernethy witches came here to settle any disputes there might be among them. This looks like a good example of imaginative reinterpretation of a name as its original sense slips out of memory.

***Quarry Burn**, a name recorded in 1829, is Snowgoat Burn GR 005095.

North Queich, a watercourse, & **Dalqueich Bridge**, both GR 080046, **Dalqueich**, a settlement, GR 080045, **South Queich**, a watercourse, & **Glen Queich**, both GR 028040. Also **Wester Dalqueich**, a settlement on record between 1796 & 1860, which seems to be at or very close to the site of the present Lynncot, GR 059038.

Earlier: 1371 'Maucuych' (ie the present Mawhill OS square 0803), 1467 'Dalquheich', 1498 'Dalquech', 1654 'Nether Cwich fluvius (ie river)', 'Over Cwich fluvius', 1685 'Skarhill of Dalqueich', 1775 'Upper Queigh Water', 1783 'Lower Queigh Water', c1796 'West Dalqueich', 'S Queich River', 1827 'North Queich Water'.

Derivation: From Gaelic 'Cuach', genitive 'Cuaich', a drinking cup, a bowl, but in placenames used also to refer to the shape of the bed of rivers; The first part of Dalqueich is Gaelic 'Dail', a dale or a meadow. WJ Watson suggests that some streams "called Quaich, Queich are probably named from pot-holes". 'Maucuych', the earlier name of Mawhill OS square 0803, is a secondary name from 'Queich', and 'Tonquey' Faulds OS square 0208 may also be one.

Glen Quey & **Glenquey Burn** both GR 974020, **Glenquey Reservoir**, built in 1903, GR 980027, **Glenquey Moss** GR 988036, **Glenquey**, a settlement, GR 983033, **Glenquey Hill** GR 981041.

Earlier references: 1333-4 'Glenkoy', 1358 & 1362 'Glencoy', 1547 'Glenquoy', 1569 'torrens (ie stream) de Glenkoy' (the modern Glenquey Burn), 1617 'Glenquay', 1761 'Cloverknows of Glenquoy', 1828 'the Burn of Glenquhey', 1836 'Glenquey Road' (which runs along the Glen of Care), 1860 'Glenquey Hill', 'Glenquey Moss', 'Glenquey Plantation'.

Derivation: Scots 'Quey' &c, a heifer, is sometimes given as the derivation of this name but Scots 'Quey' appears on the scene later than the glen name, and in any case the word order of the glen name is Gaelic not Scots. Gaelic 'Gleann Coimhich', stranger's or foreigner's glen, would be one suggestion to take account of the earliest forms I have.

Quilts GR 025120, a settlement. It earlier was part of Pitmeadow OS square 0212.

Earlier references: 1530 'Cultis', 1738 'Kilts of Pittmeadie' (ie Pitmeadow OS square 0212), 1783 'Little Cuilt', 'Mickle Cuilt', 1855 'Quilts'.

Derivation: Gaelic 'Cùillte', a place set apart or tucked away, with the later addition of the Scots plural showing division of the lands. The holding would be named from its position in relation to another site, perhaps Pitmeadow. The farmhouse doesn't look 'tucked away' now but it must be remembered that names can quite possibly have shifted location in the course of the 600 to 700 years that separate us from the end of the Gaelic period in this area.

Quoigs House GR 836054, **Quoigs Wood** GR 831058. **Dam of Quoigs** GR 837068, **Upper Quoigs** GR 825060, settlements.

Earlier: 1477 'Bereholme Coig', 'Littil Coig', 1503 'Reterne-Strivelin alias Coygis de

Strathalloun', 'le Wester Coyg', 'le Welcoyg', 1526 'Fyve Coigis', 1650 'Little Quoiges', 1657 'Milnehill of Quoiges' (ie Millhill OS square 8307), 'Gaitsyde of Quoyges', 1716 'Paffill of Quigs', 1723 'Dam of Quigs', 1755 'Pafle of Quogs', 1767 'Bearholme', 1855-6 'Nether Wester Quoigs', 'Townhead of Quoigs' (ie Townhead OS square 8306), 'Upper Wester Quoigs', 'Pendicle of Quoigs', 'Well Pendicle of Quoigs', 'Townhead Pendicle of Quoigs', 'Lower Dam, Quoigs', 'Dam Pendicle', 'Whitehill Pendicle, Quoigs', 1860 'Upper Quoigs', 'Townhead'.

Derivation: This is a much divided holding as befits one named from Gaelic 'Còig', five, here a fifth, a division of land. The 1526 form quoted, 'Fyve Coigis', may imply that an awareness of the origin of the name persisted until that time at least. In the references I have, spellings remain reasonably close to Gaelic 'Còig' until the 17th century. Judging by the early references Quoigs ('Coygis' &c) and Rottearns ('Reterne') OS square 8407 &c made up a single unit in the early 16th century held by the Stirlings of Keir. 'Paffill' in the 1716 form quoted is Scots 'Paffle' &c, a small piece of land, a croft, an allotment, in placenames late 13th century on.

A scene near Coul, looking towards Craig Rossie and Ben Effray, photographed by Magnus Jackson in the late 1800s. Reproduced by permission of Perth Museum and Art Gallery.

R

Rab's Burn GR 995032, on record since 1860.

Raemore GR 218143, a settlement, ***Ramour Hill** recorded in1827. Earlier: 1535 'Ramoir', 1731 'Ramore', 1812 'Raemore'.

Derivation: Gaelic 'Rèidh Mòr', big meadow or level site, is not inconsistent with the location. For the first syllable Gaelic 'Ràth', fortress, dwelling, would also be possible.

The Ramsheugh Waterfall above Dron. Drawing by Ken Laing.

Ram's Heugh GR 136152. A semicircular precipice over which the Dron Burn runs.

Derivation: Scots 'Heuch' &c, a precipice, 15th century on.

***Ramsay's Loup** "A beauty spot in the North Ochils" (Auchterarder Community News Letter, May-June 1985), not so far identified by me.

Derivation: Scots 'Loup', a leap, late 14th century on, a place where a river has been, or is thought to have been, crossed by leaping, late 18th century on.

***Ranshill**, on record between 1830 & 1855, a settlement at GR 882083 approximately? This is described in 1830 as the site of "a intake" (sic) – Scots 'Intak' &c, the place where water is diverted from a river by a channel, frequently to supply a mill, late 15th century on.

Earlier: 1830 'Runshill'.

Derivation: Scots 'Rin', 'Run', a stream, rivulet, water channel, late 16th to 19th centuries.

***Rashie Forrat**, recorded in 1723 in approximate OS square 8603. See Greenforet Hill OS square 8601.

Rashiefauld GR 132095, a settlement. Earlier: On record since 1860.

Rashiehill GR 042092, a settlement, **Rashie Hill** GR 042087, **Rashiehill Burn** GR 039080.

Earlier references: 1594 'Easter Letgrene called Raschehill', 1610 'Rashiehill', 1860 'Rashie Hill', 'Rashiehill Burn'. The 1594 reference makes it clear that this holding evolved from part of Late Green OS square 0308. Between about 1811 & 1822 part of Rashiehill was given the name 'Glentyre' (q.v.). I am told it was abandoned as an independent holding c1890.

***Rashielee**, a settlement, GR 052128. Another holding now abandoned.

Derivation: Scots 'Rashie' &c, overgrown with rushes, 18th century on.

*__Rattlingford__ on record between 1617 & 1828, a settlement at GR 246142 approximately.

Earlier: 1617 'Ratilling-fuird', 1676 'Ratlinfoord of Lumquhat' (ie Lumquhat OS square 2413).

*__Raws__, a settlement in approx OS square 0413 on record between 1717 & 1783.

Earlier: 1717 'Raw of Boghall'.

Derivation: Scots 'Raw' &c, a row of farmworkers' cottages, 15th century on.

Ray Burn GR 060086, on record since 1796.

Derivation: Possibly the relic of a Gaelic 'Allt an Rèidh', the burn by the cleared ground? It runs past Stronachie Hill, the point of the 'field', so the sense would suit here.

Reacleuch Burn GR 938030, on record since 1860.

Derivation: Scots 'Cleuch', a gorge, a ravine, in placenames late 12th century on. The first syllable is not clear – Gaelic 'Rèidh', meadow, level ground, would be very contradictory here!

Red Brae GR 843993. A red scar on the ground on the West side of the Third Inchna Burn caused by a landslip exposing the underlying rock and soil. Less apparent now as it becomes overgrown.

Red Carr GR 829969, a settlement. 'Carr' here is perhaps to be regarded as a Scots loanword from Gaelic 'Càrr', rocky projection.

*__Red Gote__. Reference: 1769 'Head of Red Gote'. This is at or very near the source of Glengreenhorn (now Greenhorn) Burn GR 897022.

Derivation: Scots 'Gote' &c, a watercourse, early 17th century on

Red Myre, a lochan, GR 254140.

Earlier: 1860 'Red Mire'

Redfordnook GR 121086, a settlement.

Earlier: 1775 'Redford Nook'.

Reediehill ('Reedie Hill Farm' on OS Pathfinder 1977) GR 209132, a settlement. This site may be related to **Reedie Mill**, on record to 1860, GR 235123.

Earlier forms: 1509 'Redy', 1823 'Reedy Mill', 1860 'Reediehill'.

*__Revar Burn__, recorded in 1723. Seemingly the burn rising at GR 858022. Derivation: Perhaps Scots 'Reiver', 'Reiffar' etc, a plunderer, late 14th century on.

*__Richard's Inche__ on record in 1627. These were lands beside the 'loch of Wodmyln' now known as Lindores Loch or the Loch of Lindores.

Derivation: Scots 'Inch' &c, a stretch of low-lying land near water, late 15th century on, a loanword from Gaelic 'Innis', an island, a meadow.

Rickle Knowe GR 238127, on record since 1860.

Derivation: Scots 'Rickle', a heap, late 16th century on.

The Rig GR 960075, **Westrig Burn** GR 957070, **Eastrig Burn** GR 962070, all on record since 1860.

Derivation: Scots 'Rig' &c, a ridge of high ground, a hill-crest, in placenames late 12th century on; a strip of arable land, 16th century on.

Muckle Rig GR 022077, **Littlerig**, a settlement, GR 013070, **Little Rig**, a small ridge on Littlerig Farm. Macfarlane (1723 – see Bibliography) describes 'The Ridge' as a "room", ie a rented holding, of Kippen OS square 0112 and says that Innerdounie Hill OS square 0307 belonged to it.

Earlier: 1723 'The Ridge', 1750 'Meickle Rigg', 'Little Rigg' (ie the settlement), 1860 'Little Rig' (ie the ridge).

Derivation: Scots 'Rig' &c, a ridge of high ground, a hill-crest, in placenames late 12th century on; a strip of arable land, 16th century on.

Rintoul GR 072055, a settlement. *__Rintoul Head Moss__ on record between 1836 & the late 19th century, appears to be near Slungie Hill OS square 0507.

Earlier references: 1616 'Rentouill', 1654 'Rentoull' & 'Rentowle', 1836 'Rintoul Head Moss'. Earliest surname form from Black (see Bibliography): 1362-7 'Rentoule'.

Derivation: Possibly Gaelic 'Rinn an t-Sabhail', point or spur of the barn – the contours at the site form a slight spur on the hillside.

*__Long Risk__. An unidentified site on Sheriffmuir on record in 1766.

For derivation see the next entry.

*__Riskfoot__ & *__Riskhead__, settlements on record in 1783 in approximate squares 0012 & 0013 respectively.

Derivation: Scots 'Reesk', 'Risk' &c, a piece of moor or marshy ground covered in natural grass, frequent in placenames, late 15th century on. The Scots term is a loanword from Gaelic 'Riasg', sedge grass or land covered in sedge grass.

*__Rochallow__, on record between 1219 & 1829.

Earlier forms: 1219 'Ruhehalache', 1444 'Rahalath', 1539-45 'Ruhalloch', 1563 'Rahalloch' & 'Rahalloche', c1609 'Rahallo', 1650 'Rachalioch', 1736 'Rochallich', 1829 'Rochallow'.

I have been working on the assumption that this is the same site as the 'Rahalrig' mentioned by Macfarlane (see Bibliography) who was quoting from material collected by Robert Gordon c1654 or Timothy Pont c1595. He says it is one mile above Drumcairn OS square 8807 and half a mile from "Achalig" ie Whaick (q.v.) OS square 8806, and this would place it somewhere between GRs 875065, 885060 and 895065 approximately. The location map in *Charters of Inchaffray Abbey* (see Bibliography under Scottish History Society), which is invaluable for the geography of medieval Strathearn (but which may have been compiled without the benefit of Macfarlane's information?), situates Ruhehalache approximately in OS square 8810, near Panholes with which it is sometimes mentioned in early documents, and some 1.5 to 2 miles North of Macfarlane's location. 'Ruhe-' looks likely to be from Gaelic 'Ruighe' which can mean both a hillslope and a shieling, senses much more appropriate to Macfarlane's location than to the one to the North. It seems then that this was a piece of hill grazing which was held by the monks of Inchaffray as part of the Panholes lands. For the second part of the name, '-halache' &c, Gaelic 'Salach', dirty, and 'Seileach', willow, willow copse, have been suggested. The latter seems more sensible!

Rommante Well GR 158083 approximately.

Earlier: 1860 'Romantie Well'.

Derivation: This is obscure to me. The only way I can see of making any potential sense of it is via Gaelic 'Ruam', Rome, used in the sense of hallowed earth, then a cemetery. Two sites with religious associations, Bannaty and Eclmurghuall, are or were nearby.

Rooking Linn GR 042046, a waterfall, on record since 1860.

Derivation: The name may refer to the noise made by the water: Scots 'Rook', a quarrel, uproar, 19th century on.

***Rose Burn**, on record in 1769, flows South South East from The Law to Gannel Burn, GR 912992 approximately.

Rossie GR 997134, a settlement, **Rossie Law** GR 997124, **Craig Rossie**, a hill name but also the name of a farm in the 16th century, GR 985121. **Easter Rossie**, on record until 1800, & **Wester Rossie**, on record until 1855, were in approximate OS square 0012.

Earlier references: 1172 'Rossi', a1300 'Rossy', 1502 'Le Myddil-thrid de Cragrossy', 1506 'the west part of Cragrossy', 1595 'East Rossie', 'West Rossie', 1727 'Dykehead of Easter Rossie', 1855 'Rossiebank', 1860 'Rossie Law'. 'Knock Kelty' recorded in 1750 and 'Lawhill' recorded in 1783 may well both represent Rossie Law.

Derivation: Gaelic 'Ros', locative 'Rosaigh', at wood or promontory place.

Craig Rossie seen from the South. (AW)

Rossie GR 256125, **Upper Rossie** GR 258125, **Wester Rossie** GR 250122, all settlements, **Rossie Braes** GR 248123, **Rossie Den**, on record between 1769 & 1860, stretches from GR 246123 to GR 248120 approximately.

Earlier references: 1488 'Estir Rossy ac aulam de Rossy cum lacu et insula' (ie and the hall of Rossy with the lake & the island), 1493 'le Nethirtoun nuncupat le Hal de Rossy (ie called the Hall of Rossy), le Ovirtoun de Rossy', 1591 'Wester Rossy', 'lie Myre-yet de Rossie', 1621 'Over Rossie', 1828 'Easter Rossie', 1860 'Rossie Braes'.

Derivation: Gaelic 'Ros', locative 'Rosaigh', at wood or promontory place.

Rossie Ochill GR 087130, a settlement. Mr George Ritchie, Dunning, tells me there used to be a shebeen here where the saying was: "A shillin for the bannocks, the whisky's free".

Earlier references: 1558 'Rossy-ochill', 1811 'the Barony of Rossie Ochill', 1855 'Home Farm of Rossie Ochill & Easter ditto' (perhaps GR 091134?).

Derivation: Gaelic 'Ros', locative 'Rosaigh', at wood or promontory place. 'Ochill' here is probably the name of the hills themselves, ie this is 'Rossie of the Ochils'.

Rosslem Cottages GR 261123. The first syllable may refer to the same 'Ros', wood or promontory, as Rossie OS square 2512.

Rossie Law South West of Dunning. Drawing by Ken Laing.

Rottearns GR 845077, **West Third** (ie of Rottearns) GR 841070, both settlements.

Earlier: Early 10th century 'o Raith Erend i nAlbain' (ie from the 'Ràth' of Eire in Scotland), 1466 'Raterne', 1477 'Ratherne', 1489 'Raterne-Strivelin', 1503 'Reterne-Strivelin alias Coygis de Strathalloun' (now Quoigs OS square 8305 &c), 1650 'Rattearns easter wester & middle & Mylns', 1664 'Burnholl of Raternis', 1714 'Holetoun of Ratearns', 1800 'Rottearns', 1813 'Williamston or Wester Rottearns, Davidston or Middle Rottearns, Charleston or Easter Rottearns', 1855 'East Third Rottearns otherwise Williamsfield', 1860 'Wester Rottearns', 'Middleton of Rottearns' (ie the present Rottearns), 'Easter Rottearns', 'West Third' (ie West Third OS square 8407), 'Rottearns TP' (ie Turnpike). The earliest reference quoted above is from an Irish account of St Fillan. This means that our name could date from the 6th or 7th century, the supposed time of that saint.

Derivation: Gaelic 'Ràth', a fortress or residence, plus Gaelic 'Eire', genitive 'Eireann', Ireland, with the later addition of the Scots plural indicating division of the holding. WJ Watson (see Bibliography) says that 'Ràth Eireann' was initially a district name. The 1489 form quoted, 'Raterne-Strivelin', refers to possession of the lands by the landowning Stirlings of Keir rather than to the town of Stirling. The 1503 reference implies that Quoigs was part of Rottearns, at that time at least.

Rough Burn, recorded in 1860, GR 022051

***Rough Burn**, recorded in 1829, rises at GR 999093 and joins the Coulshill Burn.

Rough Cleuch & **Rough Cleuch Burn** both GR 956026.

Earlier: 1569 'Rouchcleuch-burne', 1860 'Rough Cleuch'.

Derivation: Scots 'Cleuch' a gorge, a ravine, in placenames 12th century on.

Rough Knowes GR 900985.

Derivation: Scots 'Know', a knoll, 16th century on.

Roughfoldslap GR 070106, a settlement. This appears to be the same as 'Rouchleslap' mentioned by Haliburton (1905 – see Bibliography).

Earlier: 1650 'Ruchfoldsloup', 1723 'Roughfald Slap'

Derivation: The 1650 form quoted looks unreliable as Scots 'Loup', a place where a river &c has been or is thought to have been crossed by leaping, dates only from the late 18th century. Nor is the original name likely to have contained Scots 'Slap', a pass between hills, since that is not recorded before the 18th century. The reinterpretation to '-slap' was probably prompted by the fact that there is a saddle on the hills to the West of the site.

The Roundal GR 903974.

Derivation: Scots 'Roundel' &c, in placenames indicating a more or less circular mound of earth or stones, 15th century on.

The Roundel GR 832068, a cairn. This is described on the 1860 OS map as "a Mote" and shown as a cairn on the 1" OS map of 1971.

Derivation: Scots 'Roundel' &c, in placenames indicating a more or less circular mound of earth or stones, 15th century on.

Rowan Heugh GR 043124, on record since 1860.

Derivation: Scots 'Heuch' &c, a steep bank, especially overhanging a river &c, 15th century on.

***Rowan Law**, also given as 'Rowing Law', on record in 1774 in OS square 0716, perhaps the rounded hill at GR 074163.

Derivation: Scots 'Law', a rounded hill, in placenames 12th century on.

Rowantree Craig GR 976074. Earlier: On record since 1860.

***Rowantree Greens**, recorded in 1819, GR 910038 approximately.

Derivation: Scots 'Green' is commonly applied to an area where grass grows well.

***Rudrie**, on record between 1795 & 1825 as an alternative name for Little Fildie OS square 1413.

Derivation: If this turned out to be an old name it could be from the Gaelic personal name 'Ruaidhri'.

***Ruglen**, a settlement in approximate OS square 0514, on record in 1783, **Roeglen Wood** GR 065142, on record since 1860.

Derivation: Gaelic 'Ruadh Ghleann', roe-deer glen or red glen.

***Rushing Linn**, recorded in 1836, seems to be in the South of OS square 9498 or the North of OS square 9497. It is on Caldron Burn, which rises at GR 939992.

Ruthven Water GR 936100. 'Egeis Water' on Timothy Pont's late 16th century map of South Strathearn may be for the Ruthven, but see remarks under Glen *Eagles*.

Derivation: Aberuthven OS square 9715, the confluence of the Ruthven, is in 1198 'Aberruadeuien'. Gaelic 'Ruadh Abhainn', red river is one possibility, though WJ Watson (see Bibliography) derives 'Ruthven' "almost certainly" from Gaelic 'Ruadh-mhaighin', red spot, from Old Irish 'Maigen'.

***Rutland**, a settlement on record in 1828, close to Reediehill OS square 2013.

***Ryecroft**, a settlement, GR 975125 approximately, on record between 1667 & 1846. This is presumably the Ryecroft where Newton and Inchbrakie plotted the murder of the Master of Rollo in 1691. Lands belonging to Inchbrakie marched with Ryecroft. Meldrum (see Bibliography) gives an account of the affair in his history of Forteviot parish, page 245-.

Ryland Lodge, formerly Kippendavie House, GR 794023, **Ryland Burn** GR 800018.

Earlier: 1722 'burn of Kippendavie' (ie the present Ryland Burn), 1860 'Ryland Burn'.

The remains of Ryecroft, where murder was plotted. Now incorporated into a field dyke. (AW)

S

Saddle Hill GR 955005, also known as Craiginnan Hill.

Earlier: 1819 'Saddlehill', 1905 'Saddleback'.

Sam's Wood GR 136120.

Sauchanwood Hill GR 875033, on record since 1860.

Derivation: Scots 'Sauchen', willow, 18th century on.

Sawmill Wood GR 188145.

Scad Hill GR 939021, on record since 1860.

Derivation: Scots 'Scad', 'Scaud' &c, a scald, 16th century on, perhaps here from a mark suggesting scalding or burning?

Scad Law GR 889035. Earlier: 1860 'Scadlaw'.

Derivation: Scots 'Scad', 'Scaud' &c, a scald, 16th century on, perhaps here from a mark suggesting scalding or burning?

***Scald Hill**, recorded in 1800, GR 962091 approximately?

For the derivation compare the previous two entries.

Scarrhill, a settlement, GR 135127, **Scarhead Cottages** GR 138113, **Scarhead House** GR 140113.

Earlier: 1860 'Scarr Hill' (ie the settlement).

***Scharamylhill**, a settlement on record between 1539 & 1618, approximate OS square 1308.

Earlier: 1539 'Schirefmilnehill ... in baronia de Cuthilgurdy', c1554 'Schyrra mylhill'. The barony of 'Cuthilgurdy' in the 1539 reference quoted is represented now by Cuthil Towers OS square 1508.

Derivation: Scots 'Shireff', 'Shirra' &c, the chief officer of a 'shire' (an area much smaller than a modern county), late 14th century on. This site may derive its name from a mill to which inhabitants of the shire had rights of usage, or to which they were 'thirled', ie obliged to have all their grain ground there.

***The Schothouis**, on record in 1574, lay between Seamab Hill & Auchlinsky Burn and so was perhaps in the southern half of OS square 9902?

Derivation: Scots 'Shot' &c, late 16th century on, a piece of ground. *The Concise Scots Dictionary* says "especially one cropped rotationally", but the site seems high for this to apply here?. The second part is Scots 'Howe' &c, a depression, a hollow, 16th century on, with the Scots plural '-is'.

***Sclatehill**, a settlement on record between 1771 & 1800, possibly near Cloan OS square 9611.

Earlier: 1752 'Sclatehall', 1771 'Sclatehill', 1800 'Sclatehall' altered to 'Sclatehill'.

Derivation: Scots 'Ha', 'Hall', a house more substantial than a cottage, in placenames 14th century on. Compare Scots 'Sclate House', house with a slate roof, late 16th century on.

***Scores**, on record between 1661 & 1783, a settlement GR 004129, now disappeared, **Scores Burn** & **Scores Den** both GR 005123, ***Scores Hill** recorded in 1829, GR 005099.

Earlier: 1661 'Scors of Keltie' (ie Keltie OS square 0013), 1860 'Scores Burn', 'Scores Den'.

Derivation: Scots 'Score', a crevice, a cleft, a gully in a cliff face, might suit the terrain but it is on record from the 19th century only. Gaelic 'Sgòr', a sharp steep hill rising by itself, or a little steep precipitous height on another hill, with the Scots plural, could therefore be behind this name.

Scouring Burn GR 785028, on record since 1654.

Scowling Craig GR 038081, a prominent rock according to the 1860 OS Name Book, **Scowling Craig Hill** GR 037079. Both are on record since 1860.

Seamab Hill GR 994016, **Seamab Foot**, a settlement, GR 005015.

Earlier: 1574 'the hill of Schemobe', 1783 'Seamab Hill', 1855 'Sea Mab Foot'.

Derivation: WJ Watson (see Bibliography) suggests that the first syllable may represent Gaelic 'Suidhe', seat, as it does in 'Seabeg' and 'Seamore' in Stirlingshire, but the 1574 form quoted above implies rather Gaelic 'Sìth', a hill, a fairy hill. '-mobe' &c is not clear to me.

The Seat GR 952062, a hill, on record since 1860.

Derivation: Scots 'Seat' can sometimes represent an earlier Gaelic 'Suidhe', a seat (of a saint or hero). St Mungo's Chapel lies some 1.5 miles to the North West and St Serf's Bridge some 3.5 miles to the South East, but any connection with this 'Seat' would probably be impossible to prove.

***Seatfold**, on record in 1750 South of Candy and near Strawyearn Burn OS square 1109.

Segg Burn GR 032120, on record since 1860.

Derivation: Scots 'Seg' &c, sedge, 15th to early 20th centuries.

Meikle Seggie GR 100063, **Seggie Bank** GR 092062, settlements, **Seggie Glen** GR 091062.

Earlier: 1505 'baronia de Segy', 1616 'lie Maynes aliasque terras de (ie otherwise known as the lands of) Mekil Segy', 'villam et terras de (ie 'toun' and lands of) Littill Segy', 1860 'Little Seggie', 'Seggie Glen'. 'Little Seggie' appears to be the present Seggie Bank. A surname may have arisen here: the earliest surname forms from Black (see Bibliography) are 12th century 'Walter junior de Seggin', 1417 'John of Segy'.

Derivation: Scots 'Seggy', sedgy, in placenames 14th century on.

***Castle Semple**, a settlement on record in 1828, approximate OS square 2316.

This is a mystery to me. The name could have been borrowed from Castle Semple in Renfrewshire?

Saint Serf's Bridge OS square 9903. It was "much dilapidated" in 1860 according to the OS Name Book and is now under Castlehill Reservoir. Also **Saint Serf's Cottages** GR 002025.

***Sanct Serf's Peat Myre** ('lie pait-myre de Sanct Serf') on record in 1591. This appears to have been at the West end of Clamieduff Hill OS square 1913.

Seven Gates GR 209154, on record since 1860. A number of tracks meet here, the 1860 OS Name Book says that "in former times" there were seven. The 'Gaits of Lumbennie' mentioned by Snoddy (see Bibliography) seem to be some at least of the same tracks.

Derivation: Scots 'Gate' &c, a way, a road, a path, late 14th century on.

***Shank**, a settlement on record in 1783, approximate OS square 8101. 'Shank of *Tongue*' (q.v.), unidentified but also on Sheriffmuir, may be a related name.

Derivation: Scots 'Shank' &c, a downward spur or slope of a hill, 17th century on.

The Shank GR 957045, a hill on record since 1860.

Derivation: Scots 'Shank' &c, a downward spur or slope of a hill, 17th century on.

Shanraw, a settlement, GR 804038, **Shanraw Cottages**, same GR.

Earlier: 1503 'Schanrow', 1650 'Shanra', 1766 'Chanra Moss', 1782 'Shanraw'.

Derivation: Gaelic 'Sean Ràth', old fortress or residence.

Shanwell GR 080049, a settlement.

Earlier: 1371-90 'Schenvale', 1372 'Schenvalle'. Earliest surname forms from Black (see Bibliography): 'John Schanwall', 'Chanwell' or 'Schanwelle', who was Abbot of Coupar Angus from 1480 to 1509.

Derivation: Gaelic 'Sean Bhaile', old steading. Orwell OS square 1105, some 2.5 miles away, is earlier: 1306-29 'Urwell', 1371 'Urwelle', 1498 'Urvell', 1650 'Orval', and looks like a matching Gaelic 'Ur Bhaile', new steading.

***Shawland**, a settlement on record in 1783, approximate OS square 9700. Derivation: If not

St Serf's Bridge in Glen Devon. Now under Castlehill Reservoir. Drawing by Ken Laing.

the surname, perhaps Scots 'Shaw', a small wood, a thicket, late 14th century on.

***Shaws**, a settlement recorded in 1801, **Shaws Wood** GR 033143, on record since 1860.

Derivation: Perhaps Scots 'Shaw', a small wood, a thicket, late 14th century on.

Ben Shee GR 952039, a hill.

Derivation: Gaelic 'Beinn Shìth', fairy mountain.

***Sheepreeve**, on record between 1769 & 1819, GR 904037 approximately. Earlier: 1769 'Rives'.

Derivation: Scots 'Reeve', 'Ree' &c, a permanent stone sheepfold used during stormy weather, shearing etc, late 17th century on.

Shepherd's Cave GR 037041.

Sheriff Muir, the moorland area centred on OS squares 8203 & 8303, also **Sheriffmuir Big Wood** GR 809020. Professor Barrow (1981 – see Bibliography) sees this as a 'Shire Muir', ie where inhabitants of the shire had grazing rights. Ross and Hume (see Bibliography) mention a distillery at the site of the **Sheriffmuir Inn** GR 827022, 1825-30.

Glen Sherup & **Glensherup Burn** both GR 952030, **Glensherup Reservoir**, built in 1875, GR 963040, **Wester Glensherup**, a settlement, GR 966051.

Earlier forms: 1540 'Glenscherop', 1602 'Glencherop', 1607 'Glenscheirop', 1650 'easter Glensheirope', 'wester Glensheirope', 1772 'Glensherup', 1860 'Glensherup Burn'.

Derivation: Gaelic 'Sìor Abh', earlier 'Ab', long-lasting river, ie not liable to dry up, or perhaps referring to the length of the glen – the 1860 OS Name Book describes it as "a long narrow glen".

Shiel Rigg GR 044048, a hill.

In 1615 this was part of the lands of Carnbo OS square 0503.

Earlier: 1615 'mons de (ie the hill of) Scheilrig'. Derivation: Perhaps Scots 'Shiel', a temporary hut, summer pasture with a shepherd's hut, a shieling, in placenames 12th century on.

Easter Shiel GR 912048, **Wester Shiel** GR 910040, burns.

Derivation: Perhaps the same as the Rivers Shiel of Moidart and Loch Duich, in Gaelic 'Seile', a very old watercourse name.

***Shilling Hill**, on record in the early 19th century, GR 991045 approximately.

Derivation: Scots 'Sheeling Hill', 'Shilling Hill', a piece of rising ground where grain was winnowed by the wind, late 16th century on.

***Shillinghill**, an unidentified settlement in Arngask parish on record in 1730. Arngask is in OS square 1310.

Derivation: Scots 'Sheeling Hill', 'Shilling Hill', a piece of rising ground where grain was winnowed by the wind, late 16th century on.

Shire End House GR 095094. This was on the Perth-Kinross county boundary. Close by must have been Patie's "shebeen" described by Haliburton (1905 – see Bibliography).

Earlier references: 1860 'Shire End', 1901 'Shirend Bungalow'.

***Shore Heads**, the hill at GR 001087, on record in 1829 and also known as Perk Hill (see Glen *Perk*).

Derivation: Scots 'Schoir' &c, steep, rugged, late 14th to 16th centuries, fits the terrain. Scots 'Heid' &c, the summit of a hill or brae, late 15th century on.

***Shotts**, a settlement on record in 1783, approximate OS square 8105.

Derivation: Scots 'Shot', a piece of ground, especially one cropped rotationally, late 16th century on.

***Shoulder End**, a hill on record in 1769, GR 906020 approximately. Also ***Shoulderend Cairn**, on record between 1769 & 1836, GR 905025 approximately, & ***Shoulderend Moss**, on record between 1769 & 1819, approximate OS square 9002.

Earlier forms: 1769 'Kairn of Shoulderend', 'Moss of Shoulderend'.

Shuttlefauld, a settlement, GR 121094.

Earlier forms: 1775 'Shittleford' (sic), c1796 'Shuttlefold'.

Derivation: A holding once occupied by weavers? Scots 'fauld', a fold, a pen, a small field, late 14th century on.

Side, a settlement, GR 823043.

Earlier: 1803 'Broadleyside', 1860 'Side'. Hence earlier associated with Broadley OS square 8304. Derivation: Scots 'Side', a sloping piece of ground, a hillside, late 17th century on.

Sillywinny Wood GR 067135. Famous for its larch trees and capercailzies and once the site of houses, as well as a mill that was worked until c130 years ago. The name is pronounced by some 'Sallywinny' (information from Mr G Ritchie).

Earlier: 1826 'the Grass Parks of Lillywinny' (sic), 1860 'Sillywinny Wood'. Derivation: The local explanation of this name is that a woman living here went mad because of the isolation. The 1826 form quoted seems to spoil that story but is not itself particularly clear.

Silver Glen & **Silver Burn** both GR 892976.

Sim's Hill GR 999076.

Earlier: 1829 'Syme's Hill', 1860 'Syme's Hill' & 'Sim's Hill'.

Derivation: Probably from the surname 'Syme'?

Simpleside Hill GR 995108.

Earlier: 1783 & 1828 'Templeside', 1860 'Simpleside Hill'.

Derivation: The placename element 'Temple' can indicate that the site in question was held by the Knights Templar during a period from the early 12th century to 1312. There were lands held by the Templars at Forteviot 5.5 miles away. Compare Temple Hill.

***Pirrack of Skershill**, recorded in 1766. The plan of Sheriff Muir on which this name appears is not accurate enough to locate the site. However it may well be related to Green Scares of Little Carim, OS square 8403 (see under Mickle *Corum*), and is probably the summit of Scares Hill approx OS square 8203, on record in 1736, which was presumably the hill land of Green Scares.

Derivation: For 'Skers', 'Scares' compare Gaelic 'Sgeir', which usually means a cliff but according to Dwelly (see Bibliography) can also mean a peatbank. Scots 'Pirrack' is a mound or pinnacle – for further information see Pirrich.

Skirlbear, a settlement on record since 1775, GR 222173. The 1860 OS Name Book describes this as two farm labourers cottages.

Derivation: Scots 'Skirl' can refer to the shriek of the wind; '-bear' is likely to be for 'bare'. Compare also Scots 'Skirl-naked', stark naked.

Skymore Hill GR 020104, on record since 1860, ***Sky Toll**, an alternative name for Blaeberry Toll, GR 024103.

Derivation: '-more' seems to be Gaelic 'Mòr', big, and the pronunciation I have heard stresses '-more' and gives it a lengthened vowel as in Gaelic. The first syllable though is obscure to me.

Skythorn Hill GR 925014.

Earlier references: 1779 'Skythorn Carn' (ie 'Cairn', presumably at the summit), 1819 'Skythorn', 1860 'Skythorn Hill'. This name is obscure to me.

The Slack GR 980128.

Earlier: 1860 'Slack'.

Derivation: Scots 'Slack', a saddle in a hill-ridge, a pass, late 14th century on.

The Slack, on record in 1860, GR 997123 approximately.

Derivation: Scots 'Slack', a saddle in a hill-ridge, a pass, late 14th century on.

***Slackdow Burn**, recorded in 1736, joins the Old Wharry Burn from the North at GR 849018.

Derivation: Gaelic 'Slochd Dubh', black hollow, pool, ditch or marsh, from a feature past or through which the burn flows. There may have been some later influence from Scots 'Slack', a saddle in a hill-ridge, since a saddle is what there is at GR 850025, above where the burn rises.

***Slate Craigs**, recorded in 1766, an unidentified site on Sheriffmuir.

Slateford Burn GR 084110, on record since 1860, ***Slateford**, a settlement on record between 1783 & 1860, GR 083106 approximately. Meldrum (see Bibliography) tentatively identifies the Water of Whitburn with Slateford Burn.

Earlier: 1783 'Slatefoord' (ie the settlement).

***Sledgate Burn**, on record in 1800, runs to the Maller Burn from the South, at GR 961099 approximately.

Derivation: Scots 'Sled' &c, a sledge, late 14th century on; Scots 'Gate' &c, a way, a road, late 14th century on.

Slungie Hill GR 058077.

Earlier references: 1727 'Slungiecarne' (ie '-cairn', presumably at the summit), c1796 'Slungy Cairn', 1860 'Slungie Hill'.

Derivation: Macfarlane (1727 – see Bibliography) describes this as a hill in the ground of Middleridge, now Middle Rigg, OS square 0608, where there was a considerable moss, and Rintoul Head Moss & Ledlanet Moss were close by. In that case Scots 'Slunge', wade through water or mud in a clumsy splashing way, would be appropriate here, though the date of its first known occurrence in Scots, late 18th century, is a bit late.

***Slunk**, a settlement on record in 1783, approximate OS square 9598. The *Dollar Chapbook* (see Bibliography) mentions the ***Slunk Road** OS square 9499 also known as 'The Roman Road'.

Derivation: Scots 'Slunk', a wet and muddy hollow &c, late 15th century on.

Small Burn GR 984100, on record since 1829.

Smillheuch Burn GR 960036.

Derivation: 'Smill-' is obscure to me; Scots 'Heuch' &c, a precipice, a crag, or a steep bank, especially above a river &c, 15th century on.

***Smithie Neuk**, a settlement on record in 1800 GR 960104 approximately?

Smithscleuch Burn GR 923043.

Derivation: Scots 'Cleuch' &c, a gorge, a ravine, in placenames late 12th century on.

Smithyhill, a settlement, GR 132103. Less than 1 mile away was Smiths Pendicle, on record in 1901 at GR 141112, so the sites may well be related.

Earlier: 1774 'Smithyhill', 1855 'Lands of Smiddyhill'.

Snowgoat Glen & **Snowgoat Burn** both GR 005095. In 1829 the burn is on record as 'Quarry Burn'.

Earlier: 1860 'Snowgoat Glen', 'Snowgoat Burn'.

Derivation: Scots 'Gote' &c, a watercourse, early 17th century on.

Sochie GR 958995, a crag. ***Sochie Falls** are close by.

Earlier: 1860 'Sauchie'.

Derivation: Scots 'Sauchie', abounding in willows, 19th century on.

Burn of Sorrow. See Burn of *Care*.

Southfield, a settlement on record since 1828, GR 150073.

The stone near Castleton from which 'Standingstone' took its name. Drawing by Ken Laing.

***Sparrmuir**. A holding on record between 1791 & 1822 as part of Pitquhanatrie OS square 0811.

Craig Sparrow GR 216166, on record since 1860. The 1860 OS Name Book describes this as a ridge of rocks.

Derivation: The order of the elements of this name may imply a Gaelic original, with 'Sparrow' as a reinterpretation. 'Creag Spearrach', cow-fetter or goat-fetter crag, would be one suggestion. The animals would be fettered to allow them to graze without going over the crag.

Craig Sparrow with Wester Clunie Farm in the foreground. (AW)

Spout Burn, on record in 1860, GR 982032.

Derivation: Scots 'Spout', a spring, 18th century on, a waterfall, 19th century on, frequent in placenames.

Spout Wood GR 798007.

Derivation: Scots 'Spout', a spring, 18th century on, a waterfall, 19th century on, frequent in placenames.

***Springfield**, a settlement on record in 1828, approximate OS square 2412.

Springhall, a settlement, GR 118090.

Earlier: 1775 'Spring Hall'.

Standingstone, a settlement on record to 1860.

Earlier: 1855 'Standystane'.

Derivation: Named from the standing stone at GR 983001.

Stank Burn, known in 1860 as 'Grey's Burn', & **Stank Bridge**, on record since 1860, both GR 085041.

Derivation: Scots 'Stank', a pond, a swampy place, frequent in place-names, 14th century on, a stream serving as a boundary, 18th century on.

Steelend GR 037139, a settlement, **Steelend Den** GR 043140.

Earlier: 1712 (an unclear entry, perhaps this site) 'Stalrond'?, 1752 'Steallend', 1824 'Easter-Steel-End'.

Derivation: Compare Scots 'Steel' &c, a steep bank, especially a spur on a hill ridge, though the date of its first use in Scots, the 19th century, is late.

Steele's Knowe GR 969080, on record since 1829.

Derivation: Perhaps from the surname, but Scots 'Steel', a steep bank, especially a spur on a hill ridge, with a plural 's' later reinterpreted as a possessive, would suit the terrain quite well.

Stewartshill GR 206159, a settlement.

Earlier: 1855 'Stewart Hill'.

***Stonefold**, a settlement on record between 1796 & 1828 in OS square 0205, at the North West end of Nether Town Hill.

Stonehill GR 802009, a settlement, **Stonehill Wood** GR 801013.

Earlier forms: 1783 'Stonyhill', 1855 'Stonehill'.

Strabanster Burn GR 880003.

Derivation: Perhaps Scots 'Stra' &c, straw, and Scots 'Bandster', the member of a party of harvesters who binds the sheaves, 19th century on, though the area seems much too steep and remote for cereals. If the name is not Scots, or is a hybrid, the path of the burn is too narrow and sloping for Gaelic 'Srath', a strath, but Gaelic 'Sruth', a stream, is possible.

***Strabo-muir** on record in 1592. This was common grazing in the vicinity of Weddersbie Hill OS square 2513.

***Straittoan**, a settlement on record in 1783 in approximate OS square 8407.

Derivation: Perhaps compare 'Straiton', Midlothian, explained by Professor Nicolaisen (1976 – see Bibliography) as 'farm on the (Roman) road'?

Strawearn Burn GR 110094.

Earlier forms: c1796, 1828, 1860 & 1901 'Strawyearn Burn'. If the first part is not Scots 'Strawy', Gaelic 'Sruth', a stream, is possible and might help to explain the presence of the 'w'. An explanation in a Gaelic context for the 'y' of the earlier forms involves a consonant such as the 'n' of the masculine or plural genitive article having been present to introduce the semivowel [j] before the 'e' of '-earn'. WFH Nicolaisen (1976 – see Bibliography) sees '-earn' in this name as possibly being cognate with (the River) 'Earn' and a number of other watercourse names of early Celtic or possibly pre-Celtic origin.

Strenton, a settlement in ruins by 1860, GR 136080 approximately.

Earlier forms: 1553 'Strentoun', 1592 'Straintoun' & 'Staintoun', 1618 'Staintoun', 1650 'Stentoune', 1686, 1745 & 1828 'Strenton'. The early forms suggest that the 'r' was original, but show alternative forms without it emerging by the late 16th century. 'Stren-' is obscure to me.

The Strip GR 899081, woodland.

***Stron**, recorded in 1769. This is the spur of hill at GR 912985.

Derivation: Gaelic 'Sròn', a promontory, a ridge of a hill. Gaelic 'sr-' in initial position resembles Scots/English 'str-'.

Stronachie, a settlement, GR 068085, **Stronachie House** GR 069086, **Stronachy Hill** GR 061084. Moss & Hume (see Bibliography) relate that a distillery opened here c1900 at GR 068085, operated until 1928 and was subsequently dismantled.

Earlier reference: c1796 'Stronachy Hill'.

Derivation: Gaelic 'Sròn Achaidh', spur field, promontory field, with 'field' in the sense of a piece of cleared ground. Gaelic 'sr-' in initial position resembles Scots/English 'str-'. Stronachie Hill forms a ridge or promontory.

Strone, a hill GR 972092, on record since 1829.

Derivation: Gaelic 'Sròn', a promontory, a ridge of a hill, describes this feature well. Gaelic 'sr-' in initial position resembles Scots/English 'str-'.

***Strude Glen**, recorded in 1848, is the foot of Alva Glen. **Upper** and **Lower Strude Mill** were here in 1860.

Mains of Struie GR 079113, **Struie Castle** (remains of) same GR, **Pathstruie** GR 076119, **Struie Lodge** 082117, ***Barnhill of Struie**, on record between 1627 & the late 19th century, GR 082119 approximately, ***Burnfoot of Strowiehill**, on record between 1788 & 1821, **Struie Hill** GR 064105, **Baulk of Struie** GR 075100, all settlements. **Baulk Hill** GR 077093 is a secondary name from this last. In 1771 &c **Whitehill**, a settlement on record since 1474, GR 083101, was 'Whitehill of Struie' so it & **Whitehill Head**, a hill, GR 077102, can be taken as secondary names from Struie.

Earlier: 1194-8 (Perhaps this site) 'Struin', 1474 'Quhitehill', 1489 'Strowe', 1505 'Lucastrowy', 1530 'Langbauk de Strowy', 1539 'Strowye-Striveling (ie held by Stirling of Keir) or Strowyehill', 1610 'Quhithill de Strowy', 1627 'Beirnhill' (ie Barnhill), 1704 'Path of Strowiehill', 1742 'Mains of Strowie', 1787 'Newbigging of Strowiehill', 1860 'East Mains of Struie', 'West Mains of Struie', 'Baulk Hill', 'Whitehill Head'.

Derivation: This looks like Gaelic 'Sruth', a stream, with locative suffix '-aigh' giving the sense' at stream place', though WFH Nicolaisen (1961 – see Bibliography) states that 'Struie' represents the old name of the watercourse itself, now Slateford Burn OS square 0811. Scots 'Baulk' &c is a ridge dividing pieces of land, or an unploughed ridge, 14th century on.

Pathstruie c1935, from a postcard. Reproduced by courtesy of Perth and Kinross District Libraries.

Summerfield GR 162110, a settlement on record since 1860.

***Burn of Summerfold**. An unidentified site on Sheriffmuir on record in 1766.

Sunnybraes, a hillside, GR 264137, **Sunnybraes**, a settlement on record in 1860, OS square 2613.

Sweel Bridge in a dry season. (AW)

Sunnylaw, a hill, GR 793982, **Sunnylaw Farm** GR 794985. Pendreich, 'portion of the sunny hillside', is in OS square 8099. Derivation: Scots 'Law', a rounded hill, in placenames 14th century on.

Susie's Plantation GR 233177.

Swallow Hole GR 192125, a hollow.

Sweel Bridge GR 020091, on record since 1860.

Derivation: Scots 'Sweel' refers to the swirling motion of water, late 18th & 19th centuries.

Sweerie GR 230180, a settlement.

Derivation: Scots 'Sweirie', rather lazy, somewhat reluctant, 19th century on. A wry comment on the nature of the land?

Black Swelth GR 975121. The 1860 OS Name Book describes this as a large deep linn.

Earlier form: 1860 'Black Swilth'.

Derivation: Scots 'Swelth' &c, a whirlpool, late 14th to early 17th centuries.

***The Syke** GR 076121. This location is sometimes known as The Blacksmith's Shop. It was the site of a smiddy which, I am told, served some 35 pairs of horses in the 19th century.

Derivation: Scots 'Syke', a cleft in the ground, 18th century on.

Sheriff Muir from Thomson's map of South West Perthshire, 1832, which was based on Stobie (see p 147). Reproduced by permission of the Trustees of the National Library of Scotland.

T

***Tackethall**, a settlement recorded in 1796, approximate OS square 0906.

***Tam Lachie's Cave**. In fact a mine boring on the slopes of Dumyat OS square 8397. Probably from a personal name?

Tambeth GR 877056, a hill, on record since 1860.

Derivation: Gaelic 'Tom Beithe', birch knoll.

Tamteethie Hill GR 133085, on record since 1796.

Earlier: 1860 'Tamteethie Quarry'.

Derivation: Gaelic 'Tom', a knoll, with an unidentified second element.

Tannerhall GR 121070, a settlement.

Earlier: 1860 'Tanner Hall'.

Tarduff Hill GR 197150, **Tarduff Burn** GR 194150.

Earlier: 1785-93 'Hill of Tarduff', 1800 'the Commonty of Tarduff', 1820 'Tarduff Hill', 'Tarduff Burn'.

Derivation: Gaelic 'Tàrr Dubh', black bulging hill.

***Tarfine Hill** on record in 1774. This was an earlier name for Drumfin Hill GR 083162 (q.v.).

Tarmangie Hill GR 942013. Earlier: 1779 'Tarmangie Carn' (ie 'Cairn', presumably at the summit), 1860 'Tarmangie Hill'.

Derivation: Gaelic 'Tàrr Mangaigh', hill at kid or fawn place.

Tarnavie, a mound below Craig Rossie GR 987131, **Tarnavie**, a settlement, GR 988131, **Tarnavie Burn** GR 990135.

The 1860 OS Name Book applies 'Tarnavie' to two nearby cottages and calls the mound 'The Ship'. The Old Statistical Account for Dunning quotes a tradition of a man cutting divots from Tarnavie being confronted by an angry old man, supposedly "the spirit of the mountain".

Earlier: 1650 'Tarnavie'.

Derivation: The name is popularly believed to be from Latin 'Terrae Navis', ship of the land, ship of earth, an etymology reinforced by the perceived inverted ship-like shape of the mound, but a Latin name would be highly unlikely to survive on the lips of the indigenous people. Nearer the mark perhaps is WJ Watson (see Bibliography): "The first part is probably (Gaelic) 'Tàrr', a paunch, belly, with reference to a bulging spur of an eminence; the second part is 'Neimhidh' (holy place, shrine) doubtless, and the site of the 'Nemed' was probably on Craigrossie".

Across the middle of the picture, Tarnavie or 'The Ship' seen from the Dunning-Auchterarder road.

Across the middle of the picture, Tarnavie seen from Craig Rossie. (AW)

Tarneybackle GR 865077, a settlement.

Earlier: 1830 'Tarneybachle'.

Derivation: Gaelic 'Tàrr na Bachaill', hill of the crozier. As a placename element Gaelic 'Bachall' (now masculine but earlier feminine) suggests that a site was held by a religious establishment. The present settlement is less than a mile from the estimated site of Rochallow which was held by the monks of Inchaffray from 1209 at least. Ben Effray (q.v.) is another site on the northern edge of the Ochils whose name appears to imply ecclesiastical tenure.

***Technad**, a settlement on record until 1821 in approximate OS square 9511, **Technad Burn** GR 952100, ***Tichnad Hill**, recorded in 1800, GR 955086 approximately.

Earlier: 1632 'Technad', 1667 'Tichnad', 1783 'Tightnaid', 1860 'Technad Burn'.

Derivation: This name may well be Gaelic 'Tigh', house, which occurred as 'Teach', 'Tech' &c in earlier Gaelic, with an unidentified second element.

Teeny Burn GR 105060, on record since 1796.

Derivation: Gaelic 'Teine', fire, could conceivably be behind this name.

Teind Knowe GR 251168, on record since 1860.

Derivation: Scots 'Teind' &c, a tenth part, late 14th to 19th centuries. This site is close to Abdie Kirk and Lindores OS squares 2516 & 2616 so the notion of tithes seems appropriate here. Snoddy (see Bibliography) says "obviously a place where heritors attended to make payment of their dues".

Temple Hill GR 106096, on record since 1860.

The element 'Temple' can indicate that the place in question was held by the Knights Templar, during a period from the early 12th century to 1312, and may perhaps do so here. Note that a charter of 1531 has "duabus terris templariis in villa de Strathmeglo" (ie two Templar lands in the 'Toun' of Strathmiglo). Strathmiglo OS square 2110 is some 6.75 miles away. Snoddy (see Bibliography) mentions part of Strathmiglo still in 1966 called 'Templelands'. Also Meldrum (see Bibliography) mentions land belonging to the Templars in Forteviot 5 miles away.

Teth Hill GR 975050, on record since 1860.

Derivation: No Scots original suggests itself. Since 'ch' and 'th' were sometimes interchanged in error in the transcription of early manuscripts this could theoretically be for an earlier Gaelic 'Tech', house, but I have no independent evidence for this.

Thane Croft GR 234165.

***Thanesfield** approximate OS square 0211. Here Dubdon, Mormaer of Athole, is said to have died after the battle of Duncrub, AD964. The Gray Stone GR 022118 is said to have been erected in his memory.

***Thainsland**, earlier called Edendunning and subsequently Glendunning, on record until 1801. This was a substantial area of ground centred on the Common of *Dunning* (q.v.).

Earlier references: 1599 'Thainsland', 1686 'Thaneslands alias vocatis (ie otherwise called) Edindonyng', 1801 'part of the Thainsland or Glendunning formerly called Common of Dunning & now Greenhill'.

Derivation: Scots 'Thane', a minor noble with fiscal and judicial authority over a tract of land, a feudal baron, 15th century on.

Thatch Burn GR 957064, on record since 1860.

***Thieves Bog**, GR 052084 approximately, recorded in 1837.

Thievesmill Bridge GR 143089, on record since 1860.

Third Hill GR 019068.

Earlier references: c1796 'Third', 1860 'Third Hill'.

Derivation: This name is likely to be a relic of the division into three of a nearby holding (compare the next two entries), though I have no evidence to show which one it was.

Middle Third GR 035130, **West Third** GR 030130 approximately, on record between 1451 & 1860, **Knock of West Third**, a hill, GR 033126, ***East Third**, on record as such between 1526 & 1794 and subsequently called Boghall, GR 042135.

These were earlier divisions of Pitcairns (q.v.). Earlier: 1451 'le West-thrid-parte terrarum de (ie of the lands of) Petcarne', 1482 'Myddilpetcarne', 1526 'Ester-thrid de Petcarne', 1794 'East Third called Boghall', 1860 'Knock of West Third'. 'Thrid' (see earlier forms quoted) is a common earlier Scots equivalent of English 'Third'.

West Third GR 841070, formerly part of Rottearns OS square 8407 &c, **West Third Cottages** GR 838068.

Earlier: 1650 'Rattearns easter wester & middle & Mylns'. 'Third' indicates that a holding is, or once was, divided.

Thirl Stone GR 196138. This is said to have been the site of markets. According to the 1860

OS Name Book a hole in the stone used to hold a beam which supported scales. Snoddy (see Bibliography) says the hole is 4" in diameter and 2" deep. He also gives the alternative names 'Borestone' and 'Pike-stane' but it looks as if there has been some confusion here with two different stones, the Borestane and the Pykstane (qq.v.) which, like the Thirl Stone itself, marked the bounds of Auchtermuchty Common.

Earlier forms: 1590 'lie Thirlestane', 1828 'Thirl Stone'.

Derivation: Scots 'Thirl' &c, a hole, an aperture, 16th to early 20th centuries.

Thomanean GR 092042, a settlement.

Earlier forms: 1371 'Tomenaygne', 1648 'Thomynane'. Derivation: Gaelic 'Tom an Ein', hillock of the bird.

***Sanct-Thomas-croftis** recorded in 1592. This was part of Lumquhat OS square 2413.

Thornton Hill GR 030036, **Thorntonhill**, a settlement, GR 032025. **Thorny Burn** GR 028026 perhaps belongs with these names.

Earlier: 1529 'Thorntoun de Fossoquhy' (ie Fossoway), 1650 'Thorntowne' (a settlement), 1775 'Thornton' (the present Thorntonhill), 1860 'Thornton Hill', 'Thorny Burn' (OS).

***Thorntree**. An unidentified site on Sheriffmuir recorded in 1766, seemingly near the Old Wharry Burn.

Thornybrae GR 242147, a hillside.

Thorter Burn & **Thorter Bridge** both GR 023113. Both on record since 1860.

Derivation: Scots 'Thorter' &c, crossing, lying across, late 15th to early 18th centuries.

Thorter Burn, on record since 1860, the burn that joins Scores Burn at GR 004118.

Derivation: Scots 'Thorter' &c, crossing, lying across, late 15th to early 18th centuries.

***Thorter Slack**, a burn at GR 925993 on record in 1789.

Derivation: It rises on a saddle (Scots 'Slack', a saddle in a hill-ridge, late 14th century on) and runs at right angles to Harviestoun Burn (Scots 'Thorter' &c, crossing, lying across, late 15th to early 18th centuries).

Threat-Moor GR 795025.

***Threep Hill**, on record in 1774, GR 102144 approximately.

Derivation: Compare Scots 'Threapland' &c, land of which the ownership is in dispute, in placenames late 13th century on.

Ben Thrush GR 987058, a hill.

Earlier form: 1860 'Ben Trush'.

Derivation: 'Ben', from Gaelic 'Beinn', a hill, a mountain, implies a Gaelic original, but I have no sensible Gaelic suggestion for 'Trush' or 'Thrush'.

Tillicoultry Burn GR 912979, ***Tillicoultry House Burn** OS square 9298, also known as Back Burn, & ***Tillicoultry Hill**, seemingly at GR 919985. For ***Eistir Tilliecultrie** see under Elistoun. These are all secondary names from Tillicoultry OS square 9197.

Nether Tillyrie GR 114059, **Upper Tillyrie** GR 112065, settlements, **Tillyrie Hill** GR 105080, **Tillyrie Glen** GR 110065.

Earlier references: 1372 'Tolyry', 1524 'Tuliriis Eistir et Westir', 1613 'Over Tilliery', 1723 'Upper Tulliery', 1750 'Little Tillerey', 'Meickle Tillerey', 1860 'Nether Tilliery', 'Tilliery Hill', 'Tilliery Plantation'. Earliest surname form from Black (see Bibliography): 1657 'Tilliery'.

Derivation: The 1372 form quoted may indicate, not Gaelic 'Tulach', a hillock, which seems the obvious explanation of the later 'Tilli-' forms, but Gaelic 'Toll', a hole, a hollow, with the first 'y' representing the Gaelic genitive article 'of the'. It may be no coincidence that the adjacent settlement is 'Holeton' (q.v), steading of the hole or hollow. '-rie' &c could be from a number of Gaelic words including 'Ruighe', a hill-slope.

Tillywhally GR 115052, a settlement.

Earlier forms: 1723 'Tillewhalle', 1748 'Tilliewhallie'.

Derivation: Gaelic 'Tulach', a hillock, with an uncertain second element.

***Tod Hill**, on record in 1774, GR 079162 approximately.

Derivation: Scots 'Tod' &c, a fox, in placenames late 13th century on.

Todfauld Well GR 154086 approximately, on record in 1860.

Derivation: Scots 'Tod', a fox, in placenames late 13th century on; Scots 'Fauld' &c, a fold, a pen, a small field, late 14th century on.

Todhill Burn GR 810057, ***Todhillburn**, on record in 1783, a settlement in the North East corner of OS square 8005 approximately.

Earlier forms: 1669 'Todilburne' (ie the settlement), 1723 'Todhold Burn' (ie the burn), 1728 'Todholeburn', 1759 'Todleburn' (ie the settlement), 1860 'Todhill Burn'.

Derivation: Scots 'Tod' &c, a fox, in placenames

late 13th century on. The earlier forms are inconclusive for the second syllable: Scots 'Hold' (see the 1723 form quoted) is a dwelling place, late 14th century on.

Tomb, on record in 1860, GR 127103 approximately.

Tombeth Hill GR 089095, on record since 1860.

Derivation: Like Tambeth OS square 8705, this is from Gaelic 'Tom Beithe', birch mound, or possibly birch clump – 'Tom' can have either sense.

Tombreak, a knowe at 066058 recorded in 1860.

Derivation: Gaelic 'Tom Breac', speckled knowe. It carried a small area of woodland in 1860 so the spelling may have been influenced by English 'Break', a thicket &c.

*__Tombrunt__, a hill on record in 1774, GR 097148 approximately.

Derivation: Seemingly a hybrid, Gaelic 'Tom', a knowe, with Scots 'Brunt', burnt

*__Tombuie__, a hill on record in 1774, GR 093150 approximately. The top & foot of its South West slope are marked 'Head of the Brae' & 'Foot of the Brae' respectively.

Derivation: Gaelic 'Tom Buidhe', yellow knowe.

*__Shank of Tongue__, an unidentified site on Sheriffmuir on record in 1766.

Derivation: This is a duplicated name since Scots 'Shank' is a downward spur of a hill, ie a tongue of land, 17th century on. It is possible that 'Tongue' here was originally Gaelic 'Teanga', a tongue, but conclusive evidence may never present itself.

Tonquey Faulds, a steep hillside also known as **Tonguey Faulds**, centred on GR 021084.

Earlier: 1860 'Tonguey Faulds'.

Derivation: Various feeder burns that form the South Queich rise near this site, so a Gaelic original 'Tòn Chuaich', back of the Queich, is perhaps not impossible, with 'Tonguey' as a reinterpretation. Subsequently a secondary name was formed with Scots 'Fauld', a fold, a pen, late 14th century on.

Topfauld GR 876082, a settlement.

Earlier: 1855 'Topsfold'.

Derivation: Scots 'Fauld' &c, a fold, a pen, late 14th century on.

Tophead, a settlement on record in 1860, GR 148091 approximately.

*__Topmain__, a hill on record between 1800 & 1811, approximate OS square 9608.

Earlier: 1800 'Tapmain Hill'.

Derivation: This name is not clear to me, but compare Gaelic 'Taip', a rock or lump, a mass.

*__Topshall__, a settlement at GR 163083 approximately, recorded in 1775.

*__Torbreakwell__ on record between 1794 & 1821. In 1794 this was a holding forming part of the lands of Pitcairns OS square 0214.

Derivation: Presumably named from a well which was itself named from a rounded speckled hill, Gaelic 'Tòrr Breac'.

Torhill GR 078155, a settlement on record since 1860.

Derivation: A hybrid name: Gaelic 'Tòrr', (rounded) hill, plus translation.

Tormaukin GR 998043, a hill on record since 1860. In the 19th century this also appears to have been the name of a farm.

Derivation: A hybrid name? Gaelic 'Tòrr', (rounded) hill, with Scots 'Maukin' &c, a hare, 18th century on.

*__Torrence__, a settlement on record between 1506 & 1828 in OS square 0715, close to the site of the now demolished Ardargie House GR 074158.

Earlier references: 1506 'Torrens', 1589 'petia terrae nuncupata (ie a piece of land called) Torrens', 1607 'Torrence', 1658 'pendicell callit Torrens with the corn mill', 1816 'Corn Mill of Torrence now demolished'.

Derivation: Perhaps Latin 'Torrens', used in Scots Latin in early maps and documents to designate a watercourse, became attached to this site beside the River May?

Big Torry GR 879983, **Wee Torry** GR 880980, both hills.

Derivation: Perhaps Gaelic 'Tòrr', a hill, used as a Scots loanword with the Scots diminutive ending '-ie', '-y'?

Touchie GR 068052, a settlement, **Touchie Mill** GR 069047, which was a corn mill in 1860.

Earlier references: c1346 (transcribed c1622-32 as 'Tochintolhe'), 1371 'Techyntulchy', 1389 'Theyntulchy', 1519 'Towquhyes', 1614 'Towchie', 1616 'Touchie-milne', 'Theyntulchy alias Tillochy or Towchy'.

Derivation: 'Techyntulchy' &c in the earliest references quoted appears to be from Gaelic 'Teach', an earlier form of 'Tigh', house, and Gaelic 'Tulach', hillock, in a form such as 'Teach an Tulachaich', house of the hillocky place? The main stress would fall on 'Tulachaich', helping to explain the loss of the first two syllables by the 16th century. Although legal documents continued to give forms of the name such as 'Tullochie' which go back to a comparatively early stage in its history, the 1519 form quoted, 'Towquhyes', shows that the 'l' had vocalised by the early 16th century at least. The Scots plural of that 1519 form suggests that by that date the holding was, or had already been, multiple.

Touchie, 'at hillocky place'. Rintoul is on the slope, to the right of the picture. (AW)

Townhead GR 054032, a settlement.

Trapmore Hill, on record in 1860. The 1860 OS Name Book also gives 'Tapmore'. This hill is on the estate of Ayton, possibly at GR 168151? It has a "precipitous rocky place" on its West side.

Derivation: I have no earlier references but Gaelic 'Taip Mhòr', great mass or rock, would fit the feature, with 'Tap-' and 'Trap-' as later reinterpretations.

***Trees** , on record between 1717 & 1855, a settlement in approximate OS square 0212, formerly part of Pitmeadow OS square 0212.

Earlier: 1717 & 1727 'Trees' & 'Trees of Pittmeadie'.

***Troon**, on record between 1710 & 1738, a settlement.

Earlier: 1710 'Troons', 1738 'Troon of Garvock'. Presumably in the vicinity of Garvock OS square 0314. Derivation: Gaelic 'An t-Sròn', the spur or promomtory.

Trooper's Dub, on record in 1860 at GR 048038 approximately.

Derivation: Scots 'Dub', a pool, especially of muddy or stagnant water, a pond, late 15th century on.

Truffy Knowe GR 958061.

Earlier: 1855 'Turfyknowe' (a settlement). Derivation: Scots 'Truffie', peaty, turfy.

***Tulliebegiswell**, on record in 1591. This was seemingly in the vicinity of Lumquhat OS square 2413 and marked the North West boundary of Whitefield Common (q.v.).

Derivation: Gaelic 'Tulach Beag', wee hillock. The Scots possessive '-is' suggests that Tulliebeg may have been a settlement when it gave its name to the well as it is far less usual to find the possessive attached to names of other kinds of features.

Tullyburn GR 179099. This is a small ridge above Morton Burn and is also known as Whinney Knowe.

Derivation: Likely to be from a lost Gaelic 'Allt an Tulaich', hillock burn. It may represent an earlier name for Morton Burn.

Tullyquhanatrie Knowe GR 022099, on record since 1860.

Derivation: Gaelic 'Tulach', a knowe. For '-quhanatrie' see remarks under Pitquhanatrie.

***Tumnick's Green** recorded in 1750, GR 015050 approximately.

Derivation: Scots 'Green' was commonly used for a place where grass grew well, so 'Tumnick' would make sense here as an earlier name for the site from Gaelic 'Tamhnach', a green or fertile field, especially in waste or heathery ground.

Turf Hill GR 999129, on record since 1860.

Derivation: Scots 'Truff', 'Turf' &c, peat, turf, late 15th century on.

Turf Hill GR 122123, on record since 1860.

Derivation: Scots 'Truff', 'Turf' &c, peat, turf, late 15th century on.

***Turf Muir** GR 110140 approximately, ***Turfhill Burn** GR 110138 also known as Glashgarie Burn. All three names are recorded in 1774.

Derivation: Scots 'Truff', 'Turf' &c, peat, turf, late 15th century on.

Turf Muir Plantation GR 077068.

Earlier: 1771 'Turfmuir' (a settlement), 1860 'Turf Muir Plantation'.

Derivation: Scots 'Truff', 'Turf' &c, peat, turf, late 15th century on.

Turflundie GR 192147, also known for a time at least as Earlsmuir, **Turflundie Wood** GR 193142.

Earlier: 1685 Tarlindy', 1687 'Turflundy', 1775 'Tarlundie', 1791-1829 'Trufflundie or Earlsmuir', 1825 'Turflundie Road'.

Derivation: The 1685 & 1775 forms quoted suggest Gaelic 'Tàrr', a rounded or bulging hill. WJ Watson (see Bibliography) explains the common name 'Lundie' as deriving from Gaelic "lunnd, meaning probably a marsh". If 1685 'Tar-' is the authentic first part of the name it has been reinterpreted as Scots 'Truff', 'Turf' &c, peat, turf, because of the nature of the ground, which '-lundie' already described. See also Earlsmuir. For 'Turf' see the previous entry.

***Turnpike Burn** GR 963000. This was a 19th century name for the Burn of *Care* (q.v.). The burn runs beside a long-standing route from Glendevon to Dollar but I do not know whether tolls were ever exacted there.

Glen Tye GR 840018, **Glentye Hill** GR 846025, **Glentye Cottage** GR 826013, ***Hold of Glentay**, recorded in 1723, a settlement in approximate OS square 8403.

Earlier: 1503 'Glenty', 1665 'Glentye' (ie a settlement), 1736 'Glenty' (ie the hill). Macfarlane (1723 – see Bibliography) describes 'Glentay' as "a shealing belonging to the House of Keir (OS square 7698) two large miles East of Dunblane", thus in approximate OS square 8501?

Derivation: Gaelic 'Gleann Taighe', house glen. Scots 'Hold', a holding, a dwelling, late 14th century on.

Glentye and Glentye Hill. (AW)

U V

Leden Urquhart GR 177111, a settlement.

Earlier references: 1505 'Ladynurquhart-Estir', 1517 'Leaden-Urquhal', 1532 'Ladinurquhart-Westir', 1616 'Leaden Urquhart', 1654 'Ledunrwhall', 1750 'Leden Urquhart', 1772 'Lednurquhart', 1775 'Linnorfal' (ie Leden Urquhart), 'Nether' & 'Upper Orphil' (ie Urquhart OS squares 1808 & 1908).

Derivation: 'Leden Urquhart' may have originally been a secondary name from Urquhart OS squares 1808 & 1908. Gaelic 'Leathadan', hill-slopes, followed by the original form of 'Urquhart', would be the equivalent of a Scots 'Braes of Urquhart'. WJ Watson (see Bibliography) states that 'Urquhart' at both sites is derived "as the old spellings show, from Gaelic 'Urchar', a cast, a shot, perhaps with reference to some real or mythological feat of casting". In a footnote he adds: "The reference may be to a spur or offshoot of rising ground". The spellings 'Urquhal', 'Orphil' &c are not consistent with Watson's explanation but do not suggest a clear derivation to me.

***Valley Green Well**, on record in 1829, GR 006078 approximately?

Wallace's Stone, Sheriffmuir. (AW)

W

Wallace Road GR 123140 &c.

A route from Lochelbank Farm OS square 1312, through the gap between Dron Hill OS square 1214 and Mundie Hill OS square 1115, and down into Strathearn. The route was traditionally said to have been often used by William Wallace.

The thin diagonal line of trees marks where the Wallace Road descends from the flank of West Dron Hill into Srathearn. (AW)

***Wallace's Cave**, on record since 1828, was in Glen Farg close to Feldie Bridge, GR 150126 approximately. It was destroyed when the railway was built c1890. Jack (see Bibliography) mentions a tradition of an underground passage from Wallace's Cave to Fordel House OS square 1213.

Wallace's Stone GR 833023. There are three traditions about this. One is that it was here that Wallace fought the Rose, another that the stone was a gathering point for part of his guerilla forces. Thirdly the 1860 OS Name Book states that it was believed to have been erected by Wallace himself to commemorate a battle against the English.

Wallhaugh, a settlement on record in 1860, appears to be on the site of modern Mount Stuart GR 003023.

***Wallhill**, a settlement on record between 1685 & 1799. Part of the barony of Gleneagles, it was absorbed into the Mains c1799.

Waltersmuir Wood GR 805005, **Waltersmuir Reservoir** GR 810004.

Wanangoat Burn GR 960057 rises in The Goat.

Derivation: Gaelic 'Uamh nan Gobhar', cave or hollow of the goats, partly translated? But compare also Scots 'Gote' &c, a trench, 16th century on, or a watercourse 17th century on.

Warroch House GR 069046, **Upper Warroch** GR 052051, **Muirhead of Warroch** GR 073046, all settlements, **Warroch Hill** GR 047057, **Warroch West Burn** GR 045050, **Warroch East Burn** GR 056060. In 1616 'Warrok' was a pendicle of Drumgarland OS square 0504. Upper Warroch is on the site of the earlier Warroch and the present Warroch House was 'Coldennook' until 1901 at least.

Earlier: 1616 'Warrok', 1654 'Warrock', & 'Warroch', c1796 'East Burn', 'West Burn', 1848 'Warroch Glen', 1860 'Warroch Hill', 'Warroch West Burn', 'Warroch East Burn'.

Washing Linn GR 056043, on record since 1860. It is one of the Golland (q.v.) Linns.

***Washing Linn**. In Menstrie Glen, OS square 8497?

Waterhead Bridges GR 053046, at the confluence of Warroch East and West Burns.

Earlier forms: c1796 'Waterhead Briggs', 1860 'Waterhead Bridges'.

***Waterloo Toll**. An alternative name for Beinsnook TP (see under Binn Hill).

***Watty-Glen**, South of the King's Seat range, thus in approximate OS square 9398. On record in 1792. The Old Statistical Account for Tillicoultry says this was a sheep farm "many years" before 1792 and mentions rich veins of iron-stone.

Derivation: Compare Scots 'Wattie' &c, diminutive of Walter, late 18th century on.

Waughenwae Knowe GR 009121, ***Wakenwae** "alias Bushes", a settlement on record in 1719-21.

Earlier: 1860 'Waughenwae Knowe'.

Derivation: Scots 'Wack', 'Wak', moist, damp, late 15th century on, & Scots 'Wae' &c, wretched, sorrowful, late 14th century on. Another wry comment on the land or location. The later spelling 'Waughenwae' was perhaps influenced by Scots 'Waugh' &c, weary, worthless, 19th century on.

Wauk Mill GR 891081, on record since 1783. It formed part of the lands of Ogilvie.

Derivation: See the next entry.

***Waukmill**, on record between 1719 & 1783, is a secondary name from Clow OS square 0511.

Earlier: 1719 'Walk-Mill of Clow'.

Derivation: The names 'Waukmill', 'Waulkmill' &c represent former fulling mills. "Up to the beginning of the 19th century the normal way of fulling or waulking new-made cloth, that is, shrinking it and making it of even texture, was by means of fulling-mills, worked by water-power. The mill was constructed so that the water-wheel operated a series of pestles which pounded the cloth, which was impregnated with urine, soap, or fuller's earth, and placed in a vat or tank" (Campbell & Collinson – see Bibliography). Scots 'Wau(l)k', 'Walk' &c, to full cloth, 14th century on.

Waulkmill Farm GR 099051, on record since 1775.

Derivation: See previous entry.

Some of the former mill buildings at Waulkmill Farm near Milnathort. (AW)

Webster's Burn GR 932090.

Derivation: From the surname, or Scots 'Wabster' &c, a weaver, 15th century on.

***The Craigs of Wedderlairs** GR 907992 approximately, on record in 1769. Derivation: Scots 'Lair' &c, a place where animals lie down, a fold, an enclosure, frequent in placenames, 16th century on; Scots 'Wedder', a wether, late 14th century on.

Weddersbie GR 261131, a settlement, **Weddersbie Den** GR 250136 &c, **Weddersbie Hill** GR 254137.

Earlier references: 1509 'Wedderisbe alias vocat (ie otherwise called) Wester Cullessy' (ie Collessie OS square 2813), 1510 'Wedderisbybank' (part of the lands of 'Wodmylne', ie Woodmill OS square 2714), 1592 'Strabo-mur de Weddersbie', 1626 'Wodhead of Weddersbie' (ie Woodhead OS square 2614), 1860 'Weddersbie Hill'. 'Strabo-mur' (see the 1592 form quoted) may have been an earlier name for the present Weddersbie Hill.

Derivation: Scots 'Wedder', a wether, late 14th century on. '-bie', usually of Scandinavian origin, seems out of place in this part of the world.

Well Eyes, a settlement, GR 134115, **Well Eyes Plantation** GR 133114.

Earlier: 1860 'Wellies' (ie the settlement), 'Wellies Plantation'.

Derivation: Scots 'Well Eye', a place in a bog from which a spring rises, 16th century, late 18th to 20th centuries.

Welley Burn GR 035118, on record since 1860. Derivation: Probably for Scots 'Well Eye', a place in a bog from which a spring rises, 16th century, late 18th to 20th centuries.

Wellfield GR 194099, **Wellfield Steading** GR 193103, settlements. Earlier references: 1827 'Wellfield House', 1855 'Wellfield Farm'.

***Wellfield**, a settlement in approximate OS square 1005, on record in 1827.

***Westburn** GR 976998. See Eastburn.

***Westerdele**. See Balquhandy.

Westerhall. See Ballieliesk.

***Westerrough Burn**. See Easterrough Burn.

Westfield, a settlement at GR 069041, on record since 1860.

***Westgate**, recorded in 1783, a settlement in approximate OS square 9008.

Westhall, a settlement at GR 098063, on record since 1860.

Westhall GR 098163, a settlement, **Westhall Hill** GR 094158.
Earlier: 1750 'West hall', 1860 'Westhall Hill'.

Westplace Burn. See Eastplace Burn.

Westrig Burn. See The Rig.

***Westside**. A settlement in approximate OS square 0712, on record in 1783.

Wether Hill GR 923059.
Earlier forms: 1783 'Weather Hill', 1860 'Wether Hill'.

Wether Law GR 042108, on record since 1860.

Whaick GR 885068, a settlement.
Earlier forms: 1664-86 'Aquhaick' & 'Awhaick', 1808 & 1824 'part of the Barony of Ogilvy viz Whaick'.
Derivation: The 17th century forms quoted make sense as Gaelic 'Achaig', 'little field burn', a diminutive of 'Achadh', a field, a piece of ground cleared for grazing or cultivation. The diminutive suffix '-aig' is not uncommon in Gaelic watercourse names. The stress must have shifted to the second syllable of 'Aquhaick', helping a later reinterpretation to Scots 'Quhaik', 'Wheek' &c, to squeak, whine, whistle at intervals, 16th century on, which is very appropriate as the site is exposed to the North at about 220 metres.

***The Whangs**, on record in 1821-29, was an earlier name for Kellybank GR 968984.
Derivation: Not clear. The only possible Scots contender here seems to be 'Wheings', 'Whangs' &c, a long narrow strip of land. The *Scottish National Dictionary* gives just a single example of this usage, from the Borders in the 18th century. A Gaelic name involving '... a' Chumhaing', genitive of 'Cumhang', a narrow, a defile, though not applicable to this precise spot, could have been transferred here from a site nearer to the spectacular Dollar Glen some 700 yards away.

Old Wharry Burn GR 850018, called '**Wharry Burn**' further downstream from about OS square 8200, **Wharry Bridge** GR 800996.
Earlier references: 1723 'Burn of Aldwharie', 'Bridge of Aldwharie', 1766 'Old Wharie Burn', 1848 'Wharry Burn'. On the outskirts of Dunblane, at GR 792008, is a building named 'Ault Wharrie'.
Derivation: 'Wh-' can represent Gaelic 'Ch-' in Scots orthography so the forms with 'Ault-' &c,

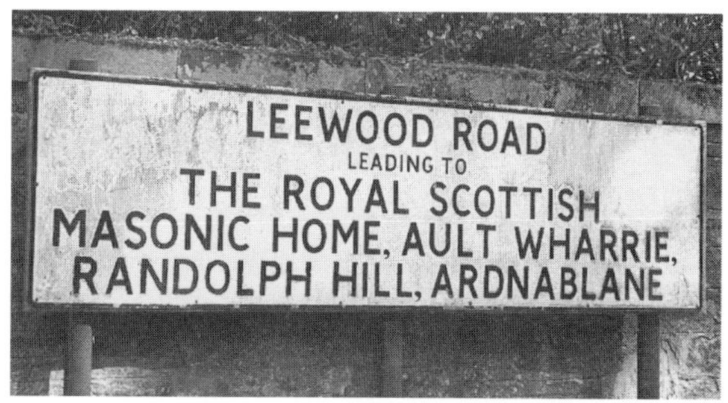

A street sign in Dunblane preserves part of the Gaelic name of the Old Wharry Burn. (AW)

reinterpreted as Scots 'Auld' & English 'Old', point to Gaelic 'Allt a' Charraigh', burn of the rock, pillar or standing stone. 'Carragh', though feminine in Dwelly's dictionary (see Bibliography), is given as masculine by others.

Whinney Knowe GR 036116, on record since 1860.
Derivation: Scots 'Whinnie' &c, overgrown with whins, gorse, 18th century on; Scots 'Knowe', a knoll, 16th century on.

Whinney Knowe GR 179099, also known as Tullyburn (q.v.).
Derivation: Scots 'Whinnie' &c, overgrown with whins, gorse, 18th century on; Scots 'Knowe', a knoll, 16th century on.

***The Whinnylaw** on record between 1774 & 1790, GR 072168 approximately.
Earlier: 1774 'Whinny Law'.
Derivation: Scots 'Whinnie' &c, overgrown with whins, gorse, 18th century on.

Whinnybank GR 229167, a settlement, appears to have been 'Glenbow' until at least 1860. See under Bow Burn.
Derivation: Scots 'Whinnie' &c, overgrown with whins, gorse, 18th century on.

The Bridge over the Wharry Burn at the foot of Glen Tye, Sheriffmuir. Drawing by Ken Laing.

***Whins**, a settlement on record in 1783 in approximate OS square 0313.
Derivation: Scots 'Whins', a clump or area of gorse, 16th century on.

Whinstone Cottage GR 983049.

Loch Whirr GR 119126, on record since 1860.
Derivation: The word order is Gaelic but in the absence of early forms my only suggestion would be 'Loch a' Chiar', loch of gloominess, dusk, darkness.

Whistlebare GR 088066, a settlement on record since 1796.
Derivation: Scots 'Fusslebare', 'Whistlebare', of land, poor, hilly, exposed, though this seems not to have been recorded in Scots until the late 19th century.

Whistlebare. The earlier building is on the right, incorporated into an enlarged dwelling. (AW)

***Water of Whitburn**. Meldrum (see Bibliography) gives this as an alternative name for Chapel Burn OS square 0708.

***White Craig**, on record in 1822, GR 930006 approximately.

White Craig GR 895036, **White Craig** GR 236178, **White Craigs** GR 032123, **White Craigs** GR 078150 and **White Craigs** GR 109084 are all on record since 1860.

White Hill GR 809976.

White Knowe GR 053134.
Derivation: Scots 'Knowe', a knoll, 16th century on.

White Law GR 039108, on record since 1860.
Derivation: Scots 'Law', a rounded hill, in placenames 12th century on.

White Stone Well, on record between 1837 & 1860, GR 063078 approximately.

The White Stone GR 805042, also **Upper Whiteston** GR 809041, **Lower Whiteston** GR 802048, settlements.
Earlier: 1656 'Quhittistoun', 1672 'Whititstoune', 1682 'Whyteheadstone', 1750 'Whitystown', 1780 'Whitetstoun', 1855 'Upper Whitestown', 1860 'The White Stone', 'Lower Whitestone'. At first sight one would expect the settlements to have been named from the White Stone, but the early forms I have contain '-stone' only once before 1860, '-toun' & '-town', ie farm steading, occurring in all other cases. The 's', then, presumably belongs to the first element of the name and is a possessive, implying that the 'toun' was named for an individual or another holding. The early forms are inconclusive as to the form of this originating name. It follows from all this that the Standing Stone appears to have been named, unusually, from the settlement, due to a reinterpretation of the earlier settlement name. The 1860 OS map may have been the 'culprit' in all this. More recent OS series have reverted to the spelling 'Whiteston' for the settlements and the 1957 OS 1" map calls the stone simply 'Standing Stone'.

***Whitefield Common**, on record until 1823. In 1591 this common covered approximate OS squares 2312 & 2313 East of Auchtermuchty Burn, squares 2412, 2413, 2512 & the South West half of 2513.
Earlier: 1591 'lie Quhitfeild', 1602 'commonty in the lands called Quhytefield'.

***White-fields**, a settlement on record between 1811 & 1905, seemingly close to the Water of May, perhaps in OS square 0510.
Earlier: 1811 'the Wester half of the back side of Strowiehill called Whitefield'.

Whitehill GR 083101, **Whitehill Head** GR 077102. Secondary names from Mains of *Struie*.

***Whitehills**, a settlement on record between 1510 & 1855, approximate OS square 9705.
Earlier references: 1510 'Quhitehill', 1540 'Eistir & Wester Quhythill', 1783 'Whitehills' ("castle in ruins"), 1819 'Easter & Wester Whitehills'. The plural 's' arose from the division of the holding.

***Whitehornduff**. See Blackthornduff Burn.

Whitelawhead GR 941979, a settlement.
Derivation: Scots 'Law', a rounded hill, in placenames 12th century on.

Whitens GR 971050, a settlement, **Whitens Burn** GR 970046, **Whittensburn**, a sheep farm in 1860.
Earlier: 1683 'Whytenstoune', 1783 'Whitensburn' (ie the settlement), 1860 'Whitens Burn'.
Derivation: Not clear to me.

Whiterigg GR 007045, a settlement.

Earlier forms: 1542 'Quhiterig', 1731 'Whiterigg', 1776 'Whiteridge', 1860 'Whiterigs'.

Derivation: Scots 'Rig', a ridge of high ground, a long narrow hill, a hill-crest, in placenames late 12th century on.

***Whiteside**, a settlement on record in 1783, approximate OS square 8098.

Whitesmoor Head GR 123058, a hill.

Whitewisp Hill GR 955014, on record since 1793. The 1860 OS Name Book first called this 'Garchel Hill' – compare Garchel Burn OS square 9601 – but withdrew that name after a correspondent protested. Locally the hill is said to be named because it holds a 'wisp' of snow later in the year than neighbouring hills. On the other hand, the 1860 OS Name Book says the name is derived from a small strip of whitish pasture on the South side of the hill near its top.

***Whitock**, a settlement on record in 1783, approximate OS square 8806.

Derivation: 'White Oak'? Black however (see Bibliography) equates the surname 'Whitock' with 'Whitehauch', from Scots 'Hauch', 'Haugh' &c, river-meadow land, late 12th century on.

Whum Hill GR 918998, **Whum Burn** GR 913000.

Earlier: 1848 'Whum Burn', 1860 'Whum Hill'.

Derivation: Possibly Gaelic 'Uamh', a cave or a hollow.

Willandale Plantation GR 203112.

***Willenbuss**, a settlement on record to 1799, approximate OS square 9308? This was part of the barony of Gleneagles, absorbed into the Mains c1799.

Earlier: 1685 'Milnebus'.

Derivation: Scots 'Buss' &c, a bush, 13th century on, a thicket, a wood, late 14th century on. In view of the 1685 form quoted 'Willen-' may be an error for earlier Scots 'Milne', a mill.

***Williamston**, a settlement on record in 1813. This was an alternative name for Wester Rottearns OS square 8406.

Williamsfield GR 852074, a settlement.

Earlier: 1855 'East Third Rottearns otherwise Williamsfield'.

***Willin Bog**. An unidentified site on Sheriffmuir on record in 1766.

***Willow Boug** recorded in 1736. This was a small expanse of bog centred on approximately the North East corner of OS square 8202.

Wind Knowe GR 045115, on record since 1860.

Windywalls GR 089066, on record between 1796 & 1860 by which date it was a ruin.

Windywalls indeed! Loch Leven is in the background, some 120 metres below. (AW)

Witch Knowe GR 053047.

Witches Hole GR 183154. A cave on the North side of Castle Law. According to the 1860 OS Name Book it was the residence of some of the Abernethy witches, but much reduced in size due to falls of earth.

Witches Road GR 188155. This is on the East side of Abernethy Glen, a "favourite haunt of witches" according to the 1860 OS Name Book.

Wizard's Stone GR 966990, on record since 1860. Said by the 1860 OS Name Book to mark the spot where a man was burnt as a wizard in the late 16th century.

***Wolbaitis fald.** This is an unidentified site in approximate OS square 0308, recorded in 1594.

Wolf's Hole Quarry GR 790981.

Wolf's Cleuch GR 972073, on record since 1860.

Derivation: Scots 'Cleuch', a gorge, a ravine, in placenames late 12th century on.

Wood Burn GR 125150.

Wood Hill GR 900985, **Wood Burn** GR 905980.

Earlier: 1790 'Wood-hill', 1860 'Wood Burn'.

Derivation: Wood Hill was planted with trees in 1725 by Sir John Irskine of Alva and this may have given rise to the name.

Woodend GR 082169, a settlement.

Earlier: 1624 'Woodend', 1684 'Woodend of Culteucher'. A charter of 1537 mentions the lands of Nether Culteuchar "cum silva et lacu", ie with the wood or forest and the loch. Woodend, and Lochend in the same OS square, may well have been named from these features.

***Woodhead** approximate OS square 0112, also

known as Craighead. Both names have now passed out of use.

References: 1719 'Woodhead alias Craighead Keltie's ground', 1783 'Craighead'.

Woodhead GR 043143, a settlement.

Earlier: 1617 'Wodheid', 1665 & 1741 'Woodhead of Garvock'.

Woodhead GR 263145, **Woodhead** GR 261153, settlements.

Earlier: 1593 'Woodhead', 1626 'Wodhead of Weddersbie', 1775 'Little Woodhad' (sic) (ie Woodhead OS square 2614), 'Mickle Wood Head' (ie Woodhead OS square 2615), 1860 'Woodhead' (for both settlements).

*__Woodhill__ a settlement on record in 1783, GR 086158 approximately.

Wood Hill seen from near Coalsnaughton. The hill was planted with trees in 1725 by Sir John Irskine of Alva. (AW)

*__Woodland__, on record between 1735 & 1783, a settlement in approximate OS square 7903.

Earlier: 1735 'Woodlands of Kippendavie'.

Woodmill House (remains of) & **Woodmill Mains** both GR 271153, **Woodmill**, a settlement, GR 271144, **Woodmill Hill** GR 264157, ***Woodmill Loch** is the present Lindores Loch GR 265165, in 1510 called 'Braidloch'. Black Loch sq 2615 belonged to Woodmill in 1510.

Earlier: 1510 'Wodmylne', 1541 'le Dene-mylne seu Wod-mylne' (ie Denmylne OS square 2417), 1607 'Grund of Wodmilne', 1618 'the Hill of Wodmilne', 1626 'Freelands of Wodmylne', 1627 'the loch of Wodmyln', 1653 'Cowdoun of Wodmilne' (compare Cowden OS square 2614), 1685 'the Louhend (ie Lochend) of Woodmylne or Frierland', 1775 'Wood Mill, Place in Ruins' (ie presumably Woodmill House GR 271153), 1860 'Woodmill', 'Woodmill Hill'.

Woodriffe, a settlement, GR 227177.

Earlier forms: 1583 'Wodruif', 1594 'Woodruff', 1644 'Woodruiff'.

Derivation: Scots 'Ruf', 'Ruif', 'Riff' &c, a roof, late 14th century on.

Woodside, a settlement, GR 951109, on record since 1783.

Woodside, a settlement, GR 094113.

Woodside, a settlement on record since 1855, GR 005022.

Wyllie Burn GR 112149.

Derivation: Perhaps Scots 'Wylie', an instrument for twisting ropes from straw, 19th to early 20th centuries. If this is the derivation it presumably refers to some perceived swirling or rotating movement of the water. Alternatively, 'Wyllie' the Scots surname.

Y

Yarra Cottage GR 798998, a settlement. From the Selkirkshire placename 'Yarrow'?

***Yeeld**, ***East Yeeld**, settlements on record in 1783 in approximate OS square 9611.

Derivation: Perhaps Scots 'Yeld', 'Yield' &c, sterile, unproductive, unprofitable, 15th to early 20th centuries, thus a wry comment on the land.

Yellow Craig, a very high and precipitous crag according to the 1860 OS Name Book, GR 818972, **Yellowcraig Wood** GR 818973.

Yellow Hill GR 154091, **Yellow Hill Road**, on record in 1860, GR 156090 approximately.

Earlier: 1860 'Yellow Hill'.

Upper Yetts, a settlement on record in 1860, GR 005018, ***Upper Yetts Inn**, on record in 1855.

These are secondary names from Yetts of Muckhart, same OS square, from Gaelic 'Muc Airde', pig height. Scots 'Yett', a gate, late 14th century on.

Woodend, formerly Woodend of Culteuchar, South of Forgandenny. (AW)

Timothy Pont's map of the district along the south side of the river Earn 1595.
Reproduced by permission of the Trustees of the National Library of Scotland.

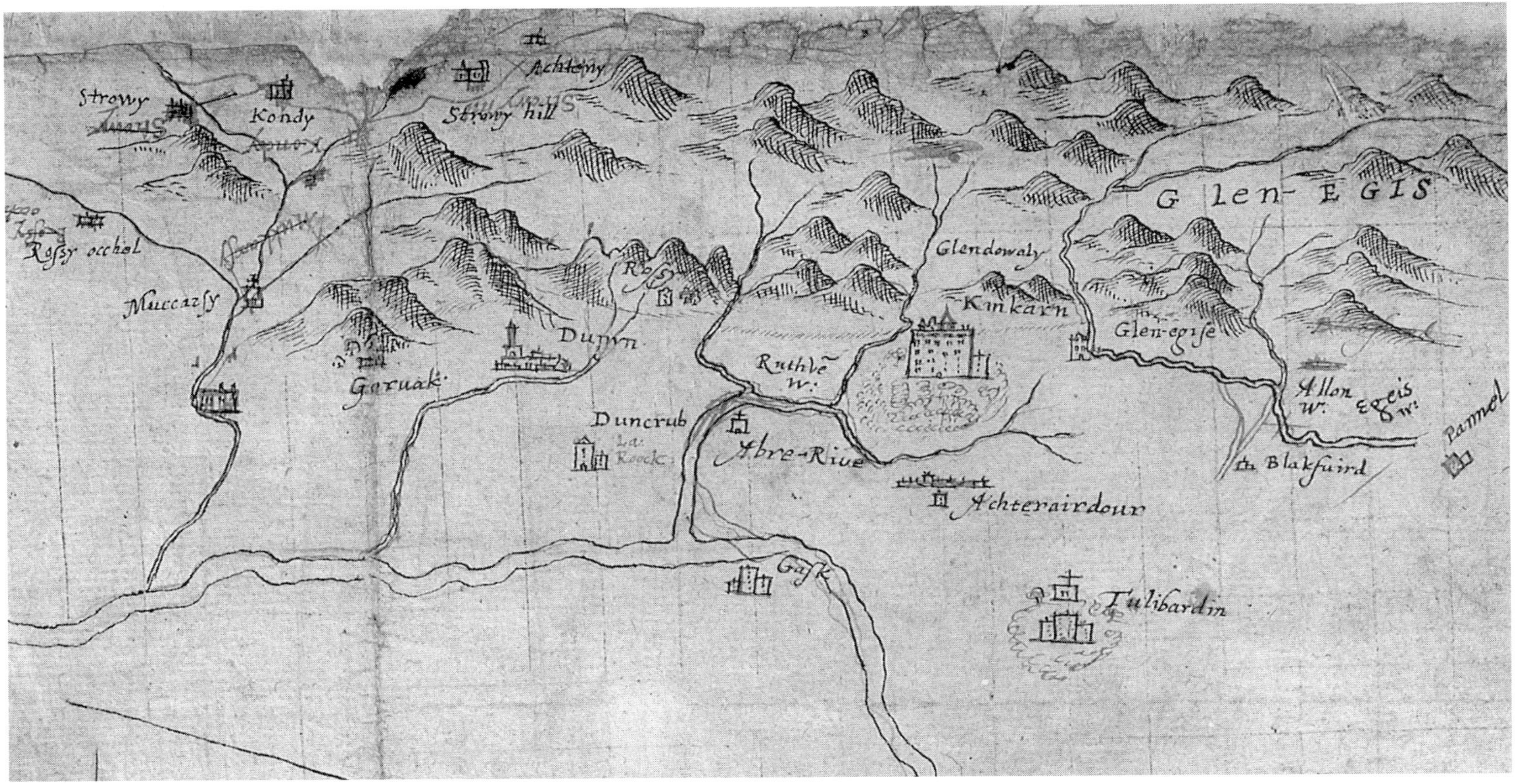

This is probably the earliest map of any part of the Ochils area. The representation of relief is symbolic. The settlements represented are burghs, feudal baronies and ecclesiastical centres, and very few natural features are shown. The orientation, with South at the top, takes some getting used to!

James Gordon: Fifae Vicecomitatus, the Sherifdome of Fyfe 1654, showing the Eastern end of the area.
Reproduced by permission of the Trustees of the National Library of Scotland.

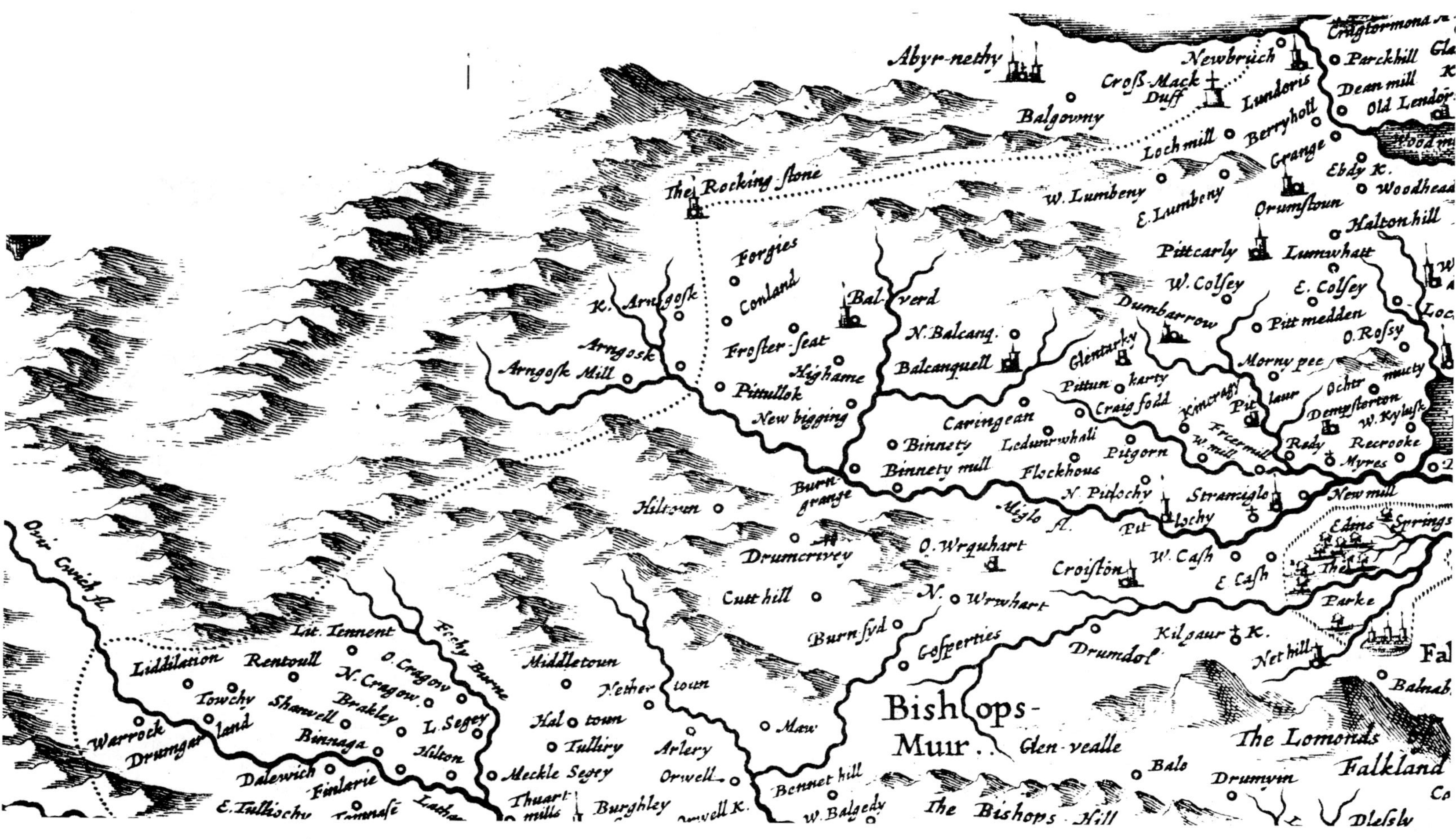

This appeared in Blaeu's Atlas of 1654. It is much more comprehensive than Pont, and humbler sites such as mills and burns are beginning to make an appearance.

From John Adair's map of Straithern, Stormount and Cars of Gourie 1720, showing the Northern Ochils between Abernethy and Dunning. Reproduced by permission of the Trustees of the National Library of Scotland.

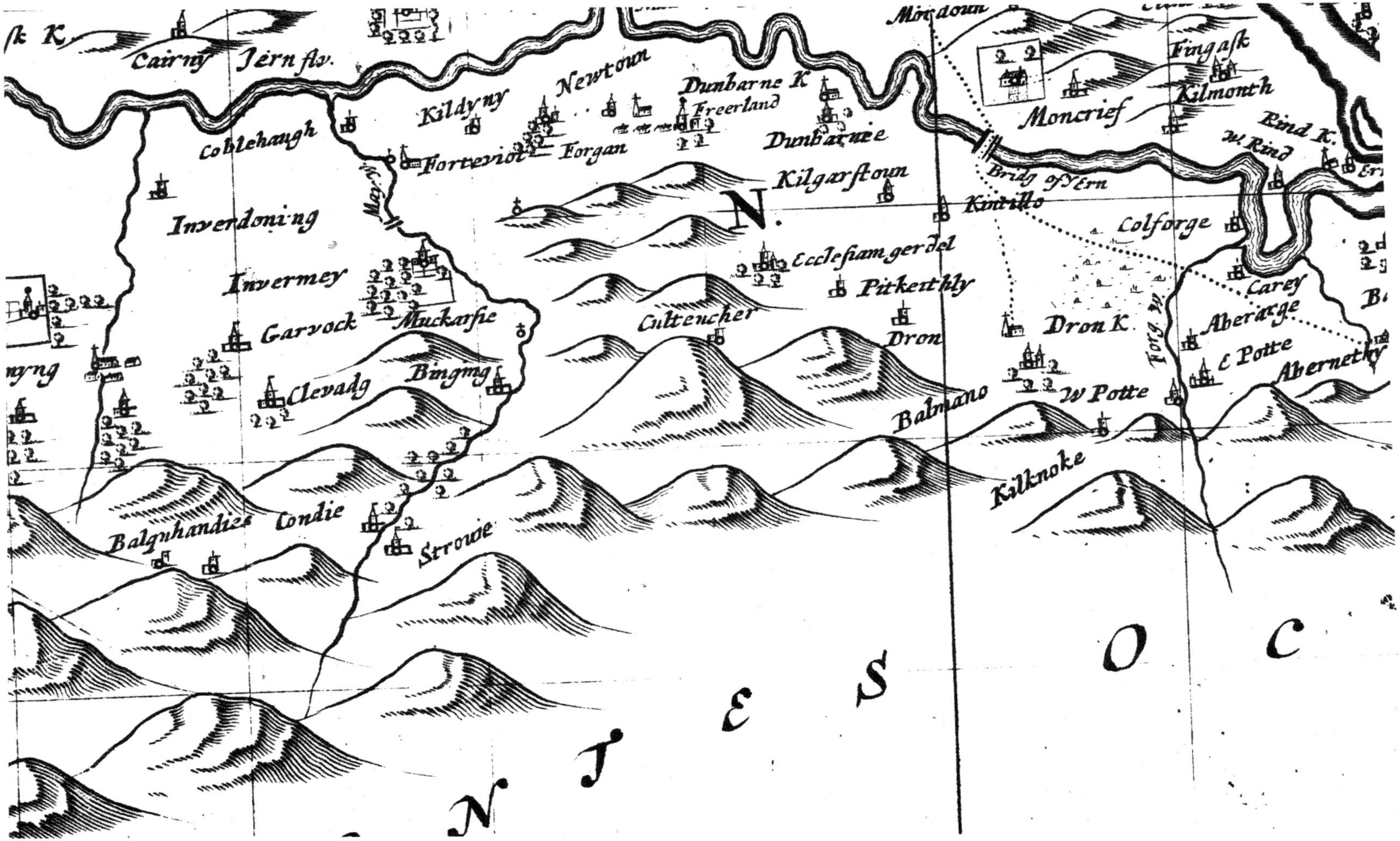

In style and content this map harks back to Pont rather than Gordon. Though the scale is bigger, coverage is still highly selective, concentrating on the more prestigious settlements. Again the relief is stylised.

Part of James Stobie's map of the Counties of Perth and Clackmannan 1783.
Reproduced by permission of the Trustees of the National Library of Scotland.

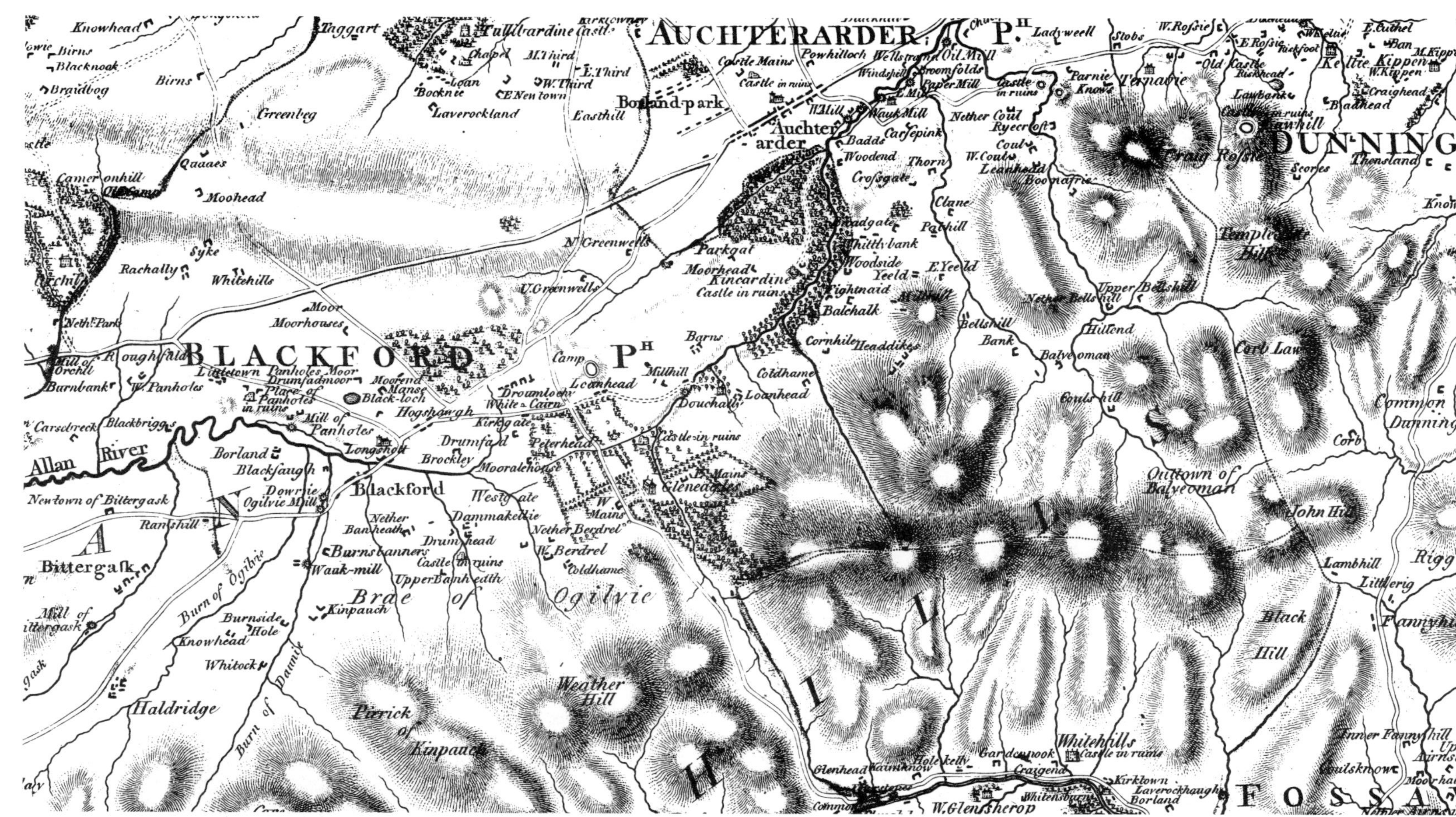

This map represents a significant advance, the fruits of improved surveying techniques. Accuracy is generally good enough for a location to be calculated to the nearest OS grid square. The bigger scale is used to give a fuller coverage of settlement names. As for natural features, many more hill names are shown. A 'bird's eye view' system of indicating relief is introduced, and a serious attempt is made to plot the shape and location of individual hills.

Appendix 1
Scots and Gaelic Names on Record, 1200 to 1950

Figure 1 shows the number of Scots and Gaelic primary names appearing between 1200 and 1950 in the maps and records consulted. The figures were plotted, not for individual years, but at 25 year intervals. In order to make some allowance for the fact that the earliest and latest records found for a given name are not likely to correspond to the true date of its first being coined or of its passing out of use, I have rounded my latest reference up and my earliest reference down to the nearest multiple of 25 years. All Gaelic names found, at whatever date, were assumed to have been in existence in 1200.

From the Scots component I have had to omit some 188 names which occur in the records only once and for which I therefore have no history. The vast majority of these names made their sole appearance in the records between 1750 and 1900 and their inclusion in the graph would distort the curve unacceptably.

Unfortunately a graph of this kind tells as much about the records available as it does about the actual number of names in use and their distribution through time. It is unlikely that any amount of searching would ever turn up the full complement of names that had existed during a given period, simply because the records themselves are neither perfect nor complete.

Generally speaking the earlier the maps and records, the more likely they are to concentrate on prestigious sites such as major settlements and land holdings, churches and other ecclesiastical possessions. With the appearance of Cess Books and the like from the mid 17th century, smaller farms and holdings begin to figure in greater numbers. In the 18th century, and particularly with Stobie's map of Perth and Clackmannan of 1783, the more modest settlements become even better represented and this is reflected by a steepening of the Scots graph line after 1725. Then progressively more and more natural features begin to appear on published maps, culminating in the appearance of the Ordnance Survey First Edition in the years around 1860. To put it another way, the Scots name list is distorted by a serious lack of names for natural features prior to the 19th century. The Gaelic name list is not as seriously disadvantaged in this particular way because a Gaelic name found at any date can safely be backdated to the end of the Gaelic period at least.

The substantial increase in coverage represented by the Ordnance Survey maps is reflected on the graph in the steep climb of the Scots curve between 1825 and 1850, the beginning of the 25 year period during which those maps appeared.

It will be seen that the graph shows a net loss of primary names since the time of the first Ordnance Survey maps, around 1860. The graph also shows the recorded Gaelic names to have remarkable staying power. Of the 351 recorded Gaelic primary names 96% survive until the mid 18th century. From that time a sharper decline sets in but even so 78% survive until 1950.

From 1860 on the main source of information has been OS maps. Comparison of the first edition with recent 6" Ordnance Survey maps shows a proportionately sharper decline in the Scots names recorded than in the Gaelic component, 12% and 6.5% respectively.

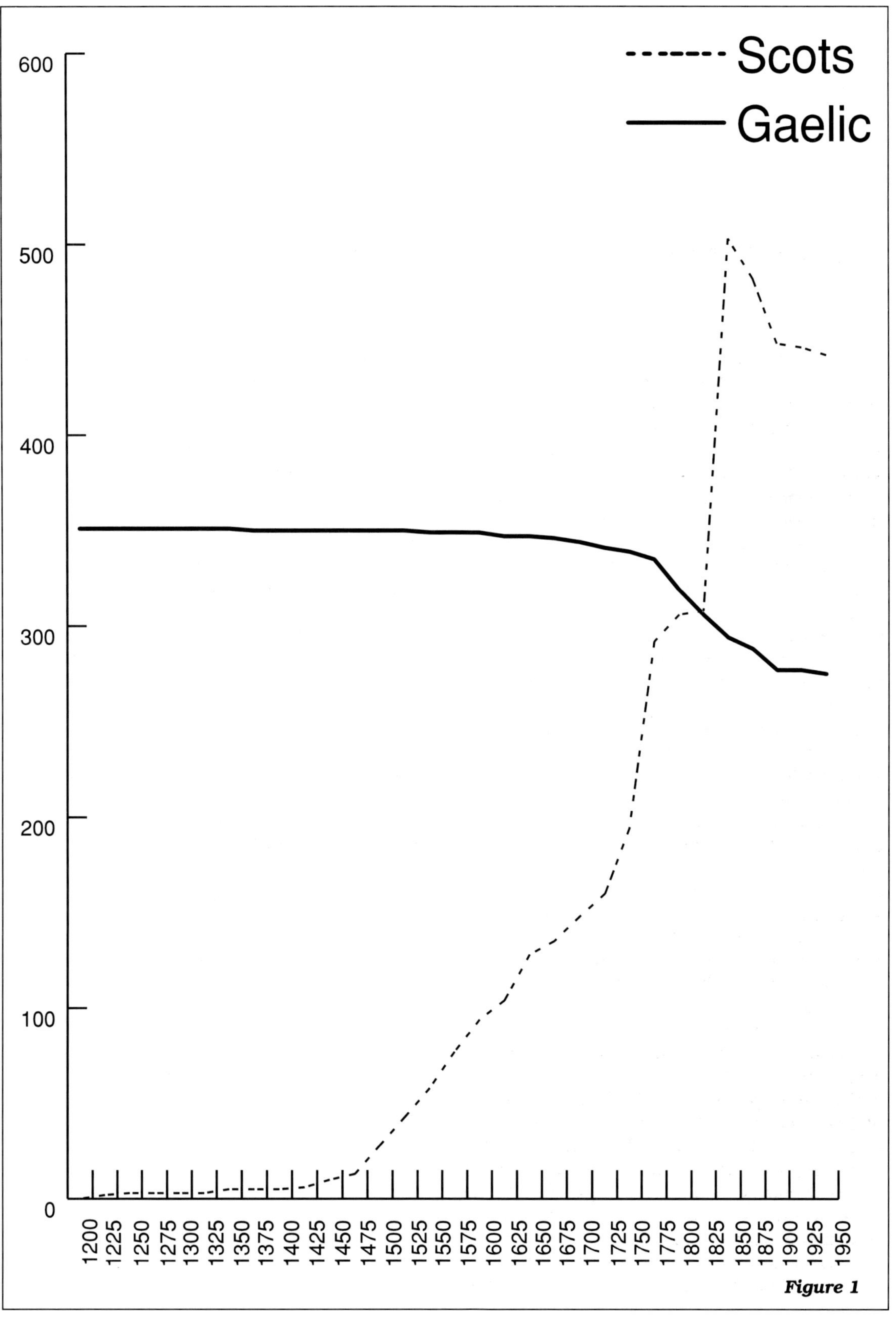
Scots
Gaelic
600
500
400
300
200
100
0
1200
1225
1250
1275
1300
1325
1350
1375
1400
1425
1450
1475
1500
1525
1550
1575
1600
1625
1650
1675
1700
1725
1750
1775
1800
1825
1850
1875
1900
1925
1950

Figure 1

Appendix 2
Settlements on Record 1200 to 1950

Figure 2 shows the settlements recorded between 1200 and 1950 on the maps and other records consulted. As with figure 1, the dates of first recorded appearances have been rounded down and the dates of last appearances rounded up to the nearest multiple of 25 years. In addition all 'Pit-' names, and all Gaelic names which appear to have been primary settlement names, ie those containing 'Baile', steading, 'Tigh' or 'Teach', house, 'Ràth', fortress, dwelling, 'Fas', level site, dwelling place, 'Both', cottage or hut, have been taken as having been in existence in 1200, whatever the date of their first actual appearance in the records consulted. In the case of Gaelic settlement names whose sense primarily implies land-use, not necessarily permanent settlement from the time of the names' creation, the recorded dates of their appearance as settlements have been adhered to (with the rounding down to the nearest 25 years already mentioned). Names of this type include those containing 'Achadh', 'field', 'Lios' and 'Lann', enclosure, 'Airigh', shieling, 'Monadh', moor or hill-land, and 'Bàrd', 'Cluan', 'Dail' and 'Fòd' (here with the sense 'sward'), which imply grazing.

There are two factors that cause the line of the graph in Figure 2 to mask what was happening to settlements in the Ochils area from the late 18th century on. Firstly, although 146 settlement names disappear from the graph between 1800 and the early 1900s, 85 appear for the first time during the same period. Secondly, this graph, like figure 1, is inevitably only as good as the records on which it is based. Between 1725 and 1800 the number of settlement names plotted is boosted by the significantly improved coverage found on the maps of Roy, Ainslie, Stobie and Bell, which between them add a substantial number of settlements, mainly small agricultural units, not previously recorded. To put this another way, the number of names recorded before 1725 is distorted downwards to an unknown degree by the comparative inadequacy of the records.

The downward turn of the graph between 1800 and 1825, when the dramatic improvement in mapping had to some extent been absorbed, shows that the true underlying curve is by this time a downward one. Then there is a similar striking upsurge from 1825 to 1850 due to the advances in coverage represented by the first Ordnance Survey 6" maps, the new names on which have been backdated to 1850 for the purposes of the graph. After 1850 it again becomes obvious that the underlying movement of the graph is downward.

The reasons for the disappearance of small agricultural holdings from c1800 onwards are not far to seek.

Many contributors to the Old Statistical Account for the Ochils area and immediately neighbouring parishes report in the early 1790s that agricultural improvements had been introduced, though with varying degrees of speed and enthusiasm. In Dollar Parish runrig had been abolished about 16 years before. In Abernethy "the ancient servitudes, so oppressive and harrassing to the farmer, (were) almost entirely abolished". What concerns us here however is the effect of this on population, and thus on settlement, the loss or survival of older place-names, the creation of new ones. Though Dunning and Auchterarder parishes had seen an increase in population, through inward migration in the latter case at least, Dron, Abdie, Strathmiglo and Fossoway had seen a decline in population, and Tillicoultry was predicting one. "The modern practice of uniting several farms into one and the suppressing of cottagers" (OSA Dron), enclosure, and "the sale of many of the feus, each of which maintains a family" (OSA Tillicoultry) are the most frequent reasons given for population loss. In Fossoway parish, for example, more than two thousand acres had been enclosed in the preceding ten years.

The contributors to the Old Statistical Account do not usually distinguish in such figures between hill and low ground, but Forgandenny's entry does make it clear that "a considerable part of the higher grounds", ie the part of the parish dealt with in this book, had been enclosed by 1792. Although a considerable part of Auchterarder parish was already enclosed the minister was able to report no decrease in the number of farms. It was also the case there that "the generality of labourers (had) as much land as enable(d) them to keep a cow" and there were still "several hundred acres upon the Hill of Foswell in common among the neighbouring feuars". But Foswell did not escape the inexorable process. I have examined a copy of the map drawn up at the time of the division, c1800, of the Common Hill of Foswell among the adjoining landowners.

In the south of the Ochils the Minister of Dollar was able to report in the New Statistical Account of 1845 that there were no undivided commons in his parish.

One symptom of this fundamental reorganisation of farming is that some 44 of the settlements disappearing from the graph between 1800 and 1900 are subsidiary units of multiple holdings such as Wester Downhill which figures in the Valuation Roll for 1855 but is described as "ruins" by 1860, or Little Jervass (ie Little Jerah), last recorded in 1822. One thing this presumably implies is that areas of land were able to be worked from a smaller number of fermtouns or steadings.

Forestry, for better or for worse a significant form of land use in the Ochils area in our own day, was to some extent a new fashion in the age of agricultural improvement. It was nonetheless to provide an increasingly significant alternative to agriculture. In the 1790s Orwell parish had little new planting "as yet come to any maturity", Auchtermuchty reports some new planting in the north part of the parish and the planting of firs on "all the waste ground", some 600 to 700 acres. In Fossoway and Tullibole planting was "becoming fashionable and . . . proceeding with rapidity" – about 800,000 trees had been planted in the previous eight years (all information from the Old Statistical Account).

Though it would be a gross exaggeration to talk of Clearances in the Ochils area in any way comparable to the Highland experience, there does seem to have been a move towards sheep farming on a fairly large scale. By the 1790s the hill part of Tillicoultry parish for example, some 4000 Scotch acres, was divided into five farms and kept about 3500 sheep. At the same period Dunning parish had "extensive sheep walks in the hills". Hugh Haliburton (1905, see Bibliography) recounts that in the early part of the 19th century many Ochils shepherds were Highlanders – MacLarens, MacDonalds, MacDiarmids, MacKilliwees, Menzieses, Gows. Proud men, they thought themselves above the Lowland shepherds, who had to do manual and arable work in addition to shepherding. When their number began to increase after the first quarter of the century they "were not always generally welcome". The ironic mirror image of the Highland situation is obvious. Haliburton also quotes a couplet from the 'poet' David Smith of Struie Mill:

If herdsmen and shepherds must only be seen
Where numerous and thriving the people have been

which shows that sheep runs were at least perceived as having helped to empty the land of people.

Further changes in farming practice coupled with economic conditions have continued to contribute to a decline in the number of working agricultural holdings in the Ochils area. Mr George Ritchie, who used to farm at Montalt, mentions the importation of cheap grain from North America as the final "nail in the coffin" for a number of small individual farming units. He remembers being told that when their holdings around the May valley were abandoned, in a period from c1890 to the 1920s, the family from Clow emigrated to Colorado, the people from Balquhandy to the Falkland Islands, those from Knowehead went to South Africa, and those from Greenhill to Chile and Peru. He was also told that a smiddy at Pathstruie served no fewer than 35 pairs of horses in the late 19th century.

These are some of the factors then, far from unique to this area of course, that help to explain the decline in the number of agricultural holdings.

Of the settlements disappearing from the graph between 1800 and c1900 that were not agricultural holdings as such, 15 were mills of one kind or another. One theory put forward for the decline of mills in the Ochils area is that the better drainage that resulted from improvements in farming practice meant that water was dissipated more rapidly, making the supply of power to mills more intermittent.

The loss of each mill would no doubt mean the displacement of at least one family. A greater number would presumably be forced to move from the five Cottowns, Cotterknowes, Raws, &c which had housed farmworkers and their families and which also disappeared during this period.

Finally, it should be said that the full number of crofts, farms &c that have ceased to be worked as independent units is masked on the graph by the fact that some of them have survived as private dwelling houses and so still count as settlement names.

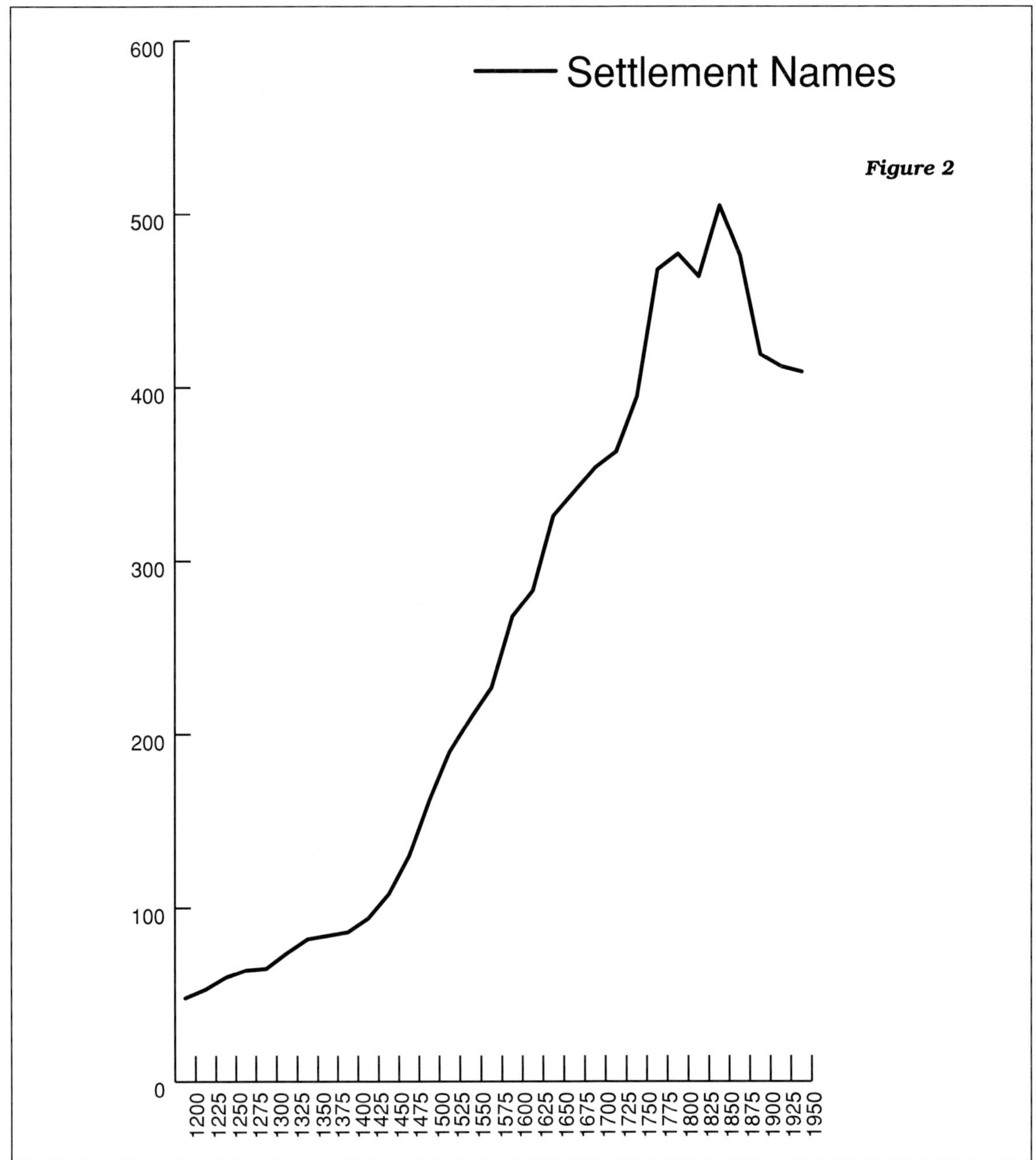

Figure 2

Appendix 3
'Pit-' Names

It will be seen from Figure 3 that the bulk of the names in the area that contain the Pictish element 'Pit-' are concentrated in the eastern third of the map. Pitgober and Pitkeathly have been omitted as they are outwith the area studied, though they contribute secondary names. They would increase the number in the central sector of the map. On the face of it then, the vicinity of Glen Farg would appear to represent a significant boundary west of which Pictish settlement, or at least the element 'Pit-', was less common, and in fact this tallies quite well with published distribution maps for Scotland as a whole.

The 'Pit-' sites have a lower average height above sea level than any of the groups of sites with Gaelic primary settlement names (ie groups sharing a particular Gaelic dwelling name-element such as the eight sites with 'Baile' names or the eight sites with 'Fas' names). This is consistent with the commonsense assumption that the lower ground would tend to be occupied by the population first on the scene. On the other hand it is of course impossible to say how many 'Pit-' settlements once existed in the area, but were abandoned before adequate records began. If a number of such settlements had come and gone it is only to be expected that they would be the ones in less favourable positions. But some evidence that Ochils 'Pit-' names tended to be on lower ground anyway is to be gleaned from the fact that the highest 'Pit-' name found in the area, 'Pitogle' at something between 210 and 250 metres, probably means 'high portion', implying that its location was unusual and worthy of comment.

Another factor we cannot know is how many other sites once had 'Pit-' names but were given new, Gaelic, names at an early stage. Of the 17 'Pit-' names plotted on the distribution map 15 have a second element that can be said with reasonable confidence to be Gaelic. The other two, 'Pitcairlie' and 'Pittendie' are still 'not proven'. This too is characteristic of the 'Pit-' names of Scotland as a whole. The hybrid nature of the names is sometimes attributed to the adoption by incoming Gaels of the Pictish system of land tenure and the 'Peit' or 'Pit' element that was part of it. But scholars such as J D Mackie and W J Watson have stated that the Picts became Gaelic speaking at an early date, and if this is so it is possible that some or all of our hybrid 'Pit-' names were coined, or gaelicised from their earlier Pictish form, by gaelicised Picts.

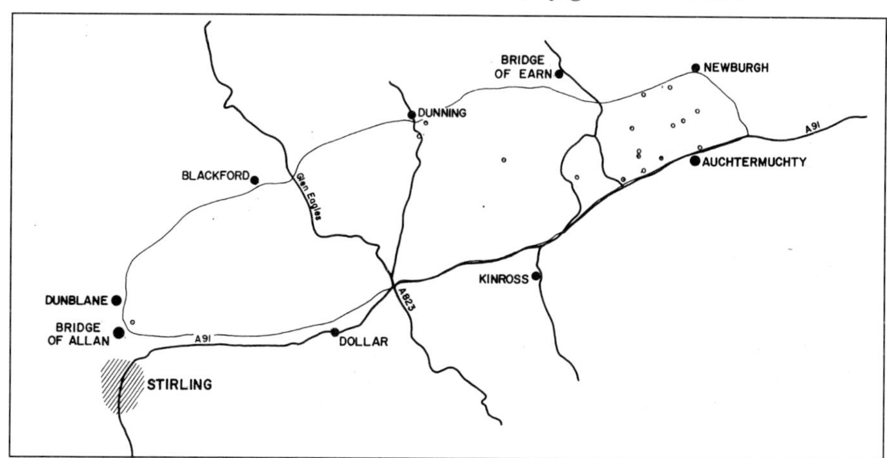

Appendix 4
A Glimpse of Gaelic Life c900 to c1300

Gilbert (see Bibliography) states that in Scotland in the Middle Ages the valleys and sheltered slopes were forested, while the uplands were mostly covered with dense scrub. As late as the 12th century the basin of the Earn was still heavily forested and badly drained, with small patches of arable land and stretches of moor, marsh and fen, and the higher ground to the south, with which we are mainly concerned, would no doubt be in a wilder state than the strath. It is in this kind of landscape that we have to situate the life of the people who gave to their surroundings and dwellings the Gaelic names listed in the Gazetteer.

The misty-eyed dreaming Gael, if he ever existed outwith the imagination of the Romantic poets and historians, the Marjory Kennedy Frasers, and those who have believed their myths, would have been hard put to it to survive in such conditions around the turn of the first millenium. Even a nodding acquaintance with the music and literature of Gaelic Scotland and Ireland shows the Gael to have a rich creative imagination. But in my experience there is also a markedly down-to-earth, practical side to the Gaelic people, and that is in fact the characteristic that emerges most strongly from an analysis of the vocabulary of the Gaelic placenames of the Ochils area that have survived in the records. The names are overwhelmingly descriptive and there is very little trace of emotion or aesthetic feeling being expressed through them.

The largest category of name-elements concerns the configuration of the landscape. There are some 29 words for different types of hills, ridges of hills, promontories and the like, and four words for hillslope. Some six elements refer to bogs and moorland, eleven to various kinds of valleys, hollows and other declivities in the ground, and four to plains and level areas. The lie of the land is also envisaged in terms of sunlight and shade and through relational elements such as 'back of', 'end of', 'middle'. The colours seen in the landscape are black, white, grey, dun, speckled, red and perhaps green. As for water, apart from lochs and pools or waterfalls there are at least five words for burn or watercourse plus a number of diminutives applied to burns.

I have detected no words for low-growing vegetation unless a reference to thorn is to be understood as the bramble rather than the thorn tree. Though there are two words for tree in general, two for wood or forest in general and (perhaps) one for scrubland, the only named tree species are hazel, elm and birch. Perhaps vegetation was of concern only as giving shelter or fuel, or as an obstruction to be cleared.

Judging from the names on record, the Gaelic people of the Ochils took little note of wild creatures unless they were of value as food. Both red and roe deer are referred to and the references to goats and pigs may well include some wild ones. Apart from that, only the wild cat and the badger are singled out for mention. It is possible that the badger's pelt was of value and that both badger and wild cat were admired as bonnie fechters.

Apart from a possible reference to the raven, birds fare even less well, appearing only in the form of 'Eun', the generic term for 'bird'. It is true that in earlier Gaelic poetry 'An t-Eun', the bird, could be used to mean the eagle, but there is no particular reason to believe that that was ever the case in placenames.

The creatures that figure principally are domesticated ones: cattle, goats, pigs, horses and dogs. It is consistent with this that some eight items of vocabulary imply grazing, giving a picture of a pastoral people moving about the hills by the routes, crossings, passes and fords their placenames also record, to visit their shielings and other grazings. It appears that they had the practice of tethering animals at steep rocky sites, conceivably to maximise use of available fodder even in dangerous spots.

On the other hand there is evidence of a more settled form of agriculture, with four references to enclosure of land, presumably for cultivation, and one reference to a barn. Yet there seems to be only one reference to a named crop, oats, and even that is not certain. The davoch seems to have been used as a unit of land measurement, some holdings were divided, into fourths and fifths for instance, and there were some set boundaries.

The interesting word 'Achadh' appears to play a part in both parts of the land use system. In the Gazetteer I have suggested that in the Ochils context 'Achadh' should be understood in the sense 'piece of ground cleared for grazing or cultivation' because it occurs at heights between c50m where cultivation would be possible and c500m where the only option would seem to be periodic grazing. All our ten 'Achadh' names are to be found either near fairly gentle hillsides, or near flattish areas some of which are among very steep slopes. They are all within reasonable distance of one or more important early holdings and it is possible that at least initially they were grazing or cultivation sites for these. It is interesting that Nochnarie (also known as Auchnarie, an 'Achadh' name) is described in 1591 as part of the arable lands of Pitlour, and the connection may go back a long time.

I have detected only six Gaelic primary settlement elements (for the hybrid names with 'Pit-' see Appendix 3). The group that appears to contain 'Ràth' has the lowest average height (though higher than the 'Pit-' names). Next come 'Fas' and 'Làrach' which imply a good level site for a dwelling. The 'Baile' group lies a little higher, but significantly higher than the rest are sites with 'Both' or 'Tigh' (or 'Teach') in their names. There is likely to be a rough correlation here between height above sea level and the prestige of the settlement type.

Activities other than agriculture referred to include conquest by force of arms, legal jurisdiction, lodging of the sick, hunting, shoemaking and the work of the smith. Non-Gaels appear to have been rare enough to merit mention in placenames.

On a less utilitarian level, the Gaelic population took note of the forts of earlier peoples. There are also four words used for standing stones. The cairns present in the namelist may well have included both ones erected in the Gaelic period and ones that predated it. The element 'Nemed', used once or possibly twice, provides some evidence for thinking the Gaels of the Ochils respected the sacred sites of their predecessors.

As regards their own beliefs and culture, little indication of pagan lore survives except one reference, perhaps two, to fairy mounds or hills. Two names which may contain reference to Fionn MacCumhail are all that seems to survive of other mythological material. At least one name shows that the Gaels followed the immigrants' practice of remembering their old homeland, Ireland, in names given to their new surroundings.

The Christian religion is represented by seven elements, three, perhaps four, of which are concerned with ecclesiastical jurisdiction and land tenure by the Church rather than with faith as such. Three sites are associated with the idea 'blessing' or 'blessed'. A cross and a priest are also referred to. In addition, up to six different saints' names could be present but unfortunately none of the etymologies concerned can be taken as certain.

The poet and the shenachie were important enough to be commemorated in Ochils placenames. The shenachie had the function of preserving the history of the race or clan and the genealogies of its leading men. The 'Eigeas' or learned man from whom Glen Eagles took the earlier form of its name may have been a poet specifically. A 'Bàrd' was probably of a lower poetic rank, but the fact that this term is used in our names at all, and that land at Balvaird was granted to one so described, implies that 'Bàrd' had not become a designation of a very inferior poet, almost a term of abuse, as it did in Ireland. In addition 'Balvaird' shows that land was granted in our area to important functionaries like the poets, whose main role was to use their art to praise the group and its leaders, thus fortifying and justifying the political and social status quo.

It should be stressed that the above remarks are based solely on the Gaelic placenames that have come down to us. We must trust that the Law of Averages has left us with a representative selection!

Bibliography

When reference is made in the text to books listed below, it is generally by means of the author's or editor's surname. If there are two or more authors or editors with the same surname the date of the publication concerned is also given, as additional identification.

Anderson J, ed: *Calender of the Laing Charters 854-1837:* Edinburgh, 1899.

Bannatyne Club: *Liber Insulae Missarum:* Edinburgh, 1847.

Bannatyne Club: *Registrum de Dunfermelyn:* Edinburgh, 1842.

Bannatyne Club: *Registrum Honoris de Morton:* Edinburgh, 1853.

BARROW GWS: *The Earls of Fife in the 12th Century:* Scottish Historical Review, 1951-2.

BARROW GWS: *Popular courts in Early Medieval Scotland: Scottish Studies 25,* 1981a.

BARROW GWS: *Kingship and Unity:* London,1981.

BARROW GWS: *Robert Bruce and the Community of the Realm of Scotland:* Edinburgh, 1976.

BARROW GWS et al, eds: *Registrum Regum Scottorum:* Edinburgh, 1960-.

BERNARD R: *Devon Valley Diary:* Clackmannan District Libraries, 1985.

BERNARD R: *Off The Beaten Track:* Clackmannan District Libraries, 1986.

BEVERIDGE D: *Between the Ochils and the Forth:* Edinburgh, 1888.

BILLINGS, ROBERT WILLIAM: *The Baronial & Ecclesiastical Antiquities of Scotland:* Edin & London, 1845.

BLACK, GEORGE F: *The Surnames of Scotland, Their Origins, Meanings & History:* New York, 1946.

BORD J & C: *Sacred Waters, Holy Wells & Water Lore in Britain & Ireland:* Granada, 1985.

BUTLER D: *The Ancient Church and Parish of Abernethy:* Edinburgh, 1897.

CAMPBELL J: *Balmerino and its Abbey;* Edinburgh & London, 1899.

CAMPBELL J: *Panoramic View from Craig Rossie in the Ochil range:* Auchterarder, 1905.

CAMPBELL JL & Collinson F: *Hebridean Folksongs,* 3 vols: Oxford, 1969-1981.

CARMICHAEL A: *Carmina Gadelica:* Edinburgh, 1900–.

CASH CG: *MS Maps by Pont, The Gordons & Adair:* Scottish Geographical Magazine 23, 1907.

Craigie, Aitken, eds: *A Dictionary of the Older Scottish Tongue:* Chicago, 1937-.

Dollar Civic Trust: *Dollar Chapbook:* Dollar, 1977.

DRUMMOND ALR: *Old Clackmannanshire:* Alva, 1953.

DRUMMOND, MRS (sic): *The History of Alva & District:* reprinted Clackmannan District Libraries, 1981

DRUMMOND The Hon Wm: *The Genealogy of the Most Ancient House of Drummond:* Edinburgh, 1831

DWELLY E: *The Illustrated Gaelic-English Dictionary, Eighth Edition:* Glasgow, 1973.

GIBSON W: *Reminiscences of Dollar:* Edinburgh, 1883.

GILBERT JM: *Hunting and Hunting Reserves in Medieval Scotland:* Edinburgh, 1979.

GRANT IF: *Highland Folk Ways:* London & Boston, 1975.

GROOME: *Ordnance Gazetteer of Scotland:* 1893.

HALDANE ARB: *The Drove Roads of Scotland:* Edinburgh, 1971.

HALDANE ARB: *The Path by the Water:* Edinburgh, 1944.

HALIBURTON, HUGH: *In Scottish Fields:* Paterson & Co, 1905.

HALIBURTON, HUGH: *Furth in Field:* London, 1894.

HILL BURTON J: *The History of Scotland, 8 Vols:* Edinburgh & London, 1873.

HUME BROWN P: *History of Scotland, 3 vols:* Cambridge, 1899.

Hunter, Rev J, ed: *Chronicles of Strathearn:* Crieff, 1896.

JACK J W: *Glenfarg and District, Past and Present:* Perth, 1906.

JAMIESON J: *An Etymological Dictionary of the Scottish Language:* Paisley, 1879-.

JOHNSTON JB: *Place-Names of Scotland:* Edinburgh, 1892.

Lawrie AC, ed: *Early Scottish Charters Prior to 1153:* Glasgow, 1905.

LIDDALL WJM: *The Place Names of Fife and Kinross:* 1896.

MACGIBBON D & ROSS T: *The Ecclesiastical; Architecture of Scotland:* Edinburgh, 1897.

MACGIBBON D & ROSS T: *The Castellated & Domestic Architecture of Scotland, 5 vols:* Edinburgh, 1887.

MACKAY AE: *A History of Fife and Kinross:* Edinburgh, 1896.

MACKENZIE DA: *Scottish Folk-Lore & Folk Life:* London & Glasgow, 1935.

MACKENZIE WC: *Scottish Place-Names:* London, 1931.

MCKERRACHER A: *The Street & Place Names of Dunblane & District:* Stirling, 1991.

MACKIE JD: *A History of Scotland, Revised Edn:* Penguin, 1969.

MACKIE J: *Annals of Arngask:* Privately Printed, 1958.

MACKINLAY JM: *Folklore of Scottish Lochs & Springs:* Glasgow, 1893.

McNeill P & Nicholson R, eds: *An Historical Atlas of Scotland, c400-c1600:* St Andrews, 1975.

MELDRUM N: *Forteviot, The History of a Strathearn Parish:* Paisley, 1926

MENZIES FERGUSSON: *Logie, A Parish History:* Paisley, 1905.

MORRIS R & F: *Scottish Healing Wells:* Alethea Press, 1981.

MOSS MS & HUME J: *The Making of Scotch Whisky:* Edinburgh, 1981.

Murray D, ed: *The Scottish National Dictionary:* Edinburgh, 1941-76.

Neville CJ: *The Earls of Strathearn from the 12th to the mid-14th Century:* Aberdeen PhD Thesis, 1983.

NICOLAISEN WFH: *Notes on Scottish Place-Names: Scottish Studies,* 5, 1961, & 6, 1962.

NICOLAISEN WFH: *Scottish Place Names:* London, 1976.

NICOLAISEN WFH: *Gaelic and Scots 1300-1600: In 'Gaelic and Scots in Harmony'*, Glasgow, 1990

NSA: *The New Statistical Account of Scotland:* Edinburgh & London, 1869.

Paton H, ed: *Abstracts of Entries relating to Campbells in the Sheriff Court Books of Perthshire:* Edinburgh, 1914.

PENNANT T: *A Tour in Scotland MDCCLXIX:* Chester, 1771.

REID G: *The Annals of Auchterarder and Memorials of Strathearn:* Crieff, 1899.

Robertson JA: The Gaelic Topography of Scotland: Edinburgh, 1869.

Robinson M, ed: *The Concise Scots Dictionary:* Aberdeen UP, 1985.

Rogers C, ed: *Rental Book of the Cistercian Abbey of Coupar-Angus:* London, 1880.

Scottish History Society: *Bagimond's Roll (in Miscellany, 3rd Series, vol vi)*: Edinburgh, 1939.

Scottish History Society: *Chartulary of Lindores Abbey 1195-1479*: Edinburgh, 1903.

Scottish History Society: *Charters of Inchaffray Abbey 1190-1609*: Edinburgh, 1908.

Scottish History Society: *Macfarlane's Genealogical Collections:* Edinburgh, 1900.

Scottish History Society: *Macfarlane's Geographical Collections:* Edinburgh, 1906 & 1907.

Scottish History Society: *Sheriff Court Book of Fife 1515-1522:* Edinburgh, 1928.

Scottish History Society: *Rentale Dunkeldense:* Edinburgh, 1925.

Scottish History Society: *Rentale Sancti Andree 1538-1546:* Edinburgh, 1913.

Scottish Records Office: *Commissariot Record of Dunblane, Register of Testaments 1539-1800:* Edin 1903.

Scottish Records Office: *Commissariot Record of Dunkeld, Register of Testaments 1682-1800:* Edin 1903.

Scottish Records office: *Commissariot Record of St Andrews: Register of Testaments 1549-1800:* Edin 1902.

SIBBALD, SIR ROBERT: *The History of the Sheriffdoms of Fife and Kinross, New Edition:* Cupar, 1803.

SIMPKIN JE: *Fife, Clackmannan & Kinross, County Folklore Series No vii:* London, 1914.

SKENE WF: *Celtic Scotland, 3 vols:* Edinburgh, 1876.

SNODDY TG: *Tween Forth and Tay:* Kirkcaldy, 1966.

Spalding Club: *Antiquities of Aberdeen & Banff:* Aberdeen,1847-9.

STEWART AG: *Buildings of Architectural & Historic interest in Clackmannan District:* Clackmannan D.C, 1981.

STONE JC: *The Pont Manuscript Maps of Scotland:* Tring, 1989.

STONE JC: *A Locational Guide to the Pont, Gordon & Blaeu Maps of Scotland:* Aberdeen, 1971.

SWAN A: *Clackmannan and the Ochils:* Edinburgh, 1987.

THOMPSON, STITH: *Motif-Index of Folk Literature, 6 vols:* Helsinki, 1955.

Thomson DS, ed: The Companion to Gaelic Scotland: Oxford, 1983.

Thomson JM et al, eds: *Registrum Magni Sigilli Regum Scotorum:* Edinburgh, 1882-1914.

Thomson T, ed: *Inquisitionum ad Capellam Domini regis Retornatarum:* 1811-16.

TIMPERLEY LR: *Directory of Landownership in Scotland* c 1771: Edinburgh, 1976.

WATSON A & ALLAN E: *The Place Names of Upper Deeside:* Aberdeen UP, 1984.

WATSON WJ: *History of the Celtic Placenames of Scotland:* Edinburgh, 1926.

WILKIE J: *The Benedictine Monasteries of Northern Fife:* Edinburgh & London, 1927.

WILSON J: *Dunning, Its Parochial History:* Crieff, 1906.

Witherington & Grant, eds: *The Statistical Account of Scotland 1791-1799:* Wakefield, 1978-.

WITHERS CWJ: *Gaelic in Scotland, 1698-1981:* Edinburgh, 1984.

Maps and Plans Consulted

Adair, John
c1680, Perthshyre
c1680, A Mapp of Clakmanan Shire
1688, The Turnings of the River Forth
1720, The Mapp of Straithern, Stormount & Cars of Gowrie
Ainslie, John
1775, The Counties of Fife & Kinross with the Rivers Forth & Tay
1827, Western Part of Fife with Kinross-shire
Bell, John
c1796, Map of Kinross County
Birniehill
1836, Plan of Birniehill by John Beveridge
Castle Campbell
1822, Plan of Castle Campbell Estate
Cloan, Cloanden (by kind permission of Mr Richard Haldane)
1772, Plan of Cloan Estate
1862, Plan of Cloanden Estate
Coul (by kind permission of Mrs Kennard)
1846, Plan of the Estate of Coul
Edgar, William
1745, Map of Stirlingshire & Clackmannan-shire
Foswell & **Foswellbank** (by kind permission of Mr John Haldane)
c1800, Plan of the Common Hill of Foswell
1829, Plan of the Estate of Foswellbank
Fraser, Greenwood & **Fowler**
1841, Map of Fife and Kinross
Gordon, James & Robert
Fyfe Shyre
Keannrosse-shyre described (a sketch map)
Fifae Pars Occidentalis, The West Part of Fife
Fyff Shire, Fifa Provincia Noviter Delineata
NB The Gordon maps date from 1642-54 approximately but in the text I have used the token date 1654 for Gordon references
Harvieston
1819, Plan of Harvieston & Castle Campbell Estates
1836, Plan of the Estate of Harviestoun, Castle Campbell &c
Knox
1828, Map of the Basin of the Tay
Morrison, S N
1848, Map of the County of Clackmannan
Ordnance Survey
c1860-1985, Sheets at 6", 2.5", 1.25" and 1" to the mile. For all references in the text to the 6" first edition I have used the token date 1860
Pont, Timothy
The Draugt (ie Draught) of Strath Erin (Pont 21b)
Part of South Strathearn (Pont 22a)
North West Fife (also known as Gordon 54b)
NB Pont's maps date from 1583-96 approximately but in the text I have used the token date 1595 for all Pont references
Register House Plans, held in West Register House, Edinburgh. They are listed below in numerical order

RHP 23	Plan of the Lands of Quigs & Balhalldies with the Muires & Hills thereunto belonging, 1736
RHP 35	Plan of Excambion & Division of the Lands of Dalquich, 1788
RHP 44	Plan of the Runridge & Rundale of Dalquigh, 1783
RHP 48	Sketch of the Division of the Commonty of Abernethy, 1820
RHP 58	Plan of Abernethy Common, 1816
RHP 59	Plan of the Commonty of Forgandenny, 1774
RHP 531	Plan of the Property in Auchtermuchty & Neighbourhood Belonging to the Burgh, 1823
RHP 688	Plan of the Common Hill of Tillicoultry, 1769
RHP 1042	A Plan of Sheriffmoor, 1766
RHP 1235	Proposed Mills on the Dollar Burn, 1836
RHP 1239	Plan of the Common Hill of Tillicoultry, 1769

RHP 3578 Plan of the Estate of Glentarkie, early 19th century
RHP 4046 Plan of the Lands of Easter Greenside, 1825
RHP 6307 Sketch of Proposed Line of Road between Yetts of Muckhart & Dunning, 1818
RHP 6748 Sketch of Newton &c from the plan by Alexr Brown, 1769
RHP 9622 Plan of the Estate of Buttergask, 1830
RHP 12658 Plan of the Lands of Culteucher, 1801
RHP 12659 Plan of Auchtenny, 1806
RHP 12661 Plan of Middlerig, 1837
RHP 12662 Plan of Auchtenny & Middle Rigg, late 19th century
RHP 12663 Plan of Culteuchar, late 19th century
RHP 12664 Plan of Binzian, Easter Gatherleys, Mains of Condie & Path Green, late 19th century
RHP 13718 Plan of Tormaukin, early 19th century
RHP 23619 A Scheme of Inclosing Easter Demperston, 1771
RHP 32993 Plan of The Mains of Condie, c1750 (poor quality photocopy)
RHP 44315 A Plan of Grounds in dispute between the Duke of Argyle & William Foot of Glensherup, 1779

Roy
1750, General Roy's Military Map

Sharp, **Greenwood** & **Fowler**
1828, Map of the Counties of Fife & Kinross

Stobie, James
1783, Map of Perth & Clackmannan

Other Material Consulted

Carpow (courtesy of University of St Andrews)
Various dates, Inventory of Titles to the Lands of Carpow, Mugdrum &c

Cess Book
Various dates 1742-, Perthshire Cess Book

Coul Disposition (by kind permission of Mrs Kennard)
1812, Feudal Disposition by John Smeaton
1850, Feudal Disposition by Patrick Smeaton

Dunning Parish Register (on microfilm, Sandeman Library, Perth)
Early 18th century, Dunning Parish Register, Births, Deaths & Marriages

Greenside (courtesy of University of St Andrews)
Eighteenth century, Instruments of Sasine of the Lands of Greenside

Leys (courtesy of University of St Andrews)
Various dates, Inventory of Papers of Hay of Leys

Name Book (on microfilm, West Register House, Edinburgh)
c1860, Ordnance Survey MS Name Books for the appropriate parishes

Perth Museum
Documents of various dates in the keeping of Perth Museum & Art Gallery.

Rent Book
Various dates 1650-, The Rental Book of Perthshire

Seisins
Various dates late18th century on, Register of Seisins for the County of Perth

Valuation Roll
Various dates 1667-, Valuation Roll, County of Perth

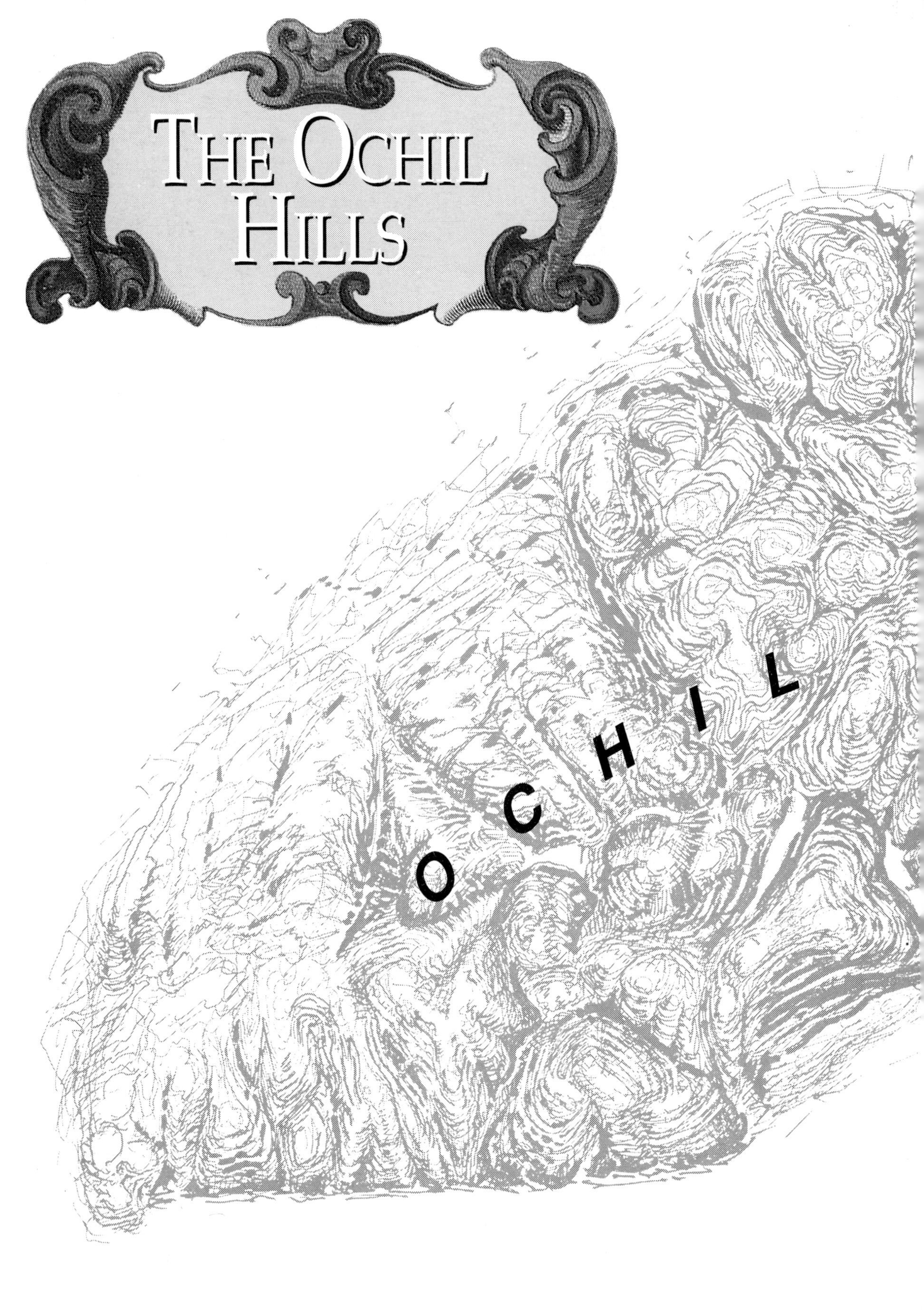
THE OCHIL HILLS
OCHIL